The Information Revolution
Current and Future Consequences

edited by
Alan L. Porter
and
William H. Read
Georgia Institute of Technology

Ablex Publishing Corporation
Greenwich, Connecticut
London, England

Ten chapters in this volume are being reprinted from the September 1996 issue of the journal *Technology, Analysis & Strategic Management* (vol. 8, no. 3). The chapters are used with the permission of the publisher, Carfax Publishing Company, Abingdon, Oxfordshire, England. They are the chapters written by: Tjaden, Read, Sassone, Riggs et al., Poehlein, Cunningham, Papp, Bandini, Balsamo, and Porter/Bostrom.

Printed in the United States of America

Library of Congress Cataloging-in-Publication Data

The information revolution : current and future consequences / edited
  by Alan L. Porter and William H. Read.
        p.   cm. – (Contemporary studies in communication, culture &
  information)
     Includes bibliographical references and indexes.
     ISBN 1-56750-348-9 (cloth : alk. paper). – ISBN 1-56750-349-7
  (prk. : alk. paper)
     1. Information technology–Management.   2. Information technology-
  -Social aspects.   3. Communication and technology.   4. Information
  society.   I. Porter, Alan L.   II. Read, William H.   III. Series.
  HD30.2.I5276   1998
  303.48'33-dc21   97-22317
                                                                         CIP

Ablex Publishing Corporation   Published in the U.K. and Europe by:
55 Old Post Road #2   JAI Press Ltd.
P.O. Box 5297   38 Tavistock Street
Greenwich, CT 06830   Covent Garden
                                             London WC2E 7PB
                                             England

Contents

Foreword

As we approach the Millennium, the developed countries are broaching a new paradigm of economic and social activity. A revolution is at hand which represents the elevation of one resource—information. Consequently, this revolution implies the diminished relative importance—but certainly not the abandonment—of managing other resources such as material processing, energy access, food production and, perhaps, access to capital. This does not mean that agriculture and manufacturing disappear; it does mean that an information-based economy must rethink and rework its structures and processes.

The implications of the transition to an information-based economy are profound because so many private and public sector institutions are "leftovers" from the Industrial Age. The traditional way we work and the way we learn are premised upon mechanical models in which repetitive, efficient manipulation of materials was the dominant motif. Policy mechanisms and international relations cast in eras where information was a limited commodity are ill-adapted to times when information access is a global reality. We have far to go to reconceptualize our economic and social mechanisms to adapt to shifting priorities centered upon enhanced information. Those reconceptualizations need to encompass both the direct implications of the changes in technology and information access, and the indirect, unintended, and delayed consequences of various possible adaptations—about which we know too little.

This volume compiles new thinking about the consequences of the Information Revolution. It is thoroughly interdisciplinary but, we trust, not undisciplined. The scope of the ramifications of "informationalization" is daunting, and we don't claim a fully comprehensive grasp of the changes and their implications. However, we do believe that by deliberately seeking multiple perspectives on this major societal shift we can identify essential issues and their interactions.

A fundamental premise of our grappling with the transition to an Information Economy is that its essence is not the introduction of information technology. Information technology is the enabler, but it is not strategic. Profound change derives from the creation and enhanced availability of information. More data become cheaply and easily shared. That contributes to enhanced value in the guise of information "at the fingertips" of workers, students, and consumers. In turn, productive "information work" must recast that information into higher value "knowledge" which yields strategic benefits. The processes to accomplish this constitute our primary focus, reflecting in our efforts to understand better:

- How to manage information technologies for information purposes.
- How best to build and provide access to information resources.
- How to transition Industrial Age institutions to knowledge-based ones.
- How to reconceptualize the workplace to facilitate information processing that generates wealth.

But we do not stop there. The pervasive influences of enhanced information access will alter our most basic societal processes (and reverberate back on information work accordingly). So, while our "Consequences of the Information Revolution" begin with work, they reach out to economic implications, then to educational and research processes, to political processes, and on to the essence of our lifestyles.

Issues include:

- How can we redefine the "work ethic" to accommodate changing societal needs?
- How can higher education adapt to distributed learning?
- How does information welfare alter international military, political, and business relations?
- How do we enlist broader participation effectively in policy formulation on matters involving, for instance, environmental risks?
- How must we retune our lifestyles?

This volume, which engages these questions, is the outgrowth of a two-year process of intellectual discovery. In spring 1994, we the editors initiated a set of informal discussions that led to a series of seminars at which Georgia Tech faculty shared views on changing information technologies and their current and future (circa 2020) impacts. In spring 1995, some twenty faculty committed to generate research papers during the summer on particular facets of the Information Revolution and its consequences. Results of that research became the content for a fall 1995, advanced seminar that engaged 40 graduate students in Public Policy, Engineering, Management, Computing, Architecture, and Psychology, along with about 100 intermittent visitors from outside academia—from companies, consultancies, and government. The interchange of ideas was strenuous fun.

The research papers presented at the seminar have passed through the "crucible of criticism" to constitute a provocative primer on the implications of *The Information Revolution: Current and Future Consequences.*

This edited volume is organized into six sections:

    I Implications for Modern Management
   II Implications for the Workplace
 III Implications for Academia
 IV Implications for Political Affairs
  V Implications for "Information Societies"
 VI Predictions

These topics pose a set of challenges to those who are curious and concerned about the implications of living in an information-based society.

part I
Implications for Modern Management

Chapter 1 tackles one of the daunting challenges of information enterprises—how do we tell how we are doing? An industry specialist attacks this by building a productivity measurement approach for information-based work.

Chapter 2 provides a conceptual framework for the Information Age business. It arrays five key management issues attendant to organizing around information as the critical resource.

To complete this section, the authors of Chapter 3 offer the case for open engineering systems, arguing that such systems can lead to a form of mass customization in the age of information.

chapter 1

Measuring the Information Age Business

Gary S. Tjaden
Georgia Tech Research Institute

INTRODUCTION

T he world (at least most of it), it is commonly agreed, is leaving the industrial age and entering a new age. Toffler[1] called it the "third wave." Drucker[2] referred to it as "post-capitalism." These scholars and a host of others who have studied the issue believe that the changes involved in this revolution are of many different types and stem from many different advances. However, each proposes that one of the most important changes has to do with humankind's dramatic new capabilities to manipulate information using modern information technology. Somehow these capabilities appear to be so powerful that some call this new age the information age.

Although not necessarily agreeing that information is the single most important characteristic of the new age, or at least so important as to justify being its name, it does seem clear that information age businesses will differ in significant ways from those of the industrial age. Discussions of such differences in general terms are quite common these days, and can be fascinating. However, as Lord Kelvin pointed out long ago, knowledge based on generalities is of "a meager and unsatisfactory kind."

The admittedly ambitious objective of this chapter is to produce a more satisfactory kind of knowledge about how information age businesses should be structured and managed. More specifically, I seek to understand what the key structural and operational characteristics of information age businesses are, and how these characteristics can be measured in order to predict and influence business performance. I argue that key operating parameters for industrial age businesses should be based on the concepts of structural effectiveness (as contrasted with operational efficiency) and knowledge productivity (as contrasted with labor and capital productivity).

The selection of the right set of metrics for information age businesses is the most crucial and fundamental step in developing a management science for them. Perhaps no better example of this point can be given than the observation about industrial age businesses by Peter Senge[3] that there is "an increasing awareness on the part of American manufacturers that while they have worked traditionally to control tightly the amount of inventory in warehouses, their Japanese counterparts have concentrated on reducing delays—a much more successful effort." As the cliché goes, what we do is determined by what we measure.

Of course, it may be many years before it can be determined if these proposed metrics for measuring the management of information age businesses are the right ones. Predicting the future is always uncertain, so let us acknolwedge that this humble attempt can at best be a step toward better understanding. It is certainly not the last step.

DATA, INFORMATION, KNOWLEDGE, AND TECHNOLOGY

In order to define useful metrics for information age businesses, it is necessary to have a clear understanding of the terms *data, information, knowledge,* and *technology.* My use of these terms is based on the discussion of this subject by Bohn.[4] He essentially defined them as forming a

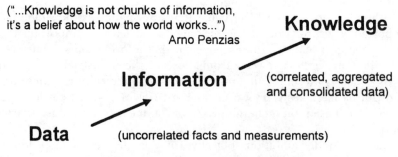

FIGURE 1.1. The Knowledge Continuum

continuum, with data at one end and knowledge at the other. Figure 1.1 depicts this continuum.

Data are facts, determined from a measurement of some kind. Information is the result of correlating or organizing data. Knowledge, finally, allows for confident prediction of future outcomes. For example, measured values for the defect rate of a manufacturing process are data. Collecting a series of such data points and plotting them together on a run chart results in information (a trend, perhaps). Knowledge is the ability to predict the future performance of the process from the information at hand (by knowing to place control limits on the chart and looking for data points outside the limits.

Another way to appreciate the difference between knowledge and information is to think of knowledge as representing a paradigm or worldview. As Arno Penzias, the Nobel Laureate in physics, said, "knowledge is not chunks of information, it's a belief about how the world works."[5] New knowledge, then, is the embodiment of a new belief about how the world works.

The discussion of knowledge is rejoined shortly. First, however, it is helpful to clarify my use of the term *technology*. I follow the spirit of macroeconomist Paul Romer[6] when he said, "technological change—improvement in the instructions for mixing together raw materials—lies at the heart of economic growth." To Romer, the "instructions for mixing together raw materials" are technology. He also uses the term *design* in the sense of a design for a good or service to be produced, to be synonymous with technology.

If one uses a liberal interpretation of the term *raw materials* to mean any basic components, logical or physical, then knowledge and technology are the same thing. That is, technology = design = knowledge, which is a belief about what will happen if a certain set of transforming operations are performed in a certain way on a certain set of basic components.

Romer, who is developing new models of economic growth that treat technology as a basic driver, made a further useful distinction here. He pointed out that a design (technology), once it "is created, can be used as often as desired in as many productive activities as desired."[7] As a result, he added "a design differs in a crucial way from a piece of human capital such as the ability to add." That is, human capital, as the term is used by Romer, is different from a design, because a unit of human capital can only be in one place, doing one thing, at a time. This means that, for example, expenditures by a business to train production workers on a new production process are not investments in knowledge (technology), but in human capital.

Thus, once knowledge is created, there is an inexhaustible supply of it, and it cannot be consumed. It can be instantiated in as many human minds as can comprehend it. Each of these minds, acting as a unit of human capital, can use the knowledge as needed and desired. However, knowledge can become obsolete when it is superseded by new knowledge. Human capital, on the other hand, can be consumed either by its knowledge becoming obsolete or by ceasing to be able to apply it. It is also replenishable, but at a cost (procreation and education).

It is not known how to measure knowledge quantitatively. A qualitative method for measuring knowledge proposed by Bohn[8] is useful here. Consider any business activity, P, which exists to produce some output, Y. P could be an entire business, or it could be merely a small subactivity of a large and complex business. If the latter, then Y is also an input to other subactivities, which operate together to produce the business's final output(s).

Bohn thinks of P as a function that transforms raw material inputs into the output, Y. Figure 1.2 illustrates Bohn's model, which he called a process. The inputs to the process consist of two types of variables in addition to the raw materials. Environmental variables, such as weather or the supply of electrical power, are (thought of as) exogenous to the process. Control variables are those that can be manipulated to affect the way the raw materials are transformed (e.g., temperature of a baking oven).

Bohn's measurement of knowledge is based on how much is understood about "the effects of the input variables on the outputs." He defined eight knowledge stages, from complete ignorance to complete knowledge. The more that is known about which input variables are important, what their effects are on the outputs, and how to control these effects, the more knowledge exists. If complete knowledge exists, the process can be fully automated so that it operates with no human

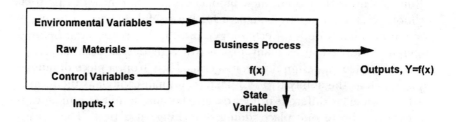

FIGURE 1.2. The Business Process Model

involvement. In reality, complete knowledge can never be obtained, but it can be approached. An interesting corollary of this proposition is that mature processes, about which much knowledge exists, tend to be based on obsolete knowledge.

According to Drucker,[9] there are three basic types of new knowledge. The knowledge metric defined by Bohn can be used to distinguish between them. *Improvement* knowledge has to do with better ways to perform a process, or make incremental improvements to an existing product. The Japanese depend on this type of knowledge in their approach to continual improvement called *kaizen*. *Exploitation* is the use of existing knowledge to develop entirely new processes or products. New knowledge that allows entirely new products or processes to be developed is called *innovation*.

If a unit of new knowledge results in a process that has the same input and output variables as another process, it is improvement knowledge. If the knowledge involves new or different output variables, but primarily the same input variables, it is exploitation. Finally, innovation knowledge would have many new or different input and output variables.

INFORMATION TECHNOLOGY

The term *information technology*, literally interpreted, means the technology of information. Because technology, as we have defined it, is knowledge, information technology is knowledge about information. That is, information technology is a belief, or paradigm, about information that allows for predictions about information. Furthermore, because information is organized data, information technology is a paradigm with predictive power for organizing data. An example of such a belief is what is called the relational model of data. This model says that information can be represented as tables of data, and that relations between tables having some common elements are also information. Additionally, the model defines basic operations for manipulating such information.

Information technology is often used to refer to tools, such as computers, computer programs, and data networking products, for manipulating data and information. Such a use of this term is incorrect, based on the preceding definition. To illustrate, a tool for manipulating information based on the relational model is what is called a relational database management system (RDBMS). The RDBMS is an information tool, whereas the relational model is an information technology.

In many cases, such a misuse may not matter. The context of the usage often serves to allow for a correct understanding of the point being made. However, for purposes of measuring information age businesses, it is important to use these terms correctly. For example, measuring a return on information tools (a component of capital equipment assets) is much different from measuring a return on information technology as we have defined it.

There are only two basic ways in which a business can use information tools: to manipulate data and information, and to automate complex processes (assuming a high degree of knowledge exists about them). In fact, information tools are available so ubiquitously that they cannot provide a sustainable competitive advantage for an information age business. It is the business' information technology (i.e., how the information tools are used by the business) that provides the competitive advantage.

KNOWLEDGE WORK

According to Drucker, there are three kinds of work: manual labor, service work, and knowledge work. It is helpful in understanding knowledge work to understand all three.

Manual labor is the work of making and moving things. It has traditionally been called blue-collar work, the most prevalent kind of work in industrial age manufacturing companies. However, the percentage of the U.S. workforce engaged in manual labor has been falling for the past 30 years. In 1960, total manufacturing employment was about 25% of the workforce. It had fallen to about 16% by 1990 (while the total workforce during that period doubled).[10]

Service work is similar to manual labor in many ways. The level of formal education required to do it is relatively low, and the skills can be easily learned with training (as opposed to education). A major difference is that, whereas much of the work in manual labor is paced by the needs of the machines or tools in the production line, the tools of the service worker serve the needs of the worker. For example, the computer terminal of the telemarketing worker is there to provide the worker with certain information when the worker requests it. In a production line, the worker is there to provide the metal stamping machine with parts to stamp when the machine needs them.

In the sense that tools serve the needs of workers, service work is similar to knowledge work. Drucker pointed out that the productivity of manual labor was improved by "applying knowledge to work" using the principles developed by Frederick W. Taylor in the late 1800s.[11] He went on to propose that this has not been done yet for service and knowledge work, and that as a result the productivity of such work is very poor (and may even have been declining).

Knowledge work, as Drucker used the term, is performed by educated people who possess specialized knowledge. To be a knowledge worker it is not enough to be educated as a generalist; for example by completing a liberal arts program at a university. Knowledge work involves doing something with knowledge, as opposed to just speaking or writing about events or interesting concepts. Knowledge work, therefore, is defined as the production of goods or services through the application of knowledge.

It is important to recall at this point that knowledge has the property that it gives the possessor predictive abilities. The master chef, who uses his or her knowledge of cooking to select just the right ingredients and prepare them in just the right way to produce a magnificent meal, is a knowledge worker. The person who sets the dining table and clears the dishes is not. Drucker used the example of the technicians in a modern minimill who produce steel through the use of their knowledge of process, chemistry, metallurgy, and computer operations to control the machines in the mill.[12]

A good or service can be, of course, almost anything. Knowledge itself is a good (the technology driving Romer's economic growth models). Thus, knowledge work can be the application of knowledge to the production of new knowledge. This is the traditional role of the applied research activities some businesses conduct.

Knowledge work to produce new knowledge is also performed by many other functional areas within a business. For example, marketing research to develop new ways to segment prospective customers, conducted by the marketing department of a high-tech computer company, falls into this category. Recall that there are three types of knowledge: improvement, exploitation, and innovation. New knowledge of each type can be produced for each activity or function in any business. Doing so requires knowledge work

Knowledge work, however, as we have just seen, is not just about producing new knowledge. One of the most important issues in an information age business is how it produces and uses information. Knowledge work determines how data can be organized to produce information, and how this information can be used to produce goods and services. In contrast, the actual production of the information and its movement from place to place (unless it is automated with information tools) is service work, because knowledge is not required to perform these activities.

Knowledge plays a new role in an information age business. It is the most important asset to be managed by such businesses, replacing labor and financial capital, which are the paramount assets of industrial age businesses. This leads to a new focus for managers. In an information age business the "right definition of a manager is one who is responsible

TABLE 1.1.   Key Business Characteristics

Industrial Age	Information Age
1. Mass production	Mass customization
2. Labor serves tools	Tools serve labor
3. Labor performs repetitive tasks	Labor applies knowledge
4. Command and control structure	Common control structure
5. Capital intensive	knowledge intensive
6. Capitalists own production means	Labor owns production means
7. Capital is primary driver	Knowledge is primary driver

for the application and performance of knowledge."[13] Management in an information age business (as in businesses of any age) is a special kind of knowledge work.

CHARACTERISTICS OF INFORMATION
AGE BUSINESSES

With a firm understanding in hand as to what is meant by information, knowledge, and technology, information age businesses can be characterized. This is done by contrasting them with the key characteristics of industrial age businesses. Table 1.1 summarizes these contrasting characteristics.

Whereas industrial age businesses focus on mass production, information age businesses focus on mass customization. That is, market differentiation and sustainable competitive advantage are achieved by identifying and serving ever smaller niche segments. Knowledge work is used to accomplish this. First, knowledge is applied to market information to produce the new knowledge of interesting, viable segments. Knowledge is also applied to design new or better products to serve those segments. Finally, knowledge is applied to the design of production processes in order to produce economically the mass-customized goods.

Information technology and information tools are the key new information age ingredients that make mass customization feasible. Information on individual purchase transactions, for example, is collected as transactions occur, forming the basis for defining niche market segments.[14] This collection was not feasible in the industrial age of mass advertising. Manufacturers are mass customizing such mundane items as household dimmer switches by designing microprocessor controls into the switches and then customizing them by simply reprogramming the software.[15] The Japanese company National Industrial Bicycle has developed a manufacturing process that allows it to produce and deliver a fully customized bicycle in three days.[16] Sadly for the United States, the Japanese have placed a special emphasis on producing and using new manufacturing process improvement knowledge, and appear to be far ahead. They spend about two thirds of their research and development (R&D) budgets on producing new process knowledge, double the fraction spent by U.S. industry.[17]

In information age businesses, the tools serve the needs of the workers, rather than the other way around. The tools consist of either pure information tools, such as computer information systems, or tools that have been made intelligent and physically agile enough to automate virtually all high knowledge stage activities. Only activities truly requiring knowledge work are left to humans, with support as needed from the tools.

It is apparent, then, that the information age business depends on knowledge workers as its key labor force, rather than manual laborers or service workers who perform highly repetitive, simple tasks. A critical issue for these businesses, as already mentioned, is improving the productivity of knowledge workers and reducing the dependence on service workers. The reengineering movement is really aimed at doing so by producing new process knowledge. Unfortunately, much of this effort is misdirected, due to a lack of appropriate knowledge by traditional, embedded management knowledge workers.[18]

Information age businesses, even those whose products are durable goods, are really in the business of delivering knowledge or value-added

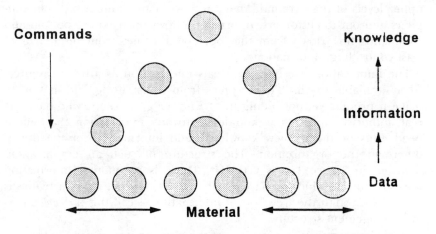

FIGURE 1.3.   Industrial Age Command and Control

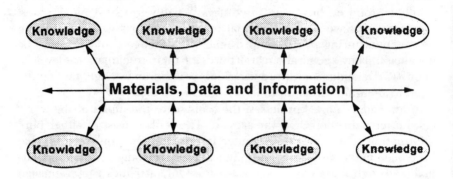

FIGURE 1.4.   Information Age Common Control

information. As Drucker pointed out, the "actual product of the pharmaceutical industry is knowledge; pill and prescription ointment are no more than packaging for knowledge."[19] Such businesses must be organized differently than traditional industrial age businesses. They must be organized around the flow of information, rather than the flow of things.[20]

Industrial age businesses are organized to keep physical items flowing from machine to machine. The organizational structure used is the command and control hierarchy, depicted in Figure 1.3. In such a structure, knowledge resides within the relatively few knowledge workers at the upper levels of the pyramid. Material flows at the bottom, in from suppliers and out to customers. Information flows up from the bottom and commands flow down from the top. Power comes from hiding, or at least controlling, information.

The information age business treats information as a basic resource, freely available to all. "Power comes from transmitting information to make it productive, not hiding it."[21] Knowledge workers, who have the real authority, apply their knowledge to any information they might need, thus producing new knowledge and information for the use of others in the organization. The structure of such an organization, depicted in Figure 1.4, is very flat. There is a common information infrastructure to which all have equal access. Coordination of activities is achieved through the free flow of information. I call this a *common control* management structure.

Intel Corporation manufacturer of the microprocessor used in the vast majority of personal computers, develops a new generation every 2 to 3 years. Each new generation basically makes the previous one obsolete. In this way, Intel remains ahead of any potential competitors that wish to develop clones of its successful products. In order to expand capacity for manufacturing existing products and bringing out new ones, Intel spends huge amounts of capital on new and upgraded integrated circuit fabrication facilities every year. However, the most important asset for Intel to manage is not this capital equipment base, but the knowledge of how to design and manufacture ever better microprocessors. As long as its knowledge assets continue to grow ahead of competitors, Intel will have no trouble obtaining the capital it needs.

The most important asset in an information age company is knowledge, not capital. That is not to say that capital is not needed or used, but that it is not the most important input on which to focus attention. Without a growing knowledge store from which to create new outputs, the information age company will become ill and die. However, in the information age, this knowledge store can be used to obtain capital or any other needed assets. Thus, measuring the performance of an information age business through the traditional financial ratio of return on capital is meaningless. More appropriate metrics are discussed later.

Human capital is the primary means of production in an information age company. However, the owners of the company do not own the means of production, as they do in industrial age companies. The means of production, obviously, reside with the knowledge workers themselves. Moreover, the ownership of information age companies is no longer restricted to a relatively few capitalists. In fact, the largest ownership stake in U.S. companies is held by pension funds, which are in turn "owned" by the workers whose retirement savings are invested in the funds. Additionally, individuals are increasingly investing more directly in the ownership of companies through mutual funds and tax-deferred retirement plans. In 1977, there were only about 4 million mutual fund investors, compared with more than 40 million in 1995.[22]

The key driving economic input of an information age business is knowledge, not capital. The more knowledge it has (including the knowledge of how to apply it), the more it will succeed. However, it is not at all clear that economic growth is (or should be) the overarching business objective and therefore the correct measure of success. The field of industrial dynamics shows us that everything (including businesses and individual business subactivities) is part of a feedback system.[23] Every such system has natural limits to growth. It is pointless and destructive to try to exceed them.

For information age businesses, "success...might mean increasing the skills of our people, our own capacity to learn, the quality of what we produce, or the quality of our workplace. The business would be rewarded for growing better instead of bigger."[24]

The Patagonia sports clothing company has adopted this approach. According to its president and founder, Yvon Chouinard:

> Most of us managed to exceed our limits. Patagonia...was not an exception. By the end of 1989 we...had nearly outgrown our natural niche, the specialty outdoor market, and were on our way to becoming much larger than we wanted to be....Last fall you had a choice of five ski pants, now you may choose between two....The fewer styles we make, the more we can focus on quality. We think the future of clothing will be less is more, a few good clothes that will last a long time. We have never wanted to be the largest outdoor clothing company in the world, we have only wanted to be the best.[25]

MEASURING INFORMATION AGE
BUSINESS STRUCTURE

The way in which a business conducts its activities is called its *business process*. A business process is comprised of the people who conduct it, the tools they use to assist them, the procedures they follow, and the flows of material and information between the various people, groups, and subactivities. The structure of a business process, be it command and control or common control, is relatively static. That is, it changes only slowly through time.

The traditional, industrial age approaches to measuring business processes are primarily focused on its real-time operation. Common metrics used are, for example, units produced per shift, work in progress, percentage of units requiring rework, and units produced per unit of labor used (labor productivity). These metrics are all measuring operational efficiency; that is, is the process utilizing all of its resources at their maximum capacity?

This measurement focus is understandable, if not necessarily entirely appropriate, for processes aimed at producing an ever-greater number of identical outputs, as are those of industrial age businesses. Such a business is driven to a relationship with its customers that can be characterized in the following way: "We supply widgets. You can have them in X different varieties at these set prices. Take them or leave them."

As we have seen, information age businesses are focused on ever smaller market niches rather than mass markets. They use a different type of labor force, with a different organizational structure from industrial age businesses. As a result, the customer relationships toward which they are driven can be characterized as: "We would like to get to know you better. Please tell us your feelings and concerns, and how we might be able to help you."

This type of relationship, of course, depends on gathering as much information about each customer as possible and turning it into knowledge. The business processes that must support it are very different in nature from traditional industrial age ones, and must be measured against an entirely different kind of metric. The appropriate metrics for an information age business process need to be focused on effectiveness as opposed to efficiency.

Effectiveness is a balance between two competing objectives: production and production capability.[26] Production is the objective of industrial age companies: increasing production, at ever lower costs, no matter what. Production capability is the resources required for production, including tools, labor, capital, and knowledge. A focus primarily on production causes the resources needed for production to be depleted.[27] The information age business is driven by its knowledge resources, which must grow, rather than be depleted. Its focus, therefore, has to be on effectiveness, a proper balance between these two objectives.

Operational metrics, as discussed earlier, measure how the process is performing through time. They tend to be meaningful only if measurements are made and recorded periodically for comparison. That is because the performance of a process will vary through time in reflection of changing demands on the process, and changes in the individual people and tools used in the process. Operational metrics deal directly with dynamic properties of business processes.

Structural metrics deal with more static, slowly changing properties. These properties, however, can strongly influence the performance of a process. They provide indirect information about it, which can be used to predict how it is likely to perform. Traditional structural business process metrics include, for example, the ratio of indirect to direct personnel, the number of management levels, and the ratio of process time to cycle time. These particular metrics are also efficiency metrics, because they deal with how well the resources of the process are utilized.

Information age businesses, as we have seen, need to be measured with effectiveness metrics.[28] In particular, in order to be able to predict performance before a new business process is implemented, management needs metrics of structural effectiveness.

Work over the past several years in the area of business process reengineering has really been all about identifying structural characteristics of business processes that result in effectiveness. Among such characteristics discussed by many authors one can list simplicity, integration, self-learning, agility, virtuality, and robustness. These concepts are often discussed at length by their proponents, but only in general terms and with anecdotal descriptions to explain and justify them. Recent research is turning these characteristics of effectiveness into metrics of effectiveness.[29] So far, three metrics have been defined and studied. They are complexity, integration, and dynamicism.

Complexity measures the degree to which the process is structured around many simple activities, resulting in many hand-offs between the people performing them. The more people, activities, and hand-offs there are in the process, the higher its complexity value. Complex processes utilize mostly service workers who need and use little knowledge to perform their work. Simple processes, on the other hand, have fewer activities, but each activity performs more of the work of the process. Thus, the people needed are knowledge workers, because they are required to exercise judgment based on their knowledge. Information age businesses should use processes that are as simple as possible.

Business process (or their subactivities) that cooperate with each other very closely to achieve a common objective are said to be highly *integrated*. Information age businesses need to be closely integrated with their customers in order to achieve mass customization. The common control structure of the information age business requires that the subactivities forming the business' processes should also be tightly integrated with each other in order for knowledge workers to have appropriate access to all needed information. The integration metric measures the degree to which the structure of a business process supports the delivery of the outputs of one activity just when they are needed by their user activities. Structures having a high integration value are more likely to achieve integrated operations than those scoring a lower value.

Change is a continuous activity in an information age business. Driven by the rapidity with which the knowledge on which they depend becomes obsolete, and by the ever-changing needs of customers, the information age business cannot tolerate business process structures that inhibit changing the processes often and quickly. The degree to which a business process structure supports such change is measured with the dynamicism metric. The parameters comprising the metric include whether targets are set for the outputs of the subactivities, whether the outputs are measured against the targets, who does the targeting and measuring, and who has the authority to change the process.

Each of the metrics defines a numerical value for the process being measured. In this way the metrics allow various business process designs to be easily compared against each other as the designer attempts to achieve desired properties of structural effectiveness. The metrics also define limits on the range the measured values could have. It is there-

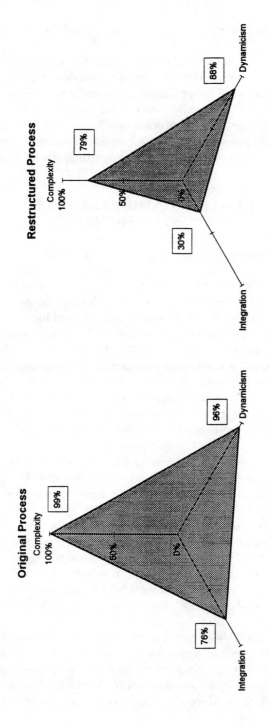

FIGURE 1.5. Using Structural Effectiveness Metrics (Scales are in Units of Percentage from Optimum)

fore also possible to evaluate a business process against a theoretical optimum.

Figure 1.5 shows the results of using the metrics to understand and improve a business process structure. The particular process that produced these data is the order fulfillment process for a small supplier of specialty clothing. The metrics were used to guide the designers to problem areas in the original process and verify that proposed changes would lead to improvement. The new process structure, according to the metric values, is much more information age than the original one.

MEASURING INFORMATION AGE
BUSINESS PERFORMANCE

Because knowledge is the most important driver and asset of an information age business, the most important measure of performance must be the return on knowledge, or what Drucker called *knowledge productivity*. As already discussed, traditional industrial age financial ratios such as return on capital are not meaningful measures to use.

Productivity is a ratio of outputs produced to inputs used. Knowledge, valued as a balance sheet asset, would be the obvious input belonging in the denominator of a knowledge productivity calculation. This would be the equivalent to the book value of invested capital in a return-on-capital ratio. Bohn's qualitative measure of knowledge described earlier, although enlightening, does not provide a numerical value expressible in dollars. It is the best metric available at this time, but it is not adequate here.

It is possible, however, to determine the fully burdened costs of a business' knowledge work. The definition of knowledge worker given earlier is precise enough to determine the person-hours spent doing knowledge work (it merely needs to be differentiated from service work and manual labor).[30] Standard accounting data will easily turn person-hours for each person into burdened costs. The knowledge work costs can be further partitioned, at least roughly, into those spent applying knowledge and those spent producing new knowledge. It is even possible to determine how much of the new knowledge work was spent on producing each of the three kinds of knowledge (improvement, exploitation, and innovation).[31]

The balance sheet of a business records the difference between the cost in financial terms of acquiring an asset and the amount the value has depreciated through time as the current book value of the asset. There is no reason why knowledge assets, determined by the cost of the knowledge work to produce them, cannot be treated in the same way.

The issue of determining depreciation schedules appears to be the same as for physical assets, and should be handled in the same fashion. Other knowledge assets required by the business (e.g., an intellectual property license) should, of course, be included in knowledge productivity calculations.[32]

If knowledge assets, represented by the book value of the costs of the knowledge work to produce them, are the inputs to the knowledge productivity calculation, what are the outputs? One of the outputs can be, of course, the value of the products produced by the business, as measured by its revenues. Another might be profits, such as operating income or net income. A business' values for the resulting productivity metrics, especially when compared to those of other businesses, might be very interesting and enlightening.

For an information age business, however, growth in revenues or profits is not the overriding objective. A better output parameter, one that reflects effectiveness as well as efficiency, is economic value added (EVA).[33] EVA is after-tax profits less the cost of equity capital. That is, it subtracts from net income the rent that the business should pay to its direct equity investors to compensate them for risking their investment.

Industrial age businesses have been able to ignore EVA because profit growth drives up stock prices, so investors receive their returns from the stock market. For information age companies such as Patagonia, discussed earlier, getting better is more important than getting bigger. Investors will need to receive their returns primarily from the business, so EVA will be the output parameter to watch. I define:

Knowledge productivity = $\dfrac{\text{Economic value added}}{\text{Knowledge assets}}$

Productivity ratios based on EVA have been studied extensively by Strassmann.[34] He defined a ratio called *return on management* (R-O-M)[35] that uses EVA as the output and a special definition of management costs as the input. An associated ratio, called information productivity, is an estimator of R-O-M that is computable from financial data readily available for publicly traded companies. Strassmann believed that management's responsibility in a company is the return of value to shareholders, and his ratios are an indicator of how productive management is in doing so. Interestingly, more than half of some 800 companies in Strassmann's 1994 sample have negative EVAs. This fact, I propose, is an indicator of a significant current business performance measurement crisis.

To the extent that management personnel perform knowledge work (Drucker and Strassmann believed that this is what management should be doing), R-O-M is a measure of a type of knowledge productivity. However, the distinction between management and nonmanagement is less clear in an information age business than it is in an industrial age one. With common control organizational structures, almost everyone, especially if they perform knowledge work, can be considered management.

Knowledge productivity as a metric for the performance of information age businesses is a new concept. Much needs to be learned about it before its value in organizing and managing such businesses can be determined. Variations of our definition, as well as other, similar metrics are being studied. It is clear, however, that metrics that enable the return on an information age business' knowledge assets to be tracked are one of the most important new tools needed to move businesses into the information age.

CONCLUSIONS

The information age is upon us, whether we like it or not. The more we understand it, the better we will be able to align our mental models with its reality. The opportunity to write this chapter has certainly helped me to appreciate what this reality might be. It has also helped me to see how rudimentary my knowledge truly is.

NOTES AND REFERENCES

[1] A. Toffler, *The Third Wave* (New York, Bantam, 1981).

[2] P. F. Drucker, *Post-capitalist Society* (New York, HarperBusiness, 1993).

[3] P. M. Senge, *The Fifth Discipline* (New York, HarperBusiness, 1993).

[4] R. E. Bohn, "Measuring and Managing Technological Knowledge," *Sloan Management Review*, Fall 1994, pp. 61–73. Bohn bases his definitions on the distinctions made by H. Cleveland in his book *The Knowledge Executive* (New York, Human Valley Books, 1995). Cleveland also distinguishes "wisdom" as a separate concept.

[5] "Software as Career Threat," *Forbes*, 22 May 1995, pp. 240–246.

[6] P. M. Romer, "Endogenous Technological Change," *Journal of Political Economy*, *98*, 1990, pp. S71–S102.

[7] *Ibid.* Economists use the term *nonrival* to refer to an input to an economic process that has this property.

[8] Bohn, *op. cit.*, Ref. 5.

[9] Drucker, *op. cit.*, Ref. 2, p. 185.

[10] *Ibid.*, p. 69.

[11] *Ibid.*, p. 39.

[12] *Ibid.*, pp. 72–73.

[13] *Ibid.*, p. 44.

[14] D. Peppers, "How Technology Has Changed Marketing," *Forbes ASAP*, April 1995, pp. 76–80.

[15] M. S. Malone, "Pennsylvania Guys Mass Customize," *Forbes ASAP*, 10 April 1995, pp. 83–85.

[16] Peppers, *op. cit.*, Ref. 15. The bicycles are actually delivered 2 weeks from when the order is placed because customers do not believe that a high-quality customized bicycle can be made and delivered so quickly.

[17] K.J. Kennedy, "The Dilemma of US Industrial Research and Development Focusing on the Short Term," *International Journal of Technology Management*, 9, pp. 15–29.

[18] J. Champy, *Reengineering Management* (New York, HarperBusiness, 1995).

[19] Drucker, *op. cit.*, Ref. 2, p. 182.

[20] T. G. Harris, "The Post-capitalist Executive: An Interview with Peter F. Drucker," *Harvard Business Review*, May/June 1993, pp. 115–122.

[21] *Ibid.*

[22] Gleckman, *op. cit.*, Ref. 24.

[23] Senge, *op. cit.*, Ref. 4.

[24] M. Goodman, "Should Growth Be a Guiding Idea for Your Organization?," in *The Fifth Discipline Fieldbook* (New York, Currency Doubleday, 1994), pp. 133–134.

[25] *Ibid.*

[26] S. R. Covey, *The Seven Habits of Highly Effective People* (New York, Fireside, 1989), pp. 52–59.

[27] Even for industrial age businesses, in the long run it does not work to provide adequate returns to invested equity at the expense of labor and knowledge.

[28] At the risk of belaboring this point, there are many examples of businesses with very efficient processes that failed miserably in the marketplace.

[29] G. S. Tjaden, S. Narasimhan, & S. Mitra, "Business Process Metrics of Effectiveness," paper presented to the Third European Academic Conference on Business Process Redesign, Cranfield University, Bedford, 21–22 February 1996.

[30] Not all the person-hours worked by an individual are necessarily spent performing the same type of work. Many knowledge workers spend some portion of their time doing service work, for example. Care must be taken to make this distinction when tallying the knowledge work person-hours.

[31] Costs for training, which produces human capital, should not be included, as knowledge work is not being performed by people undergoing training.

[32] Costs for training knowledge workers to do knowledge work and service workers to use new knowledge should be included as knowledge assets.

[33] Economic value added is a trademark of Stern, Stewart Management Services, Inc.

[34] P. A. Strassmann, *The Business Value of Computers* (New Canaan, CT, Information Economics Press, 1990).

[35] Return-on-management, R-O-M, and information productivity are trademarks of Strassmann, Inc.

chapter 2

Knowledge Capital: Management Principles for Every Organization's Five Most Valuable Assets

William H. Read
School of Public Policy
Georgia Tech

A NEW MODEL

Hardly a day goes by without some business publication, some CEO speech, or some consultant study invoking management expert Peter F. Drucker's adage that knowledge is now "the basic economic resource."[1] Suddenly, everyone seems to be discovering a new way of business: treat employees as knowledge workers, and innovate, innovate, innovate.

Favorable results flowing from reengineering, self-directed teams, and the creation of learning organizations all suggest a new business model is at hand.

The intellectual capital for this new model can be found in the work of economist Paul Romer. A proponent of "new growth theory," Romer contended that the emerging economy is based on ideas more than objects and that there is "enormous scope for discovering new ideas."[2]

To illustrate, Romer offered the "simple manufacturing process that requires you to attach 20 different parts to a frame."[3] When added together, he calculated, there are a near infinite number of different possible sequences. Where U.S. car manufacturers once thought they had figured out just about all they needed to know about assembly line production, Japanese competitors achieved advantages by empowering their workers to experiment—after all, the possibilities were nearly limitless.

The bottom line of "new growth theory" is that if we keep finding new ideas, keep innovating, and keep discovering, then there are no limits to growth. The theory holds that the process of creating ideas and innovative techniques will fuel long-run improvements and sustain an ever-improving standard of firm competitiveness.

The idea deviates from classic economic theory in which wealth creation is the result of the efficient allocation of scarce resources—financial capital, land, and labor. Moreover, it contradicts *The Principles of Scientific Management*,[5] the venerable treatise published in 1911 by Frederick Winslow Taylor. Efficient industrial organization, Taylor argued, came with the "substitution of a science for the individual judgment of the workman." By separating the planning of work from the actual work itself, Taylor believed that managers could analyze all the parts of the process and then decide on the "one best method" that workers should employ in order to guarantee maximum efficiency.

If "Taylorism" has informed earlier generations of managers, what are the principles that are to inform today's generation? One commentator wrote that "The majority of new managerial ideas—like cross-functional teams, self-managed work groups, and the networked organization—are either direct or indirect responses to the inadequacies of Taylor's original model. Yet," this commentator found, "for all the proliferation of specific techniques, the fundamental principles of a new managerial paradigm are far from clear."[6]

Perhaps. My own view is that five principles can be distilled from a study of contemporary writings and cases, and that these principles can serve the modern manager well as she or he strives for sustainable competitive advantage.

My list of principles is derived from a 3-year effort to articulate for graduate students at Georgia Tech (where I teach), concepts and practices for successful managers in the economic age of information. In developing a new course, called Knowledge-Based Management,[7] my objective was to enable students to conceptually think about the modern enterprise as a knowledge-based, information-processing organization and to further enable the students to acquire the analytical skills necessary to be successful managers of knowledge capital.

Knowledge-based organizations are the leading type of enterprise in postindustrial societies.[8] They are distinctive from industrial age organizations in that they rely principally on the intangible intellectual capital of their employees, not on the manual efforts of semiskilled workers.

They also rely on advanced information technologies to modernize their business processes. Their orientation is to the future, with emphasis on models, simulations, and system analysis. The modern firm, wrote Daniel Bell, no longer is the product of a "talented tinker" like Thomas Edison, but is the enterprise of the "postindustrial society [in which] knowledge and information become the strategic and transforming resources."[9]

My definition of a successful manager of the modern, knowledge-based firm is an individual who is capable of accomplishing two goals:

- Building and managing a firm's knowledge capital.
- Transforming the firm's industrial age processes to the postindustrial age using information technologies.

Contemporary case studies and management literature reveal that these goals are achievable when managers apply five principles:

1. Conceptualize the business.
2. Create high value enterprise know-how.
3. Organize the business around information.
4. Productively manage knowledge workers.
5. Use information technology as a *transforming resource*, use *know-that information* to create value.

These principles vary greatly from the core concepts of Taylor, who strove to impress on managers that control was the ultimate objective. Why control? Without control, Taylor saw money, materials, energy, and labor being wasted, and waste was the enemy of productivity. With control, productivity would increase and indeed with Taylorism the country experienced massive increases in productivity and standard of living. Increasingly, Taylor's scientific principles are being abandoned as "a recipe for disaster."[10] The arguments against Taylorism are that markets change too fast, rigid organizations cannot respond fast enough, and planning and execution must go hand in hand.

Although tactically valid, these criticisms miss a strategic point. If labor and capital were to be used efficiently, Taylor believed that his challenge was to empower management with a set of principles so that limited supplies of materials and energy could be put to productive use by semiskilled workers.

Materials and energy are still limited resources, but in the new economy, business theorists argue that the intellect of all knowledge workers should be tapped in order to acquire an abundance of entrepreneurial know-how. Drucker suggested that the new economy began in the

United States after World War II with enactment of the G.I. Bill,[11] which opened higher education to millions of Americans. Others cite the computer as the underlying force of the new economy, creating an information age in which the fundamental particle is the bit—not the atom.[12] Both are right. And the two work together.

Alan M. Webber, whose magazine *Fast Company*, focuses on the new economy, explains it this way:

> The revolution in information and communications technologies makes knowledge the new competitive resource. But knowledge only flows through the technology; it actually resides in people—in knowledge workers and the organizations they inhabit.[13]

Because knowledge is becoming *the* key wealth creating asset, and because high value knowledge is hard to accumulate in organizations— and even harder to organize and effectively deploy—mangers need to learn how to master the process of knowledge management. They need to become innovators in creating knowledge capital in order to achieve competitive advantage.

Typically, managers begin this process by trying to better understand all the new information and communications technologies. That is, they start with the "tools." The tools, as we know, continue to experience soaring performance and plunging cost as information technology improves by about an order of magnitude every 5 years.

However, tools are just a part of the story. Witness the very large fraction of working people who are engaged in innovative processes, as opposed to production. As Walter B. Wristen observed: "A piece of steel, whether raw or as part of a new automobile or skyscraper, is very different today from what it was a generation ago. It still contains a lot of iron mixed with other metals, but it contains a great deal more information."[14]

This paradigm shift to knowledge capital as strategic resource has been going on long enough to yield some patterns. Entry barriers are broken down, costs go down, and new things become possible. The priesthood of suppliers and experts is undermined. Power moves to customers, consumers, and users. The perception of uncertainty grows, and a sense takes hold of being on the threshold of an unpredictable future.[15]

All this suggests that managers need a new set of guideposts; a framework for thinking and acting in this new era. The five principles offered here for managing knowledge capital may be of some value in that regard (see Table 2.1).

TABLE 2.1   Growth Models for Managers

	Industrial	Post Industrial
Wealth creation	Primary managerial activity is to efficiently allocate scarce resources (land, labor, financial capital)	Primary managerial activity is to foster acts of innovation (ideas, discovery, inventiveness)
Firm structure	Hierarchy organization with command and control	Flat organization around the flow of information
Workforce	Supervised subordinates	Teams of knowledge workers
Nature of work	Tasks are planned and executed separately for mass production	Projects are integrated and outputs customized

CONCEPTUALIZE THE BUSINESS

In the industrial age, business progress was born of experimentation. The results shaped an organization's behavior, informed decisions about what to do and what not to do, and above all produced a set of assumptions about what worked and what did not. What evolved was what Drucker termed, a company's *theory of the business*.[16] Often it took years for such a theory to emerge, but when it did it could produce wondrous results.

General Motors' (GM) 70 years of prosperity and a nearly equal number of years for AT&T attest to this. GM's knowledge of the car-buying market and efficient manufacturing process, and AT&T's monopoly network-building capability were powerful and long-lasting formulas for success. However, eventually, like every business theory, these became obsolete. When that occurs, there can be a costly mismatch between what a company knows how to do and what it should do. Whereas "how-to" tools abound, the "what-to-do" issue can be devilishly difficult to address. If anything, the longevity of any *theory of the business* seems to be lessening. Arguably, the proliferation of all the many new major management techniques, of all the "how-to" tools, is a response—however effective—to the quest for winning theories on what to do.

In recent times this divide between how and what has been dramatized in corporate battles between such firms as GM and Toyota, CBS and CNN, Pan Am and British Airways, RCA and Sony. As Gary Hamel and C.K. Prahalad pointed out, "competitiveness is born in the gap between a company's resources and its manager's goals."[17] GM, CBS, Pan Am, and RCA, they noted, all had more of everything than their competitors—except "aspirations."

However, the central challenge facing knowledge-based organizations goes beyond the mere ability to articulate lofty goals, or to dream the impossible. Hamel and Prahalad agreed. To them, today's managers must be much more than experimenters in search of successful business theories; they must acquire "frames of reference"[18]—the assumptions, premises, and accepted wisdom that bound or frame a company's understanding of itself and its industry.

They must, in short, conceptualize the business; and they must conceptualize it in a way that leads to initiative and trust among their employees. In head-to-head competition, Hamel and Prahalad wrote, "competition is not just product versus product, company versus company, or trading block versus trading block. It is mind-set versus mind-set, managerial frame versus managerial frame."[19] In this sphere of competition, individual initiative is critical, and trust is crucial to achieving the participation of every individual in the organization. President Kennedy embraced these requirements when he declared that America would "put a man on the moon by the end of the decade," and thereby accelerated a technology and knowledge race, with immense implications. Komatsu's goal of "encircling Caterpillar" triggered a similar competition, as did Ted Turner's launching of CNN.

Because concepts count, managers are faced with the hardest job of all—thinking ahead. Intellectual energy, not phrase making, is needed to provide *conceptual answers* to questions like: What new products or services should we pioneer? How should we shape the future of our industry? What competencies must we build or acquire?

For every business, there are particular individuals who strive to answer such questions. In start-ups, the answers usually come from an entrepreneur, often using intuition, and a personal sense of commitment. In large organizations, the CEO, with the help of a planning staff, holds the responsibility. In times of crisis or chaos, a "czar" sometimes arrives to take command. In each case, point of view gets expressed, and the organization operates on this premise.

In the knowledge-based organization, a different model is recommended, in part because the organization's strength relies on its intangible assets, and in part because people of intellect tend to do their best work when they are intellectually motivated and involved. This does not mean that top management should avoid a unilateral conceptual statement. When Jack Welch, the CEO of General Electric (GE), said that every GE division should be number one or two in its industry, he clearly conceptualized the performance he expected. At the same time, he signaled his managers that he believed they were smart enough to achieve that goal and now had the mandate to sustain or achieve it.

One of the best illustrations of conceptualizing the business comes from Electronic Data Systems, which revisited its assumptions and direction by involving 150 key managers who, through an enormous and thoughtful effort, restated EDS's strategy in these words: globalize, informationalize, and individualize.

The EDS experience is reminiscent of efforts by successful Japanese companies. NEC's concept of "Computers and Communications" seeks synergy between industries, and "Optoelectronics" helps Sharp define new technologies and markets.

In his report on "The Knowledge-Creating Company,"[20] Ikujiro Nonaka argued that "the best Japanese companies offer a guide to organizational roles, structures, and practices that produce continuous innovation" by successfully managing the creation of new knowledge.

At the top, he said, management provides a conceptual framework. The framework may address one or more critical questions: What are we trying to learn? What do we need to know? Where should we be going? Who are we? Answers provide conceptual umbrellas ("Computers and Communications" and "Optoelectronics") or perhaps a more equivocal statement to give employees freedom of opportunity (Honda executives launched a new car initiative with the phrase, "Let's gamble").

Frontline workers, Nonaka reported, are full of tacit knowledge—expertise at the fingertips—and they are constantly encouraged to share that knowledge by making it explicit to others in the company. The role of the middle manager is to facilitate, or mediate between a company's grand concept, like Matsushita's "Human Electronics," and the efforts of frontline workers. These managers frequently use figurative language to bridge the worlds of what should be and what is. When senior Honda management said, "Let's gamble," the project team leader responded with the concept of the "theory of automobile evolution," thus challenging his colleagues to ask if a car were an organism, how would it evolve. Sometime later, this concept gave birth to the term "Tall Boy," which in turn eventually led to the Honda City, a distinctive new urban car.

There is a risk here that "Let's gamble," "Tall Boy," and "theory of automobile evolution" will ring of "sound bite" solutions to the challenge of managerial responsibility. Clearly, much more is involved, but no firm can long be successful without having a successful concept or theory of its business. That concept will have to be communicated in a way that its workforce of knowledge employees can respond to with initiative—and respond wholeheartedly because they trust that management has done its homework in this critical realm. A lack of trust incurs the worst of all responses—phony, even destablizing initiative.

Drucker instructed senior management to periodically "abandon" every organizational assumption, to study noncustomers for early signs of problems, to recognize when a firm has outgrown its theory, and to change theories before there is a crisis.[21] In an era when too often companies are catching up rather than getting out in front, this is sage advice. However, a commitment to decisive action is not enough. In Drucker's words, "To establish, maintain, and restore a theory does not require a Genghis Khan in the executive suite. It requires hard work."[22]

The effort at conceptualizing the business looks first at the industry and the environment in which it does—and will—operate. It looks next at what the firm is attempting, or should be attempting, to do. Finally, it examines the issue of firm know-how. All must fit together, and all must pass a "reality" test; that is, all must yield, what Drucker termed, "a *valid* theory of the business."[23]

Of equal importance, concepts about how to run the business must be constantly evaluated so that the business has the ability to change itself. When conceptual change is lacking, corporate culture—"the way we do things around here"—turns from being a strength to an impediment to acquiring those new competencies needed to reinvent a firm that has outlived its original concept of the business. Symptoms of having outlived an original and successful concept appear in the form of arrogance and excessive bureaucracy, and too often the treatment is a combination of defensive action and "fixes." These seldom work for long, as GM, among others, learned so painfully.

Conceptualizing is akin to the work of inventors: Great inventors, it is said, achieve their greatness with 10% inspiration and 90% perspiration. Business theories for great knowledge-based organizations require similar efforts of conceptualization and articulation.

CREATE HIGH VALUE ENTERPRISE KNOW-HOW

"In a world of increasingly global competition...the basis of competition has shifted more and more to the creation and assimilation of knowledge." So wrote Michael E. Porter, a leading theorist on business competition.[24] "Companies achieve competitive advantage," according to Porter, "through acts of innovation [that] always involve investments in skill and knowledge, as well as in physical assets and brand reputation."

Too often, however, firms view their knowledge investments narrowly, focusing mainly on proprietary intellectual assets for which they can obtain governmental protection through patents, copyrights, and trademarks. This is not to imply that intellectual property is unimportant; to the contrary it can be commercially quite valuable. The task of mangers is to use these assets wisely, deciding, for instance, when to engage in licensing agreements and under what terms.

Intellectual property is a form of what may be called migratory knowledge[25]—knowledge that can be packaged, and distributed. Unless protected, this type of knowledge cannot be relied on for sustainable competitive advantage. Competitors can engage in intelligence gathering practices, reverse engineering exercises, and hiring away key personnel in order to access this type of knowledge.

When innovation rests on this kind of knowledge, a firm must constantly strive to upgrade it, lest competitors first catch up and then bypass it. When knowledge can be packaged and distributed, it is easily transferable and can diffuse rapidly, thus yielding only temporal advantage. Relentless upgrading is the only remedy to this challenge.

There is, however, another form of knowledge that is superior in terms of competitive advantage: I call it high value enterprise know-how. High value enterprise know-how should be a principal knowledge asset of every organization.

When a firm has high value know-how, it has capabilities and competencies that are longer lasting and not easily replicated. Through investment and experience, Boeing has acquired high value enterprise know-how about commercial jet aircraft, Toyota about the production of automobiles; Microsoft about the development of software.

High value know-how can reside in individuals (a master violin maker), in groups of individuals, or teams (the scientists of the Manhattan Project), and in companies. A company, in fact, is usually a large team, or, what one observer termed, "a confederation of teams, in which enormously complex skills and knowledge are embedded in the minds of its members and in the formal and informal social relationships that orchestrate their efforts."

High value enterprise know-how goes hand in hand with a good theory; that is to say it directly complements the managerial ability to conceptualize the business. How then does a firm with a winning concept acquire high value know-how? Three possibilities can be considered: contracting with another organization, merging with or acquiring another organization, and building know-how internally.

Contracting is the least feasible method. To begin, we are not talking about knowledge that is easily packaged and distributed. Moreover, the idea of even trying to write a contact for a capability-creating relationship, with all its uncertainties and contingencies, would be exceedingly challenging, even to the most gifted attorney. Hiring a consultant might help, but in the end consultants can only advise or recommend courses of action. Put differently, you can contract for teaching, but not for learning.

Mergers and acquisitions seem more promising, although the record of such transactions presents a sober picture.[26] Alliances—something less permanent, and more focused—have become fashionable, especially when the firms involved are seeking know-how about supporting capabilities. As one executive advocate of alliances commented, "It's a dangerous thing to think we know everything."[27]

The leading option then is to build high value know-how internally, that is within the enterprise. Intuitively, every manager probably knows this. It would be reckless to think and act otherwise. However, the basic problem with autonomous efforts is that they are often too slow in a world that is too fast. This is particularly true for an established firm whose internal know-how is experiencing eroding value.

A number of good techniques have been proposed and are in use to address this problem. They include benchmarking, sharing of best practices, and the use of new technologies like groupware. Xerox, Philip Morris, and Hughes are among the companies who have used such techniques and reported favorable results.

As good as these new techniques may be, one wonders whether they will have long-lasting effects, that is, whether they will yield sustainable competitive advantages. My guess is that they will not, because most of the knowledge gained is migratory in nature and therefore is or will quickly become available to competing companies.

In searching the literature for evidence of competitively sustainable high value know-how that resides within an enterprise, I came across research on the pharmaceutical industry by Rebecca Henderson and Iain Cockburn in which they reported:

> The longevity of pharmaceutical companies attests to a unique managerial competency: the ability to foster a high level of specialized knowledge within an organization, while preventing that information from becoming embedded in such a way that it permanently fixes the organization in the past, unable to respond to an ever-changing competitive environment.[29]

This is a remarkable achievement.

In effect, these researchers found that pharmaceutical companies understand both how to create high value know-how and, equally important, how to avoid becoming prisoners of eroding know-how. Henderson and Cockburn report:

> The managers of these companies, did all the things that business pundits recommend: they used sophisticated resource-allocation procedures, hired the best people, and encouraged cross-functional and cross-disci-

plinary communications. [Moreover]...they focused on continuously refurbishing the innovative capabilities of the organization. They actively managed their companies' knowledge and resources.[30]

What was their paradigm? First, they "kept connected" to external knowledge sources including their peers, because no one company can hope to master all of its knowledge environment. Second, they allocated financial resources in a contentious, intellectual process, foregoing last-year-plus-five-percent thinking, and substituted stimulating debates that in turn stimulated the rapid transfer of information across the company. Finally, they actively managed the tension in choosing organizational design, with the most successful companies never being satisfied with any single answer. One senior manager was quoted as saying, having tried every organizational model, "We know nothing works as well as being continually aware of the need to be both at the leading edge...and in total command of the important developments in other areas."

In simpler words, high value enterprise know-how means how we do things in this company and achieve success. Of course, every good manager should adopt contemporary good business practices and processes. However, to constantly maintain high value know-how, to be in a position that enables the manager to say, "Yes, the way we do things around here gives use a competitive advantage!" requires a special managerial competency.

First, management must reach out for knowledge, internally and externally. Second, management should sponsor intellectual exercises, in which ideas are debated and constructive confrontation produces both a flow of new information and support for projects based on that information flow. Third, management should never accept an organizational design as perfect (more is said on this topic in the next section).

In combination, these steps yield high value enterprise know-how. They can produce a winning how-to formula, while lowering the risk that the formula becomes static and outmoded. With such a formula in place, a firm becomes a true learning organization—"an organization skilled at creating, acquiring, and transferring knowledge, and at modifying its behavior to reflect new knowledge and insights."[31]

This definition, offered by David A. Garvin of the Harvard Business School, brings to mind companies like Corning, GE and Honda—each of which has learned how to translate new knowledge into new ways of behaving, which is to say, into acquiring high value enterprise know-how that yields competitive advantage.

Garvin recommended a few simple steps a company can take to change itself.[32] One is to "foster an environment that is conducive to learning"—the intellectually driven budget planning of the pharmaceutical companies being an example. Another is to "open up boundaries and stimulate the exchange of ideas," because, he said, boundaries not only inhibit the flow of information, they isolate individuals and reinforce old assumptions. He also suggested creating "learning forums"— programs or events designed with explicit learning goals in mind. Again, these are ideas long embraced by the successful pharmaceutical companies and championed by some thoughtful CEO's like GE's Welch.

Garvin's principal point, embraced here, is that "high philosophy and grand themes" are—by themselves—inadequate to the challenge. Managers must engage "the gritty details of practice." Until they do, their organizations will muddle along in their "how we do it" world of yesterday, and not acquire the ability to create for themselves the unique know-how for competitive success they will need tomorrow.

ORGANIZE AROUND INFORMATION

The third principle for managing the knowledge-based organization addresses the question of organization itself.

In *Through the Organizational Looking Glass*, Charles Handy argued that "You can't plan tomorrow's organizations with today's assumptions." Writing in 1980, he foresaw a period of discontinuous change during which the assumptions we have been working with as a society and in organizations are no longer necessarily true. At issue, in Handy's view, were three questions: What causes efficiency? What work is? What value organization hierarchy has?[33]

In the 1990s, many firms were still struggling with these questions. In the intervening years, however, several clear trends have developed— levels of management have been reengineered out of existence and teams focused on projects have emerged as a model that goes beyond the matrix form of organization. Handy would hardly be surprised. He predicted that a new set of assumptions would take hold in which management viewed contractual organizations as the most efficient, that labor would be considered an asset, and organizations would evolve into communities.

The recent interest in *outsourcing* and *fees for work done*, instead of *wages for time spent*, are signs that many managers do view contractual organizations as efficient. Although some managers still believe that their employees need them more than they need their employees, that style of thinking is in fact yielding to the perception that knowledge workers are a firm's most valuable resource—and retaining those resources are critical for success. In financial service firms, for example, some "star" money managers are compensated more handsomely than top management. Perhaps the most important shift is to the concept of an organization as a community, which implies unit or team sizes in which everyone knows everyone else, and all participants share a sense of ownership (whether financial or psychological), and where authority stems from consent, not command and control.

Max Weber, the German social scientist and father of organizational theory would be appalled. At the turn of the century, Weber outlined and described the features of the bureaucracy as the ideal form of organization. Drawing on the structures of the military and the church, Weber sought to make organizations rational and efficient using four prescriptions: (a) differentiation of tasks, (b) coordination by a hierarchy of authority, (c) separation of planning and execution, and (d) the use of technical criteria for recruitment and promotion.[34]

Weber's influence is still felt today, but it has come under attack as the need for organizational learning and faster decision making have become competitive imperatives. As a consequence, decentralization is required to promote continuous self-improvement and innovation. All this has led to the evolution of teams that are assigned projects. Hence the requirement to organize and reorganize around information.

In determining what projects need to be undertaken, management must address the issue of information flow and decision making. The issue is critical because decision making improves with the quality of information. "We are rebuilding organizations around information," according to Drucker,[35] and that means information becomes a structural element. One fallacy, he warned, is reliance on the chief information officer (CIO) to determine what information is required. To Drucker, CIOs are mere toolmakers.

In knowledge-based organizations, "everyone takes[s] information responsibility...everyone asks [or should ask, in Drucker's opinion], 'Who in this organization depends on me for what information? And on whom, in turn, do I depend?'"[36] It should be the responsibility of every knowledge worker to do a personal information audit, and it should be the responsibility of every manager to act on the results of such audits.

Personal information audits can open an organization's eyes to the need to abandon the Weberian bureaucracy that has served as the foundation for traditional organizational structures (functional, divisional, and matrix). The concept of the knowledge-based organization, some say "networked" organization, differs from the traditional models in that workers with specialized know-how provide the building blocks of the organization. Cross-functional teams are assembled to address specific problems, opportunities, or needs. Autonomous work groups on assembly lines are relatively permanent. A Hollywood film production is a one-time project. Yet each is discrete with its own organizational mission. The role of top management primarily is that of strategic direction and oversight.

In this new type of organization, all kinds of boundaries get blurred, most importantly the inside and outside boundaries. Everyone is expected to deal with the environment, for there is no core to seal off the external world and thereby attempt to lessen uncertainty. Informality flourishes and expertise is valued. The main advantage of this organizational model is adaptability, and adaptability is essential in the new economy.

The challenge of the new economy is to innovate and that means entrepreneurship. This requires the new structure—the knowledge-based organization. In this organization, the individual who holds tactical and specialized knowledge will have to exercise a high degree of self-discipline, as hierarchical authority, and therefore managerial accountability, is diminished. Moreover, the knowledge worker must be responsible for communications and relationships within the context of projects, not traditional departments, as since much of the firm's work is not done there anymore.

Expected benefits of this new type of organization include increased time efficiency, improved responsiveness, adaptability as a competency, and flourishing innovation.[37] However, to achieve these benefits management must recognize that the division of labor is no longer measured by inputs and outputs, but rather by knowledge; that coordination is a team responsibility, not one of hierarchical supervision; that decision making is highly decentralized; that boundaries are porous and changing; that the organizational structure is highly informal; and that, above all, the basis of authority is knowledge.

Because all organizations exist to enable a group of people to effectively coordinate their efforts and get things done, the shaping of a knowledge-based organization is a top priority of management. Executives need to focus on identifying what the informational requirements will be to achieve the objectives of the projects at hand, and then to organize around those requirements. In Hollywood and on Wall Street, in Japanese factories and in research universities, in consulting firms and many entrepreneurial firms, the concept of the knowledge-based organization with its unifying flow of information is the norm. Yet it is far from being widely accepted. There is some peril in this, for as Handy concluded, when he peered through the "organizational looking glass" more than a decade and a half ago, "Many traditional operators will wake up one morning to find themselves obsolete."[38]

PRODUCTIVELY MANAGE KNOWLEDGE WORKERS

The fact is, more and more jobs—no matter what the title—are taking on the contours of "knowledge work." People at all levels of the organization must combine the mastery of some highly specialized technical expertise with the ability to work effectively in teams, form productive relationships with clients and customers, and critically reflect on and then change their own organizational practices. And the nuts and bolts of management— whether of high-powered consultants or service representatives, senior managers or factory technicians—increasingly consists of guiding and integrating the autonomous but interconnected work of highly skilled people.[39]

How far different is today's managerial challenge than in the era of Frederick Winslow Taylor, the turn of the century expert on work, who considered workers as nothing more than "dumb oxen?"

Of course, Taylor's harsh judgment has been considerably modified over the years, first in the classic Hawthorne Experiments of Elton Mayo,[40] who concluded that worker output was affected not only by a job's scientific design, but also by social norms, and later by Frederick Herzberg's pioneering research on motivation and job satisfaction.[41]

If Mayo and Herzberg's findings weakened the influence of the classic school, the sociotechnical systems theory that originated with a group of British researchers at the Tavistock Institute of Human Relations provided the breakthrough to new thinking about involving employees in the planning as well as the execution of work.[42] Early experiments of this theory were successfully conducted in the United States at plants in Topeka, Kansas by General Foods, in Jamestown, New York, by Cummins Engine, and Lima, Ohio, by Procter & Gamble.

As the contours of *knowledge work* was spreading to the factory floor, another phenomenon was also becoming evident: The professional worker was growing in numbers and occupations. What historically had been known as the learned professions (clergy, educators, lawyers, and physicians), now included proliferating numbers of accountants, brokers, consultants, data processors, engineers, financial analysts, and so on. Workers who made and moved things were declining in number as workers who talked on the phone, used computers, wrote reports, and attended meetings were on the rise. In short, a new balance was being struck between the workforce of traditional blue-collar employees and knowledge workers. With this new balance came two questions: First, how should management adjust? Second, how should the worker adjust?

For both management and knowledge workers, these are difficult questions. Both may agree that increased productivity would serve their mutual interest, but measuring the productivity of a knowledge worker can be difficult, if not impossible. Is a surgeon to be judged on how many operations he or she performs in a month, or how many patients recover to live long, useful lives? Quality of performance is therefore often more important than quantity.

Even more challenging is the fact that knowledge workers cannot easily be supervised, for by definition they possess specialized knowledge; that is, they know better than their "superiors" how to do what they are most qualified to do—write a software program, trade futures, prepare a tax filing, create advertising copy, or repair a nuclear reactor. This undermines traditions of hierarchical authority and managerial control. Studies have shown that knowledge workers do not perceive themselves as subordinates. To the contrary, they highly value operational autonomy, their preferred option being to have freedom to work within a set of rules.[43]

How then is a manager to go about guiding and integrating the work of knowledge workers in ways that are beneficial to the firm's successful performance? The answer is to productively manage the knowledge worker—our fourth principle for managing the knowledge-based organization. To act on this principle, a set of recommendations is offered.

- *Focus* the knowledge worker on doing what she or he does best—and eliminate the rest. Engineers who spend more time doing paperwork than at their workstations will underperform, and probably be less happy.

  One technique to achieve *focus* is to use the "best work" method,[44] in which the knowledge worker provides a quarterly letter to management. The employee answers four questions: What was your best work of the last quarter? What was its objective? Why was this your best work? How could you have done better? The best work method is simply a technique to help insure that the knowledge worker stays focused because in the end concentration counts.
- *Establish a partnership* with your knowledge workers, so that both parties have clear responsibilities. Ask knowledge workers, for example, to take responsibility for results, and you in turn take responsibility for providing the knowledge worker with the information and tools she or he will need to do the job.

  Having the right information is particularly important, as Benjamin M. Compaine and John F. McLaughlin reported in their study, "Management Information: Back to Basics." In a new job, they wrote

[You] should recognize the need to adjust the sources of information [you] are receiving from that which had been flowing to the previous holder of the job. The individual's personal information system is determined in large measure by that person's own knowledge, which is probably different from his predecessor's.

• *Team knowledge workers* with colleagues that fit each particular project. This is important for two reasons. First, management's job is to provide strategic direction. It has to say what needs to be done, and what it needs its workers to accomplish, and why. When these questions are fully answered, the right kind of knowledge team can be assembled. Second, highly skilled knowledge workers value achievement and are more likely to remain committed to a firm where that value is fulfilled.

In building a team, management must be good at both managing individuals and at being able to combine different kinds of knowledge. The latter is important to create effective cross-functional teams; the former requires individual placement based on an individual's unique competencies, as opposed to just credentials. There can be a major difference in deciding a team placement between, say, two senior engineers with identical credentials, but with different competencies (viz., one is decisive under pressure whereas the other tends to procrastinate).

Studies of team performance stress urgency and direction, skills over personalities, setting clear rules of behavior, paying particular attention to the kick-off phase, getting some early results, getting good feedback, and challenging the team with new information and fresh facts. When managed well, teams of knowledge workers can and do achieve high performance.[46]

• *Provide training and educational opportunities* so that every knowledge worker can maintain and improve her or his skills and competencies. In addition, Michael Hammer, coauthor of *Re-Engineering the Corporation*, advised companies to "quintuple their investment in education...[because] everybody who works in a company needs to understand the business."[47]

Workers themselves understand the need for training and education; indeed one study found that personal growth was the highest motivation among knowledge workers. In recognition of this, companies like Motorola and Intel operate their own "universities" where employee knowledge workers often serve as instructors. Asking knowledge workers to teach others is an excellent idea, for teachers reap many rewards, not the least of which is that it compels them to deepen their own expertise.

• *Understand that knowledge work is different* than the work of management. Too often firms fail to recognize the difference and make the mistake of promoting a very good knowledge worker into the ranks of management, only to find that he or she is not cut out for it. Knowledge workers have specialized expertise, which usually is very different than the skills required of a good manager. Of course, some individuals possess both—but not all.

The problem here is with the traditional promotion system. When the corporate ladder is the only means to get ahead, the risk is real that a knowledge worker will be promoted beyond his or her competence. It happens all the time. To deal with this issue, firms will have to adopt pay policies based on knowledge or skill, not just on the number of people supervised or level of corporate responsibility.[48]

For their part, knowledge workers will have to understand that "a successful career will no longer be about promotion." Said Hammer, "It will be about mastery."[49]

Each of these techniques—focus the knowledge worker on what she or he does best, establish partnerships in which each party accepts responsibility, form teams that fit the task, provide learning opportunities, and understand that knowledge workers do not necessarily have managerial skills—will enable the knowledge worker and the firm to collectively work smarter and thereby work more productively.

USE INFORMATION TECHNOLOGY AS A TRANSFORMING RESOURCE, USE *KNOW-THAT INFORMATION* TO CREATE VALUE

Over the past 30 years, the design and management of IT [information technology] resources concentrated on the "T"—technology—and largely ignored the "I"—information. This approach reflects the roots of IT architecture and management in the mainframe era, when technology processed "data" and people processed "information" and "knowledge."[50]

As information technology has evolved and continues to evolve—it has two significant implications for management of knowledge capital. First, IT can be used as a resource to transform the nature of work. Second, IT can be used to create value through the timely sharing of what I call *know-that information*. Work transformation and *know-that value creation* can come together as is illustrated by the following excerpt from *The New York Times*:

Workers like John A. Cruz are the great hope for old corporate center cities like Hartford, and perhaps their greatest threat as well: He's been liberated from his office. Rootless, mobile, armed with 120 megabytes in his briefcase, Mr. Cruz—a 32-year-old account executive at Travelers Insurance—is one of the new breed of high-tech nomads who are changing the face and the culture of many companies....They specialize in being anywhere and nowhere. Mr. Cruz has done computer insurance audits in parking lots and at restaurant counters. His laptop computer is actually used on his lap....

Under fierce pressure to cut costs, insurance executives say that two important insights make the mobile workforce irresistible. First, insurance is essentially a disembodied product anyway, ideally suited to being electronically blipped, faxed and phoned from one place to another, without regard to place. The second is that all the apparatus of modern telecommunications—laptops, modems, cellular phones, voice mail, electronic mail and beepers—keeps everyone in touch all the time and lets managers tract non-office workers and their performance even more closely than people sitting just down the hall.[51]

A key lesson to be learned here is that every organization has storehouses of *know-that information*, the kind of stuff that lets John Cruz do insurance audits by tapping into a remote company database. Besides financial data, a typical database might hold valuable *know-that information* on a firm's best customers and their buying habits. Employees themselves can be valuable storehouses of *know-that information* on what works and what does not. Information technology can help "mine" the first, and facilitate the timely transfer of the second.

One illustration is the American Express program to build customer loyalty. The company "mines" its "data warehouses" and learns that among its best customers, Joe Smith regularly dines at fine French restaurants. In Joe's next bill, he receives a "thank you" coupon from American Express good for a complimentary dinner at one of his favorite French bistros.

Another, albeit somewhat different example, can be found at McKinsey & Company, which has over 12,000 documents in its computerized Practice Development Network (PDNet). When a McKinsey director in Sydney recently needed to quickly start up an engagement for an important new consulting client, PDNet yielded 179 relevant documents that put at his fingertips the *know-that information* of more than 60 of the firm's consulting professionals worldwide.

As every manager knows, information technology continues to sweep through the economy. Moreover, there is a general understanding that the information revolution is not just about computers, but rather about a spectrum of convergent computer and communications technologies that increasingly can be networked.

For some time, business people have sought to understand the implications of this revolution. Some have focused on the way it alters the rules of competition, others on how it creates competitive advantage, and still others on how information technology can create a new business opportunity, or even a new business.

With technological advances in IT constantly yielding improving price–performance ratios, managers face an ever-changing technological marketplace. Just when the general manager seemed to have grasped the concepts of mainframe computing, PC-networked and client-server architecture burst on the scene. Meantime, at the leading edge are even more powerful new tools like knowledge-based systems, an application that can store, retrieve, and analyze vast amounts of information and data to accomplish such tasks as forecasting stock trends, diagnosing equipment problems, and designing new products.[52]

In 1958, a year when large companies were installing their first computers to automate routine tasks, Harold J. Leavitt and Thomas L. Whisler made some predictions about what corporate life with the computer would be like in the future. Their article, "Management in the 1980s,"[53] foresaw that the role and scope of middle managers would change and that top management would take on more responsibility for innovating, planning, and creating. Leavitt and Whisler, in retrospect, were pretty good at predictions.

Looking ahead, what can be expected about corporate life and information technologies in the 21st century? Based on what we know about the previously discussed dimensions of the knowledge-based organization, we can expect that IT will serve to focus corporate energies on projects, not tasks and on processes, not procedures. We can expect that IT will contribute to innovation and to the redefinition of how work is done.

One group of experts expects that "companies of the future will closely resemble professional service firms today. The most successful firms attract and retain employees by providing an environment that is intellectually engaging. The work is challenging, the projects diverse, and the relationships with clients fairly independent."[54]

I agree. In the course I teach at Georgia Tech on Knowledge-based Management, one of the first cases my students read is about Mutual Benefit Life, the country's 18th-largest life insurance company, which abandoned its rigid, sequential applications process and substituted a case manager system. Instead of the old multistep process involving credit checking, quoting, rating, underwriting, and so on, Mutual Benefit created a new position, a single individual to handle all these matters, with the support of powerful PC-based workstations that run an expert system and connect to a range of automated systems on a mainframe.

The result: These knowledge workers, called case managers at Mutual Benefit, can complete an application in hours, not weeks; they handle twice the volume of new applications the company previously could process; and the company was able to eliminate 100 field office positions.

Mutual Benefit Life is a clear example of how work can be transformed using information technology. However, it is also clear from this case, as well as others, that technology is only a tool—a piece of infrastructure that enables (some prefer "empowers") knowledge workers to attain high performance results.

Michael Hammer, a leading theorist and advisor on reengineering work, recognized the value of information technology as a tool. His key reengineering principles include having the organization that produces information also process it; having the classic conflict between centralization and decentralization reconciled using online databases, telecommunications networks, and standardized processing systems to get the benefits of scale and coordination, while maintaining the benefits of flexibility and service; and by having workers become self-managing and self-controlling by using IT that has built-in monitors and controls.

All this suggests the potency of IT in the knowledge-based organization, but it should not suggest that *technology* alone will become the 21st-century "silver bullet" of competitive advantage. Indeed the paradox of information technology is that, although technology becomes ever more important, it cannot become, as one observer concluded, "management's primary solution."[56] The reason is straightforward: Technology is "every competitor's potential solution," as well. This is especially true as the technology rapidly diffuses as a consequence of continuous scientific advancement.

On the other hand, *know-that information* that is associated with technology can create significant value for the postindustrial firm, even competitive advantage. Examples would include electronic commerce and new information-based products, such as financial derivatives.

In their research on "Managing in the Marketspace," J. F. Rayport and J. J. Sviokla[57] noted: "Information technology adds or alters content, changes the context of the interaction and enables the delivery of varied content and a variety of contexts over different infrastructures."

Consider what happens, for instance, when a newspaper is no longer a printed product, but an electronic service—and the disaggregated content of the "newspaper"—the newspaper's *know-that information*—is distributed by an intermediary like America Online. A different technological infrastructure is used, a different context is provided, and the consequence is a different value proposition from that of the traditional newspaper.

Clearly, managing in marketspace will require new thinking and a better understanding of what is possible by managers. Anthony G. Oettinger's study of the "Information Evolution"[58] finds that changing

TABLE 2.2.   Checklist: Knowledge Capital Management

	Ask	Act
Business concept	Is my part of the business conceptually sound?	Form an "A Team" to evaluate the current business concept; form a "B Team" to propose alternate business concept(s).
Know-how	Does my part of the business have know-how that is competitively sustainable?	Have "A Team" evaluate; have "B Team" propose alternatives.
Organization	Does the flow of information in my part of the business foster or hinder innovation?	Make two lists. List the innovations in your organization during the last year. Make a second list of innovations you wish your organization had achieved during the year. Now, ask again the question about the flow of information.
People	Do I supervise subordinates, or do I coach a team of individuals who have specialized knowledge?	If you "supervise," get help learning how to coach. As a good coach, focus not only on the team but on the personal growth of each team member, as well.
Information technology	Is our IT focus on the "T" (technology) or on the "I" (information)?	Commit to developing three value creating know-that information projects in the next 90 days.

technology offers new possibilities in business for different "bundles" of information (e.g., printed vs. electronic newspapers) and that decision makers will need to focus carefully on the basic information "building blocks" as they seek to create information value.

In sum, information technology and *know-that information* are vital to the knowledge-based organization, and the two are more and more closely associated. From a technological perspective, opportunities are at hand to transform the way individual and organizational work can be more effectively and efficiently accomplished. From the perspective of information substance associated with technology, the challenge for managers is to harness the organization's *know-that information* so that it creates value for the firm (see Table 2.2).

A FINAL WORD

For traditional industrial organizations there exists a set of well-defined metrics to measure firm performance. Accounting and financial measures have been developed in considerable detail, they are well understood, and they are widely applied. For postindustrial organizations, ways to measure performance are at best emerging.

Important work in this regard is underway at Georgia Tech by my colleague, Dr. Gary Tjaden. Elsewhere, an interim approach, called the "balanced scorecard,"[59] has been developed by Robert S. Kaplan and David P. Norton. The "scorecard" recognizes that, although financial measures worked well in the industrial era, by themselves they are insufficient tools for providing performance feedback in the postindustrial firm. "They are out of step," Kaplan and Norton said, "with the skills and competencies companies are trying to master today."

Their solution is to marry financial measures with operational data on customer satisfaction, on internal processes, and on the firm's innovative and improvement activities. This kind of scorecard, they found, "tracks the key elements of a company's strategy—from continuous improvement and partnerships to teamwork and global scale."[60]

Without fully developed new measuring tools, those who prefer to manage by the numbers ("If you can't count it, you can't manage it!!!") may be frustrated. Still, these are truly exciting times in business.

New found commitments to initiative, creativity, and entrepreneurship are underpinning a quiet revolution that is taking place in many firms, even as cost-cutting, downsizing, and de-layering attract greater attention, particularly in the media. Quietly the command and control organization is giving way to the knowledge-based organization, and both the firm and its workers will be better for it.

Work becomes more rewarding when firms adopt policies that enable employees to grow personally and professionally, and to take responsibility for the success of their projects. At the same time, the firm's leadership must take responsibility for creating the environment in which this can occur. To do this, I have recommended five principles that managers can use. They can conceptualize the business, create high value enterprise know-how, organize around information, productively manage knowledge workers, and use information technology as a transforming resource; use *know-that information* to create value.

These principles constitute a new paradigm for a new age—the age in which knowledge capital is the strategic wealth-creating resource.

NOTES AND REFERENCES

[1] P. F. Drucker, *Post-Capitalist Society* (New York, HarperCollins, 1993).

[2] See interview with P. Romer, *Forbes ASAP*, (June 5, 1995), p. 66(6).

[3] Ibid.

[4] "If you calculate all the possible different sequences for attaching those 20 parts, you get 10(18)," according to Romer. "That number is about the same as the number of seconds since the big bang. So you get these amazingly large number of possibilities out of even extremely simple systems." *Forbes ASAP* (June 5, 1995), p. 68.

[5] F. W. Taylor, *The Principles of Scientific Management* (New York, Harper, 1911).

[6] D. H. Freedman, "Is Management Still a Science," *Harvard Business Review*, November/December 1992, pp. 26–35.

[7] "Knowledge-Based Management" is a second-year course offered by Professor William H. Read in the Graduate Schools of Management and Public Policy at the Georgia Institute of Technology. Copies of the syllabus are available on request.

[8] See D. Bell, *The Coming of the Post-Industrial Society* (New York, Basic Books, 1968).

[9] D. Bell, "Communications Technology for Better or for Worse," *Harvard Business Review*, May/June 1979., pp. 76–79.

[10] Freedman, *op. cit.*

[11] Drucker, *op cit.*

[12] Nicholas Negroponte, Director of the MIT Media Lab, is credited with the observation that the "bit, not the atom" is today's fundamental particle. See Special Issue, "Welcome to Cyberspace," *Time*, Spring 1995, pp. 23–29, 62.

[13] A. M. Webber, "What's So New About the New Economy?," *Harvard Business Review*, January/February 1993, pp. 24–34.

[14] W. B. Wristen, *The Twilight of Sovereignty: How the Information Revolution is Transforming Our World* (New York, Charles Scribner's Sons, 1992).

[15] See, for example, J. C. B. LeGates, "The Sound, the Fury, and the Significance," *Incidental Paper*, Harvard Program on Information Resources Policy, January 1995.

[16] P. F. Drucker, "The Theory of the Business," *Harvard Business Review*, September/October 1994, pp. 95–105.

[17] G. Hamel, & C. K. Prahalad, "Strategy as Stretch and Leverage," *Harvard Business Review*, March/April 1993, pp. 75–85.

[18] *Ibid.*, pp. 75–85.

[19] *Ibid.*, pp. 75–85.

[20] I. Nonaka, "The Knowledge-Creating Company," *The Harvard Business Review*, November/December 1991, pp. 96–85.105.

[21] Drucker, *op cit. 16*.pp. 96–85.105.

[22] *Ibid.*, pp. 96–85.105.

[23] *Ibid.*, pp. 96–85.105.

[24] M. E. Porter, "The Competitive Advantage of Nations," *Harvard Business Review*, March/April 1990, pp. 73–94.

[25] For a discussion of "migratory knowledge," see J. L. Badaracco, Jr., *The Knowledge Link* (Boston, Harvard Business School, 1991), Ch. 2.

[26] See, for example, M. E. Porter, "From competitive advantage to corporate strategy," *Harvard Business Review*, May/June 1987, in which a select record of corporate diversification is examined, pp. 43–59.

[27] J. Kuehler, President of IBM, quoted in Badaracco, *op cit.*, p. 107.

[28] Prepared presentations, "The Knowledge Imperative Symposium," organized by Arthur Anderson and The American Productivity & Quality Center, Houston, September 1995.

[29] R. Henderson, "Managing Innovation in the Information Age," *Harvard Business Review*, January/February 1994, pp. 100–106.

[30] *Ibid.*, pp. 100–106.

[31] D. A. Garvin, "Building a Learning Organization," *Harvard Business Review*, July/August 1993, pp. 78–92.

[32] *Ibid.*, pp. 78–92.

[33] C. Handy, "Through the organizational looking glass," *Harvard Business Review*, January/February 1980, pp. 56–63.

[34] M. Weber, "The Theory of Social and Economic Organization, Ed. A. D. Henderson, & T. Parsons (New York, Free Press, 1946 translation).

[35] P. F. Drucker, "The Coming of the New Organization," *Harvard Business Review*, January/February 1988, pp. 45–54.

[36] *Ibid.*, pp. 45–54.

[37] See "Note on Organization Structure," *Harvard Business School*, 9-491-083, 24 March 1992, Exhibit 7, p 19.

[38] Handy, *op. cit.*

[39] C. Argyris, "Teaching Smart People How to Learn," *Harvard Business Review*, May/June 1991, pp. 99–110.

[40] E. Mayo, *The Human Problems of an Industrial Civilization* (New York, Viking, 1933).

[41] F. Herzberg, *et al.*, *The Motivation to Work* (New York, Wiley, 1959).

[42] E. L. Trist, "The Sociotechnical Perspective," in A. H. Van de Ven, & F. J. William, eds., *Perspectives on Organization Design and Behavior* (New York, Wiley, 1981), Ch. 2.

[43] See, for example, M. Tampoe, "Motivating Knowledge Workers—The Challenge for the 1990s," *Long Range Planning*, Vol. 26, No. 3., 1993.

[44] B. R. Helton, "The Best Work Method of Knowledge Worker Assessment," *IM*, September/October 1988, pp. 36–47.

[45] B. M. Compaine & J. F. McLaughlin, "Management Information: Back to Basics," Program on Information Resources Policy, Harvard University, Cambridge, MA, July 1986.

[46] J. R. Katzenbach & D. K. Smith, *The Wisdom of Teams* (Boston, Harvard Business School Press, 1993).

[47] *Wall Street Journal*, 24 January 1995, p. B1.

[48] See, for example, E. Ingram, "The Advantage of Knowledge-Based Pay," *Personnel Journal*, April 1990, pp. 138–141; M. White, "Linking Compensation to

Knowledge Will Pay Off in the 1990s," *Planning Review,* November/December 1991, pp. 15–18.

[49] *Wall Street Journal, op. cit.* 47.

[50] L. M. Applegate, "Designing and Managing the Information Age IT Architecture," *Harvard Business School Note,* 9-196-005, 26 September 1995.

[51] "High-Tech Mobile Workers Transform Face of the Culture of Companies," *The New York Times,* 8 February 1994, p. C19.

[52] See, for example, S. Hedberg, "New Knowledge Tools," *Byte,* July 1993, pp. 106–112.

[53] H. J. Leavitt & T. L. Whisler, "Management in the 1980s," *Harvard Business Review,* November/December 1958, pp. 62–71.

[54] L. M. Applegate, J. I. Cash, Jr., & D. Q. Mills, "*I*nformation Technology and Tomorrow's Manager," *Harvard Business Review,* November/December 1988, pp. 128–137.

[55] M. Hammer, "Reengineering Work: Don't Automate, Obliterate," *Harvard Business Review,* July/August 1990, pp. 104–113.

[56] K. B. Clark, "What Strategy Can do for Technology," *Harvard Business Review,* November-December 1989, pp. 94–99.

[57] Rayport, J. F., J. J. Sviokla, "Managing in the Marketspace," *Harvard Business Review,* November/December 1994, pp. 141–151.

[58] A. G. Oettinger "The Information Evolution: Building Blocks and Bursting Bundles," Harvard Program on Information Resources Policy, P-89-5, August 1989.

[59] R. S. Kaplan & D. P. Norton, "The Balanced Scorecard—Measures that Drive Performance," *Harvard Business Review,* January/February 1992, pp. 71–80.

[60] *Ibid.,* pp. 71–80.

chapter 3

Mass Customization in the Age of Information: The Case for Open Engineering Systems

Timothy W. Simpson
Uwe Lautenschlager
Farrokh Mistree
Systems Realization Laboratory
Georgia Institute of Technology

OUR FRAME OF REFERENCE

T he United States, despite possessing abundant resources of all kinds and having at one time "made half the manufactured products sold anywhere in the world,"[1] now faces an agile and unforgiving global marketplace in which the formerly all-important concept of economies of scale is now a thing of the past. To be effective in today's market, companies must have an intimate *knowledge* of their customers' changing demands and wishes and be flexible enough to quickly respond to them; *flexibility only comes when information feeds the ability to exploit it.*[2] It is only with the advent of the Information Revolution that we have begun to harness the power of the nearly limitless amounts of information which exist. Take for instance Kao Corporation, Japan's biggest soap and cosmetics company—the sixth largest in the world. Kao's network and information system allows them to deliver goods to any of 280,000 shops, whose average order is just seven items, within 24 hours; their information network "virtually eliminates the lag between an event in the market...and the arrival of hews to the company."[3]

One of the consequences of the Information Revolution is that information is virtually limitless. Given that we can access the necessary information then, we as designers must ask ourselves, *how can companies such as Kao provide increased product variety at less cost in a highly competitive, rapidly changing marketplace?* We believe that the key to future U.S. competitiveness lies in the development of open engineering systems and the infrastructure to sustain them. We define open engineering systems as follows.

> Open engineering systems are systems of industrial products, services, and/or processes that are readily adaptable to changes in their environment which enable producers to remain competitive in a global marketplace through continuous improvement and indefinite growth of an existing technological base.

We believe that inherent benefits of designing open engineering systems include *increased quality, decreased time-to-market, improved customization,*

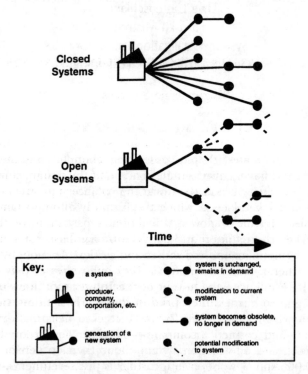

FIGURE 3.1   Open and Closed Engineering Systems

and *increased return on investment* which are enhanced through the system's capability to be adapted to change.

Consider the following analogy: Like a species that cannot adapt itself to a changing environment, a system that cannot be adapted to changing customer demands becomes extinct. (See Figure 3.1.) In Figure 3.1, the behavior of open and closed engineering systems is depicted in the context of a marketplace with rapidly changing consumer demands. When customer demands change, the company producing open engineering systems can quickly adapt their products to meet these new demands; the company producing closed engineering systems must create entirely new systems. The flexibility of open engineering systems enables them to satisfy a variety of customer demands, and their adaptability eliminates the need for new systems to be produced to accommodate a shift or change in the market. In addition, the company producing open engineering systems has the advantage of *quickly*, and more importantly *economically*, adapting to change and responding to the new market than does a company producing closed engineering systems. The *capability to adapt* enables the company producing open engineering systems to decrease its time-to-market and increase its return on investment while also increasing quality.

OUR FOUNDATION FOR OPEN ENGINEERING SYSTEMS

Examples of the Open Engineering Systems Philosophy in the Literature

Our philosophy of open engineering systems is echoed throughout the literature, whether it be in operations research, computer science, marketing and management, or design itself.[4] In design, for example, Wheelwright and Clark[5] suggest designing "platform projects" which are capable of meeting the needs of a core group of customers but are easily modified into derivatives through addition, substitution, or removal of features. Similarly, Uzumeri and Sanderson[6] emphasize standardization and flexibility as a means for enhancing *product flexibility*. At Black & Decker, marketing executive Gary T. DiCamillo stresses that the key is *commonality;* "We don't need to reinvent the power tool in every country, but rather, we have a common product and adapt it to individual markets."[7] Take, for example, the Black & Decker heatgun which, in its third generation, evolved into a comprehensive design family of variants, ranging from a basic single temperature/air flow version to a top-of-the-line version with several controllable heat settings and airflow rates.[8]

The variety-importance cost map was introduced recently by Ishii and his coauthors[9] to help minimize the life-cycle cost associated with offering product variety. This work has been further elaborated to include metrics for measuring the costs of offering product variety.[10] Chen and her coauthors[11] suggest designing *flexible products* which can be readily adapted in response to large changes in customer requirements by changing a small number of components or modules. Meanwhile, Rothwell and Gardiner[12] advocate robust designs as a means to improve system flexibility. They assert that robust designs have sufficient inherent design flexibility or "technological slack" to enable them to evolve into a *design family of variants* which meet a variety of changing market requirements. In a later article, Rothwell and Gardiner[13] give several examples of robust designs and show how they "allow for change because essentially they contain the basis for not just a single product but rather a whole product family of uprated or derated variants."

Some Basic Elements of Open Engineering Systems Design

The basic premise in designing an open engineering system is to get a quality product to market quickly and then remain competitive in the marketplace through continuous development of the product line. This can be done by developing a common baseline model where continuous improvement of the product allows several generations (i.e., *families*) of systems to be developed around the baseline model. The IBM PC is an excellent example of this; however, the success of the IBM PC as an open engineering system was more serendipitous than planned. In order to reproduce this type of success for future open engineering systems, a foundation needs to be developed for designing, realizing, sustaining, and retiring a *family* of systems which satisfy the changing needs of customers.

We believe the design of open engineering systems relies heavily on three things: (a) increasing design knowledge in the early stages of design,[14] (b) maintaining design freedom in the early stages of design, and (c) increasing efficiency throughout the design process (see Figure 3.2). Particular attention should be paid to the change in shape of the design knowledge and freedom curves in the figure. The design knowledge curve is compressed because we want to get the product to market more quickly. Notice, however, that we want to maintain design freedom longer; thus, the design freedom curve is drawn differently with only a gradual decrease at the beginning.

By spending a larger portion of time in conceptual design as shown in Figure 3.2 and by maintaining design freedom and increasing design knowledge, design changes (especially those that occur during later design stages) can be avoided, and a potential time savings and greater return on investment can be achieved. Moreover, *rework* can be elimi-

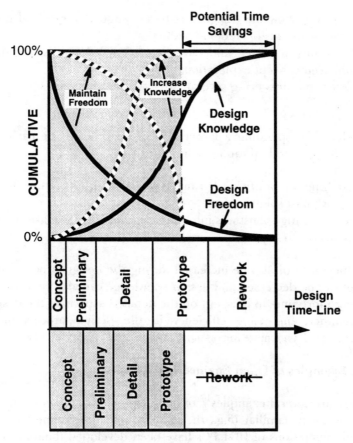

**FIGURE 3.2.   Reducing Time-to-Market by Increasing
Design Knowledge and Maintaining Design Freedom**

nated from the design process because maintaining design freedom and increasing design knowledge helps prepare for unforeseen changes in the later stages of design and facilitates adaptation to these changes. By maintaining design freedom and increasing design knowledge, *system flexibility is enhanced.*

In our work, we have identified the following ways to increase design knowledge and maintain design freedom in the early stages of design. By spending a larger portion of time in the early design stages, design knowledge can be increased by:

- determining how the design variables affect the system performance by identifying key design drivers and the significance of the design variables;

- examining how the design variables change as a result of different design scenarios or trade-off studies;
- developing a better understanding of the design space through enhanced concept exploration; and
- posing and answering several "what-if" questions during the design process.

Similarly, by spending a larger portion of time in the early design stages, design freedom can be maintained by:

- searching for satisficing,[15] ranged sets of solutions rather than optimal or point solutions; and
- incorporating robustness into the design process to make the design insensitive to adjustments or changes.

If efficiency can also be increased during the design process, time-to-market can be decreased and design knowledge can also be increased by allowing more time to be spent on the detailed aspects of the design. In this manner, increasing efficiency in the design process increases effectiveness[16] and, more importantly, improves the quality of a design.

Some Examples of Open Engineering Systems

There are several examples[17] of open engineering systems with which many of us are familiar (e.g., the IBM PC and the Boeing 747 series). Several generations of IBM PCs have been developed (built around the Intel 80286, 80386, and 80486 chips), and the modularity of the components allows many variations to occur within each generation. Similarly, the Boeing 747-200, 747-300, 747-400, and 747-SP share a strong technological family resemblance; few would argue with Boeing's view either of the family or the models within the family.[18]

Another example of an open engineering system is being developed at the University of Illinois at Urbana-Champaign (UIUC). They have established the Machine Tool Agile Manufacturing Research Institute (MT-AMRI)[19] which offers several software testbeds available over the Internet. The modular design of the testbeds allows industrial users running "in-house" software packages to augment their resources and capabilities using various computer resources from UIUC across the Internet. Open engineering systems such as these are becoming more and more prevalent; they have only been made possible by the Information Revolution.

Characteristics of Open Engineering Systems

We assert that open engineering systems can be readily adapted to changes in their comprehensive environment. Ideally, the system (which includes the product, process, and/or service as well as the producers and the customers) should be readily adaptable to any or all of the following changes:

- *Changes in the market*—includes any change in taste of the average consumer. For example, consumer taste changed from excess in the 1980s to eco-consciousness in the 1990s. In a highly commercialized culture such as ours, companies themselves are largely responsible for fueling this type of change.
- *Changes in customer needs/requirements*—includes any changes inflicted by the customer separate from those inflicted by the market. For example, a person owns a simple desktop copy machine and then wants a copier which can sort and collate copies as well as have an automatic document feeder. In this case, customer requirements have changed and the original copier is no longer sufficient even though it still works.
- *Changes in technology*—include any advancements that can improve a system's function. In this way, a faster chip represents a change in a computer's technological environment, but at the same time CD innovations do not represent a change in a phonograph's technological environment. The advent of CD technology, in fact, forced a change in the phonograph's market environment.
- *Changes in resources*—includes those that affect the manufacture of a product and those that affect the performance of a product. Resource changes that affect manufacturability include changes in the availability of manufacturing materials, manpower, etc. Resource changes that affect performance include changes in the availability of fuel (cells) needed to power a product, availability of mating products, etc.
- *Changes in the system environs*—includes all changes in the immediate physical environment of a system. Examples of such changes are the increased temperature on a machine shop floor during a hot day, the changing tides of a body of water by a dock, and a temperature drop in an automobile which is driven from Death Valley to Alaska.
- *Changes in the government/legislation*—includes changes in state and federal regulations, such as air quality standards, as well as changes in any laws that might restrict consumer use (e.g., changing FAA

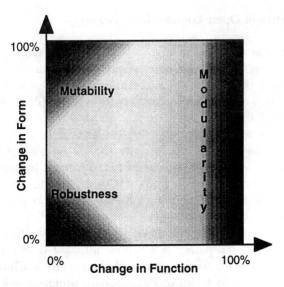

**FIGURE 3.3.   Relationship Diagram for Open
Engineering System Characteristics**

regulations which affects the aircraft industry or increased safety standards for the automotive industry).

Only some of these changes can be predicted; therefore, flexibility of options must be maintained to enable systems to be adapted to change successfully. There are several ways to realize this flexibility in an open engineering system, but remember, this *flexibility comes only when there is sufficient information to exploit.* We believe that this flexibility can be achieved through one of three characteristics—modularity, mutability, and robustness—as depicted in Figure 3.3. These three characteristics can be classified according to their influence on the system's form and function as illustrated by the two axes in the figure. The horizontal axis is **change in function** which ranges from 0% to 100% and indicates how much the function changes. The vertical axis is **change in form** which also ranges from 0% to 100%, indicating how much the form changes. The gray shading indicates the influence of each characteristic with regard to either a change in function or a change in form. We define each of these characteristics as follows:

- *Robustness* is the capability of the system to function properly despite small environmental changes or noise. Robustness implies an insensitivity to small variations and does not dictate a change in form nor a change in function.

- *Modularity* is the relationship between a product's functional and physical structures such that there is (a) a one-to-one correspondence between the functional and physical structures, and (b) a minimization of unintended interactions between modules.[20] Modularity allows the product to be used in different ways (i.e., changing functions) and may facilitate the rearrangement/replacement of physical components (i.e., changing form).
- *Mutability* is the capability of the system to be contorted or reshaped in response to changing requirements or environmental conditions. Mutability implies a change in form but does not indicate a change in function.

TWO ENGINEERING APPLICATIONS OF OUR OPEN ENGINEERING SYSTEMS PHILOSOPHY

To better anchor our philosophy of open engineering systems, we present two engineering applications. We first discuss the implications of our open engineering systems philosophy on the field of structural design. Then we describe the use of the open engineering systems philosophy for designing families of products.

Creating Open Structural Design Models Using the Open Engineering Systems Philosophy

We use structural design examples to illustrate the aforementioned characteristics of open engineering systems in this area; structural design refers the process of geometric modeling, structural analysis, and design optimization. In a computer-aided design environment, solid modeling is often used to construct a precise mathematical description of the shape of the real object. Then, the finite element method is widely used for analysis—after loads, boundary conditions, material properties, etc. are modeled—and a mesh is generated. An important goal of engineering activities is to improve and to optimize technical designs, structural assemblies, or components. The task is to support the engineer in finding the best possible design alternatives of specific structures, where the "best possible" or "optimal" structure is the one that corresponds to the designer's desired concept, while meeting multidisciplinary requirements relating to manufacturing, operating, etc.[21] We focus on geometric modeling and optimization to highlight examples of flexibility in structural design. We call structural designs that have these analogies to open engineering systems *open structural design models*.

Parametric Models in Geometric Modeling

We ignore the possibility to model each new geometry from scratch, which is of course possible in a computer-aided environment, and believe that the minimum requirement for flexibility is equal to having a *parametric* model. The primary issue to do structural design effectively is to develop such a parametric structural analysis model. By modifying the model's design variables such as geometric dimensions, the structural model (i.e., geometry, finite element mesh, boundary conditions, etc.), has to have the ability to be altered according to new variable values. Parameters, relations, or functions are introduced to specify fully the model's geometry, thereby enhancing flexibility, the core characteristic of an open engineering system. In order to develop a parametric model, a larger portion of time has to be spent in the early design stages (i.e., geometric modeling). A considerable amount of time is needed to introduce and model all of the variables which may change quantitatively during the design process. However, a parametric model allows us to maintain design freedom because the computer easily performs the tasks required to update the model according to specified parameter values.

An example from the field of blow molding is given in Figure 3.4. It represents the geometric model of a thermoplastic bottle with handle. The purpose in the blow molding example is to analyze the behavior of the bottle under internal pressure, compression, and impact. Only half of the bottle is modeled because of symmetry. The surface shape is highly complex because of all the curvature in the model, especially

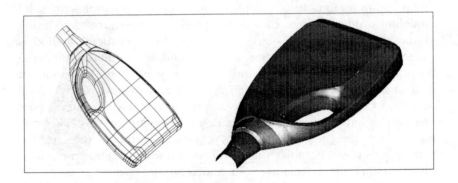

FIGURE 3.4. Geometric Model of Bottle with Handle

around the handle. The modeling process itself has been difficult and time-consuming; therefore, a parametric model has not been implemented. This means that this model represents one kind of a bottle and the only value that can be modified easily is the wall thickness. Another flexibility aspect exists through scaling since the basic shape remains the same if the model is supposed to change in size only.

In order to represent system modularity, we could assume that each single surface in the model represents a module, but there is no real functional distinction as defined for modularity between adjacent surfaces. We could assign groups of surfaces being modules such as the lid area, the handle, or the bottom, but this model is actually not developed to serve modularity, even though it is possible to do so. A change in geometry can only be done if surfaces are deleted, new ones are generated and connected to the remaining system/model. New surfaces can be treated as new modules which have to fit the interfaces of the remaining model. It is easy to see that this model is very inflexible and that the effort put into the modeling process does not provide a good "return on investment" if product changes are necessary. If flexibility can not be achieved, a designer is highly involved in time-consuming remodeling tasks and the investment becomes even larger.

A step toward creating a more flexible model is shown in Figure 3.5. A round bottle is modeled as a 90° section. According to the technical draft, the geometry is perfectly symmetric and could therefore be modeled as a line model, but the blow molding process results in a wall thickness distribution of the actual product which varies extremely with the section angle. The geometric model can be easily created by specify-

FIGURE 3.5.   Parametric Flexibility in a Round Bottle

ing five vertex points, four connecting lines, and rotation of the line section by a specified angle. The parametric model dimensions can be specified to improve model flexibility. We define three height dimensions h_1, h_2, h_3, two diameters d_1, d_2, and the radius r_1 to smooth the corner on the bottom of the bottle. Constraints can be put on the model to ensure parallel lines. The bottle model shown in Figure 3.5 consists of six parameters which can easily be modified to create a variety of new shapes and sizes. *Thus, when customer needs are specified, we can quickly generate the necessary shapes at very little cost to us.*

The parametric model representation enhances flexibility, but this is only a starting point since the model still has many limitations. A *change in form* is possible through a change in parameters. Changes in shape are achieved through modifying the corners into arcs or replacing the straight lines with more flexible splines. For modularity, each corner point could be identified as the interface between modules (e.g., lid and bottom). Additionally, a new module which is connected to the model via two new geometric points (module interfaces) is introduced in Figure 3.6. We further assume that the formulation of the new module enhances flexibility so that we can model many different shapes (e.g., use a B-spline as opposed to a straight line). That way, if requirements change, we could easily use the capabilities of the new module to adapt to the new needs and adjust the shape of the bottle. Thus, in this context, modularity provides model interfaces to account for changing requirements, enabling us to prepare a variety of models with little added effort. But how do we know where to put the interfaces and if it is worth the effort? Our current answer is to evaluate carefully each new

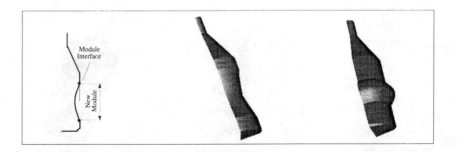

FIGURE 3.6.   Designed-in Modularity and Mutability

design, estimating how much time and effort should be invested into the modeling process and what benefits would arise in the future. We believe that this example of designed-in modularity is a long-term investment necessary to maintain design freedom and achieve a flexible design.

Several analogies exist between structural optimization techniques and the characteristics of open engineering systems. The development of a parametric structural analysis model is a must before design optimization can be applied. This simplest form of flexibility can be referred to as *parameter optimization* where mathematical programming procedures are employed to find the "best" parameter values. By employing other strategies such as shape, topology and stochastic optimization, or model decomposition, a large amount of flexibility can be achieved.

Shape and Topology Optimization

As stated before, mutability is the capability of the system to be reshaped in response to changing requirements, as seen in Figure 3.3. A corresponding analogy can be identified in shape optimization. In contrast to parameter optimization problems (where we search for optimal design variable values or parameter configurations), in shape optimization problems, we search for optimal functions that describe the shape of a structure.[22] For practical solutions to shape optimization problems, today the so-called *direct* methods, which transform the original shape optimization problem into a parameter optimization problem, usually through the introduction of special shape functions, are preferred. For direct shape optimization, the choice of the shape functions is extremely important because the original solution space will be reduced and the optimization result will also be influenced. We want to have high flexibility with a small number of free parameters to describe surfaces or lines. *Flexibility is important when rendering a large variety of possible shapes during optimization to meet customer specifications.*

Topology optimization deals with making decisions regarding the position and layout of structural elements. The objective of topology optimization is to substitute the existing intuitive design of variants by mathematical–mechanical strategies in the design phase to make it more efficient. Topology optimization involves starting with little information (e.g., applied forces and feasible solution space (topology space)), and finding solutions for structural designs, as in Figure 3.7.[23] Thus, since only little information is required for this technique, it is a valuable tool for use in the early stages of design. One of the applied topology optimization methods is the so-called "Homogenization Method" or "Bubble-Method" which simultaneously combines shape optimization and topology optimization.[24] The procedure is very flexi-

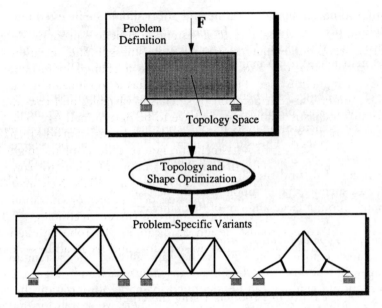

FIGURE 3.7.   Topology Optimization in Structural Design

ble since it can be easily adapted to changing environmental conditions or design requirements. A change in form is obvious; a change in function is also possible since there are no initial limitations other than the initial definition of the topology space.

Model Decomposition

In the field of structural design, the structural model as well as the optimization model can often be decomposed. The phrase *decomposition strategy* describes what is decomposed for the solution of structural optimization problems.[25] The most important decomposition strategy is model decomposition since it involves the separation of the mathematical model into equations and/or variable vectors. The application of model decomposition leads to a reduction in simultaneously treated system variables.

Modularity can be achieved through decomposition of the original system into several smaller subsystems. By using this strategy, subsystems or modules can be replaced by other modules. The less coupling there is between the subsystems, the less effort there is to make changes; however, coordinating the interactions between modules always remains of utmost importance. A change in form is also possible when modularity exists (refer to Figure 3.3). The key for this concept is to develop the proper interfaces and coupling in the design model.

Stochastic Optimization

Robustness is the capability of a system to function properly despite small environmental changes or noise. Robustness implies an insensitivity to small variations and does not dictate a change in form nor a change in function (see Figure 3.3). Stochastic optimization can be applied under the consideration of stochastic variables and constraints, where (a) stochastic failure criteria have to be determined (e.g., ceramic materials), or (b) various stochastic variables and constraints of stochastic state variables which are not stochastic failure criteria of the material, have to be modeled. The first point is important when we consider "new" materials which replace previously used materials. New materials can be developed through new processes, design, and optimization and can be used in new applications or improve current technology.[26] The second point covers robust design applications. In robust design, we deal with stochastic variables and noise factors and try to address quality issues in a design.

Designing a Family of Products Using the Open Engineering Systems Philosophy

Having anchored our open engineering systems philosophy in structural engineering, we now shift our focus to designing families of products. Specifically, we focus on the design of a family of General Aviation aircraft using the open engineering systems philosophy. The term General Aviation encompasses all flights except military operations and commercial carriers. General Aviation aircraft in the U.S. account for approximately 62 percent of all flight hours, 37 percent of all miles flown, and 78 percent of all departures. Its potential buyers form a diverse group that include weekend and recreational pilots, training pilots and instructors, traveling business executives, and even small commercial operators.

Satisfying a group with such diverse needs and economic potential poses a constant challenge for the General Aviation industry since it is impossible to *satisfy all the market needs with a single aircraft*. The present financial and legal pressure endured by the General Aviation sector makes small production runs of specialized models unprofitable. As a result, many General Aviation aircraft are no longer being produced, and the few remaining models are beyond the financial capability of all but the wealthiest buyers. Combined with the harsh legal environment to which General Aviation airplanes and component producers have been subjected, the General Aviation sector is in a deep recession as shown in Figure 3.8.

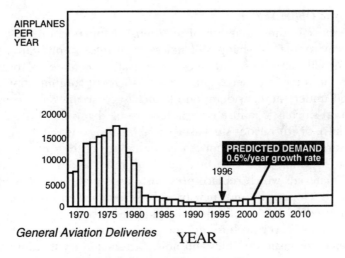

FIGURE 3.8. Airplanes Per Year

In an effort to revitalize the General Aviation sector through the introduction of state-of-the-art design techniques and construction materials,
the National Aeronautics and Space Administration (NASA) and the
Federal Aviation Administration (FAA) sponsored a General Aviation
Design Competition.[27] A General Aviation aircraft (GAA):

• is a single-engine, single-pilot, fixed wing, propeller driven aircraft
• carries 2-6 passengers
• cruises at 150-300 kts, and
• has a range of 800-1000 n.mi.

A reasonable solution to the GAA crisis is to develop an aircraft which
can be easily adapted to satisfy distinct groups of customer demands. To
do this, a family of General Aviation aircraft is designed around the 2-,
4-, and 6-seater aircraft configurations. The general dimensions of each
aircraft are developed such that a significant number of top-level design
specifications[28] can be shared by the different aircraft to facilitate the
development of a common baseline model. If a common baseline model
can be developed and maintained, *a family of aircraft which fulfills the market demands can easily be realized* and, as a result, the General Aviation
industry can profit from its production. Consequently, the problem
statement for the example problem is as follows:

Given the GAA competition guidelines and relevant GAA data, it is
required to develop a *ranged* set of top-level design specifications for a

family of General Aviation aircraft capable of satisfying the diverse demands of the General Aviation public at an affordable price and operating cost while meeting desired performance, technical, and economic considerations.

We have utilized two different approaches to design this family of three aircraft. First, we designed each aircraft individually and looked for commonalties between the top-level design specifications for each aircraft. These aircraft serve as the benchmark aircraft, and the top-level design specifications—cruise speed, aspect ratio, sweep angle, wing loading, seat width, engine activity factor, tail length-to-diameter ratio, and propeller diameter—for each aircraft are shown in the top half of Table 3.1. For example, the desired aspect ratio is 7.56 for the 2-seater aircraft, 7.1 for the 4-seater and 7.7 for the 6-seater. The corresponding ranges of the system performance variables of interest are also given in Table 3.1 (e.g., the maximum cruise range varies from 2,360 to 2,496 n.mi.) for the three aircraft based on the given top-level design specifications.

For our second approach, we employed the Robust Concept Exploration Method[29] to design all three aircraft simultaneously rather than individually. The final configurations for these aircraft are given in the lower half of Table 3.1 along with the corresponding ranges of the system performance variables. Notice that we specify a range for each top-level design specification for all three aircraft rather than individual values for each aircraft. This is because these values are "common and good" for all three aircraft as determined by using the Robust Concept Exploration Method. It is encouraging that there is considerable overlap between the top-level design specifications and system performance ranges for these aircraft and the benchmark aircraft.

The specific details regarding how these solutions were obtained are given elsewhere,[30] as is a lengthy comparison of the robustness of the solutions, individual performance of each aircraft, and variation between design variables. Suffice it to say that while we increase our efficiency by designing all three aircraft simultaneously and make our designs more "robust," we lose some individual system performance for each aircraft (i.e., the individually benchmarked aircraft can fly further with less fuel but have a much wider spread in terms of price). The question that remains to be addressed is, when is this tradeoff worthwhile and when it is not? The answer can only be found through knowledge of customer wishes and demands.

In both cases, we sought to find a ranged set of top-level design specifications (design variables) which was "common and good" for all three aircraft which comprise the family. By finding a ranged set of specifica-

TABLE 3.1. The 2-, 4- and 6-Seater Family of Aircraft

Top-Level Design Specification	2 Seater	4 Seater	6 Seater	Corresponding System Performance Range	
		Benchmark Aircraft			
Cruise Speed	Mach 0.242	Mach 0.24	Mach 0.24		
Aspect Ratio	7.56	7.1	7.7	Fuel Weight	350-450 lbs
Prop Diameter	5.72 ft	5.86 ft	5.76 ft	Empty Weight	1895-1983 lbs
Wing Loading	22.1 lb/ft^2	20.9 lb/ft^2	21.1 lb/ft^2	Operating Cost	\$60/hr-\$62/hr
Sweep Angle	5.75°	5.95°	6.0°	Max. Lift/Drag	15.2-16.0
Engine Activity Factor	86.2	88.5	87.5	Purchase Price (1970's Dollars)	\$42310-\$43956
Seat Width	18.2 in	18.5 in	19.2 in	Max. Speed	190-198 kts
Tail Length/Diam	3.7	3.75	3.75	Max. Range	2360-2496 n.mi.
		Simultaneously Designed Aircraft			
Cruise Speed	⇦ Mach 0.24-0.34 ⇨				
Aspect Ratio	⇦ 7-8.8 ⇨			Fuel Weight	435-487 lbs
Prop Diameter	⇦ 5.5-5.96 ft ⇨			Empty Weight	1845-1896 lbs
Wing Loading	⇦ 20-25 lb/ft^2 ⇨			Operating Cost	\$59/hr-\$60/hr
Sweep Angle	⇦ 6.0° ⇨			Max. Lift/Drag	15.2-15.5
Engine Activity Factor	⇦ 85-92 ⇨			Purchase Price (1970's Dollars)	\$41665-\$42556
Seat Width	⇦ 14-20 in ⇨			Max. Speed	197-199 kts
Tail Length/Diam	⇦ 3.75 ⇨			Max. Range	2261-2341 n.mi.

tions rather than a point set of specifications, we have more design freedom which allows us to readily adapt our baseline design to meet a variety of customer demands.[31] In essence, we have created a "robust design" (using Rothwell and Gardiner's terminology) which is flexible and adaptable with respect to external changes in the market and customer demand. Once additional customer information is known, we can tailor our baseline model to better suit those needs.

SUMMARY AND CLOSING REMARKS

Before closing, let us first return to the question we posed at the start of this chapter; namely, *how can product realization teams provide increased product variety at less cost in a highly competitive, rapidly changing marketplace?* Clearly, the answer lies in how we deal with information and how we use it and manipulate it to achieve our objectives. A new form of competitive advantage lies in harnessing the nearly limitless information which now exists and being able to adapt quickly to changing customer demands. Embracing our open engineering systems philosophy and the ideas of modularity, robustness, and mutability will enhance system flexibility and help maintain flexibility of options to accommodate the multitude of changes which occur in both design and the market.

Our intent in this chapter is to introduce the notion of open engineering systems and describe key characteristics for both the design process and the product sides of open engineering systems. On the design process side, our primary concern for designing open engineering systems is to maintain design freedom, increase design knowledge, and increase (computational) efficiency during the early stages of design. *This enables better decisions to be made before the freedom to make these decisions is eliminated.* On the product side, we have described several characteristics for open engineering systems including modularity, robustness, and mutability. These characteristics are selected as descriptors for open engineering systems because they *promote flexibility and facilitate continuous growth and improvement in the face of change.*

Having identified core characteristics of open engineering systems, our next step is to develop *metrics* to assess the extent to which a system is modular, robust, or mutable (i.e., the extent to which a system is open). Our initial efforts are aimed at measuring the design freedom and information certainty of a system,[32] but several questions remain unanswered:

- *On openness*: How can we measure openness? Do we either have it or not have it? Is there a relationship between design freedom and openness and if so, what? Can we increase openness or just maintain openness of a system? If we can increase it, how? If not, why?
- *On later design stages*: How do we maintain design freedom in the later design stages? Do we want to? How (and when) do we narrow our ranged sets of specifications? When do we go for point solutions?
- *Design freedom*: How can we measure design freedom? Can we increase our design freedom or just maintain it? Does a larger performance/variable range mean more freedom than a smaller one and if so, how much more?
- *On small vs. large, complex systems*: The examples we have had are for large, complex systems such as aircraft and ships. What about smaller, less complex products like disposable cameras, copiers, stereos, a tractor, a chair, a pencil? How will our open engineering systems philosophy apply to these? Is it readily applicable or must it change? If so, how?
- *On metrics*: What are metrics for modularity, mutability, robustness, and flexibility?

More generally, we should also contemplate:

- What are the consequences of this limitless information on the physical products (systems), the associated product realization processes, and the organization of the company?
- What are some examples of open systems that support our principal theses? How has the Information Revolution affected their development and implementation?
- Are open engineering systems worth pursuing? Or are there alternate approaches which we should consider in the face of the Information Revolution?
- What further impact does the Information Revolution have on realizing open engineering systems? How does it affect their design and management as well as their support and retirement?

Now that we have identified some of the "whats" and "whys" for open engineering systems, we need to look more at the "hows." In particular, we can begin developing design methods and tools for realizing open engineering systems, and this task has already begun.[33] The proposed design process, rooted in Decision-Based Design,[34] employs several mathematical tools and constructs which are part of the Robust Concept Exploration Method (RCEM).[35] The RCEM helps maintain flexibility of options to facilitate continuous improvement and technological growth of a common baseline model and increases knowledge about a system. In a world where customer needs are constantly changing, flexibility can only be achieved when information is available, and designers and managers are willing (and able) to adapt. With the advent of the Information Revolution, implications such as these can no longer go unheeded.

ACKNOWLEDGMENTS

Timothy W. Simpson has been supported by an NSF Graduate Research Fellowship. We gratefully acknowledge NSF grants DMI-94-20405 and DMI-96-12327 and NASA grant NAG-1-1564. Uwe Lautenschlager is funded by the German Academic Exchange Service (DAAD) with a "DAAD Post Graduate Fellowship supported by the Second Special University Program." We acknowledge the intellectual contributions from our classmates in *ME6171: Designing Open Engineering Systems* taught at the Georgia Institute of Technology. The cost of computer time was underwritten by the Systems Realization Laboratory of the Georgia Institute of Technology.

NOTES AND REFERENCES

[1] L. Dobbins & C. Crawford-Mason, 1991, *Quality or Else*, Houghton Mifflin, New York.

[2] T.A. Stewart, 1992, September 21 "Brace for Japan's Hot New Strategy," *Fortune*, Vol. 126, No. 6, pp. 62–74.

[3] Stewart, *op. cit.*, Ref. 2.

[4] For examples from (a) operations research see: N. Gaithen, 1980, *Production and Operations Management: A Problem-Solving and Decision-Making Approach*, The Dryden Press, New York; (b) computer science see: G.J. Nutt, 1992, *Open Systems*, Prentice Hall, Englewood Cliffs, NJ; and (c) marketing and management see P. Kotler, 1989, "From Mass Marketing to Mass Customization," *Planning Review*, Vol. 17, No. 5 (September/October), pp. 10(5); M.H. Meyer & J.M. Utterback, 1993, "The Product Family and the Dynamics of Core Capability," *Sloan Management Review*, Vol. 34 (Spring), pp. 29–47; and B.J. Pine II, 1993, *Mass Customization: The New Frontier in Business Competition*, Harvard Business School Press, Boston, MA.

[5] S.C. Wheelwright & K.B. Clark, 1992, "Creating Project Plans to Focus Product Development," *Harvard Business Review*, Vol. 70 (March-April), pp. 70–82.

[6] M. Uzumeri & S. Sanderson, 1995, "A Framework for Model and Product Family Competition," *Research Policy*, Vol. 24, pp. 583–607.

[7] G.T. DiCamillo, 1988, "Winning Turnaround Strategies at Black & Decker," *Journal of Business Strategy*, Vol. 9, No. 2 (March/April), pp. 30–33.

[8] R. Rothwell & P. Gardiner, 1988, "Re-Innovation and Robust Designs: Producer and User Benefits," *Journal of Marketing Management*, Vol. 3, No. 3, pp. 372–387.

[9] K. Ishii, C. Juengel, & C.F. Eubanks, 1995, "Design for Product Variety: Key to Product Line Structuring," *9th International ASME Design Theory and Methodology Conference (A.C. Ward ed.)*, Boston, MA, ASME, DE-Vol. 83 No. 2, pp. 499–506.

[10] M. Martin & K. Ishii, 1996, August 18-22, "Design for Variety: A Methodology for Understanding the Costs of Product Proliferation," *10th International ASME Design Theory and Methodology Conference*, Irvine, CA, ASME, Paper No. 96-DETC/DTM-1610.

[11] W. Chen, D. Rosen, J.K. Allen, & F. Mistree, 1994, "Modularity and the Independence of Functional Requirements in Designing Complex Systems," *Concurrent Product Design (R. Gadh ed.)*, ASME, DE-Vol. 74, p. 31–38.

[12] Rothwell and Gardiner, *op. cit.*, Ref. 7.

[13] R. Rothwell & P. Gardiner, 1990, "Robustness and Product Design Families," *Design Management: A Handbook of Issues and Methods (M. Oakley ed.)*, Basil Blackwell Inc., Cambridge, MA, pp. 279–292.

[14] The early stages of design are characterized by *uncertain* or *ambiguous* information which is "soft" compared to information in the later design stages.

[15] Satisficing solutions are solutions which are "good enough" but not necessarily the "best", from H.A. Simon, 1981, *The Sciences of the Artificial*, Second Edition, The MIT Press, Cambridge, Mass.

[16]*Efficiency* is a measure of the swiftness with which information, that can be used by a designer to make a decision, is generated. *Effectiveness* is a measure of the quality of a decision (correctness, completeness, comprehensiveness) that is made by a designer.

[17]Additional examples can be found in: (a) Rothwell and Gardiner, *op. cit.*, Ref. 12, (b) S. Kotha, 1995, "Mass Customization: Implementing the Emerging Paradigm for Competitive Advantage," *Strategic Management Journal*, Vol. 16 (Summer), pp. 21-42; and (c) S. Maital, 1991, "The Profits of Infinite Variety," *Across the Board*, Vol. 28 (October), pp. 7–10.

[18]Rothwell and Gardiner, *op. cit.*, Ref. 7.

[19]MT-AMRI can be found on the World Wide Web at http://mtamri.me.uiuc.edu/mtamri.html.

[20]K.T. Ulrich & K. Tung, 1991, "Fundamentals of Product Modularity," *ASME Winter Annual Meeting*, Atlanta, GA, ASME, pp. 73–80.

[21]H.A. Eschenauer, "Multicriteria Structural Optimization as a Technique for Quality Improvement in the Design Process," *Microcomputers in Civil Engineering*, Blackwell Science Inc., Cambridge, MA, pp. 257–267.

[22]H.A. Eschenauer, J. Geilen, & H.J. Wahl, 1993, "SAPOP—An Optimization Procedure for Multicriteria Structural Design," *Software Systems for Structural Optimization (H.R.E.M. Hörnlein and K. Schittkowski eds.)*, Birkhäuser Verlag, Basel.

[23]Figure 3.7 is from A. Schumacher, 1996, "Topologieoptimierung von Bauteilstrukturen unter Verwendung von Lochpositionierungskriterien.," Ph.D. Dissertation, University of Siegen, Siegen, Germany.

[24]Ibid.

[25]M. Weinert, 1994, "Sequentielle und parallele Strategien zur optimalen Auslegung komplexer Rotationsschalen," Ph.D. Dissertation, University of Siegen, Siegen, Germany.

[26]T. Vietor, 1994, "Optimale Auslegung von Strukturen aus sprden Werkstoffen.," Ph.D. Dissertation, University of Siegen, Siegen, Germany.

[27]NASA and FAA, 1994, "General Aviation Design Competition Guidelines," Virginia Space Grant Consortium, Hampton, VA.

[28]Top-level design specifications are used to define the overall system configuration, e.g., wing area, aspect ratio, sweep angle, etc., and subsystems at an abstract level. They can be either continuous (e.g., aspect ratio = [7–11], sweep angle = [0°–6°], etc.), or they can be discrete (e.g., single- or twin-engine, high or low wing, etc.)

[29]W. Chen, J.K. Allen, D. Mavris, & F. Mistree, 1996, "A Concept Exploration Method for Determining Robust Top-Level Specifications," *Engineering Optimization*, Vol. 26, pp. 137–158.

[30]T.W. Simpson, W. Chen, J.K. Allen, & F. Mistree, 1996, September 4–6, "Conceptual Design of a Family of Products Through the use of the Robust Concept Exploration Method," *6th AIAA/USAF/NASA/ISSMO Symposium on Multidisciplinary Analysis and Optimization*, Bellevue, WA, AIAA, pp. 1535–1545.

[31]Developing this ranged set of top-level design specifications and a lengthy comparison of the baseline models against the individual benchmark aircraft is also presented in Simpson, et al., *op. cit.*, Ref. 29.

[32]T.W. Simpson, D. Rosen, J.K. Allen, & F. Mistree, 1996, August 18–22, "Metrics for Assessing Design Freedom and Information Certainty in the Early Stages of Design," *10th International ASME Design Theory and Methodology Conference*, Irvine, CA, ASME, Paper No. 96-DETC/DTM-1521, to appear in Journal of Mechanical Design.

[33]T.W. Simpson, 1995, "Development of a Design Process for Realizing Open Engineering Systems," M.S. Thesis, Georgia Institute of Technology, Atlanta, GA.

[34]F. Mistree, W.F. Smith, B. Bras, J.K. Allen, & D. Muster, 1990, "Decision-Based Design: A Contemporary Paradigm for Ship Design," *Transactions Society of Naval Architects and Marine Engineers (H.R. Paresai and W. Sullivan eds.)*, Jersey City, New Jersey, pp. 565–597.

[35]Chen, et al., *op. cit.*, Ref. 28.

part II
Implications for the Workplace

Part II begins with an a chapter written by industrial psychologist who identifies the challenges attendant to reorganizing around information. In particular, he brings to bear research on change processes and work groups to disabuse the reader that these adaptations will come smoothly or quickly.

In Chapter 4, an economist digests 20 in-depth case studies of office productivity in major U.S. corporations. These lead to explicit recommendations on how to boost information work productivity by altering the mix of professional and support workers.

Chapter 6 focuses on group work. The authors conceptualize how information enables a team of workers in different locations to function, leading to a model of how groupware can make a difference. This model is explored by tracking a groupware implementation project and the authors draw practical conclusions about how to manage such implementations.

chapter 4

Workplace Changes: Psychological Perspective

C. Michael York
School of Psychology
Georgia Tech

THE RAPID COMPUTERIZATION OF WORK

About 40 years ago, development of the integrated circuit permitted a large amount of information to be processed or stored on a single microchip. The information age was driven by that technological advance. Just 30 years ago, faint voices were mentioning the significant changes on the horizon in work and organizational life. Although the impact was apparently modest, numerous theorists forewarned us that the nature of work would be altered and that the perspectives and expectations of the future workforce would be different. Even the definition of work was unraveling.

Futurists Bell, Kahn, and Cornish were getting good press in the 1960s and 1970s era. The business press quoted behavioral scientists such as Argyris, Leavitt, Levinson, Likert, McGregor, and Schein, but they left the potential technology impact argument—and appropriate cautions—to the futurists. Tomeski, in his book *The Computer Revolution*, gave the clarion call that a maelstrom of change was underway in society in the form of a new powerful management tool, already beneficial in budget and inventory control function. As early as 1970, he argued that the people problems (i.e., staffing, supervision, setting up objectives) would be more severe than the technical challenge. Later, others have expressed concern for the societal impact.[1] To be accurate, Leavitt[2] and Whisler did hint in 1958 in the *Harvard Business Review* at coming events when they considered technology as a target for change interdependent with alteration of organization structure and the people involved. In fact, they may have coined the term *information technology*.

EVERYONE'S CHALLENGE INTO THE NEXT CENTURY

Let us move quickly to the current scene in terms of workplace changes. The timely writings of behaviorists Steers and Black[3] reveal the conviction that any person in today's workforce must concurrently deal with issues such as:

- International competition (i.e., loss of clout and profitability as companies in Western Europe and Asia have gained significant market share in automobiles, home electronics, telecommunications, medical equipment and ship building, to name a few areas).
- New technologies (i.e., advances in most industries, including the explosive growth in microcomputing) are forcing managers to adapt to the technological imperative while maintaining and developing the organization's human resources.
- An increasingly diverse workforce (i.e., an accelerating pace of change in gender, race, and age with unforeseen consequences, such as only 15% of the new workforce entrants in Year 2000 being White males).
- Quality enhancement (i.e., products and service that are customer oriented).
- Employee motivation and commitment (i.e., in an era of job insecurity and lack of trust, revision of reward systems, the emerging elite vs. "have-nots" schism).

These authoritative organizational psychologists also express grave concern for pervasive unethical behavior as a cancer working on the fabric of society. Information security is one example. Although the intensity of these issues will vary at the local level, experience suggests as a minimum that all executives and managers must promote the prerequisite fact of continuous learning in relation to the interplay of these complex relationships. Note that advances in information technology are embedded in the schema of challenges (viz., new technologies) adding to the proliferation of new devices for handling, entering, retrieving, and manipulating data.

Space permitting, we could elaborate on numerous dramatic developments in the areas of information technology and knowledge production. Where went the typewriter? The software industry hardly existed 25 years ago. Cellular phones did not exist in 1970, when today's undergraduates were not yet born. Therefore, a climate of change is the constant phenomenon in work organizations and in society at large.

POTENTIAL CONSEQUENCES FROM A PSYCHOLOGICAL PERSPECTIVE

Concern for behavioral consequences predates the science and profession of psychology. With the omnipresence of computers, including E-mail, fax, paging, and electronic bulletin boards, our challenge is to conceptualize favorable functions and dysfunctions in an effort to understand the current information revolution. But to be candid, we know that computerization is masked in part by the larger technological advance.[4]

The intent here is to highlight several plausible consequences of the computer revolution, which has emerged in so short a time frame. Be reminded that the perspective is psychological rather than economic, engineering, or other conceptualization framework.

The Demographic Shifts and Employment Trends

Workforce composition is changing dramatically in the United States and elsewhere. This phenomenon alone will frustrate employment practices and will prompt a heated forum (e.g., relating to immigration legislation). In the information technology context, think of the larger human capital implications that the U.S. Census projections suggest:

- An aging workforce (i.e., more experienced, stable, and reliable vs. increase in health care costs, pensions paid longer, and potentially less flexibility among older workers).
- Greater feminization among employees (i.e., women are faring well as information workers, and are experiencing more advancement in cutting-edge industries, to be 47% of the workforce by the year 2000)
- The baby boomer age bulge (i.e., information technology contributes to declining middle management opportunities, and plateaued employees whose motivation may decline)

How can we forecast and avoid gaps, age bulges, and surpluses in job categories as organizational demands change? If the long view is logical, are the forecasts of altered customer behavior and the competition valid enough? The computer represents a useful tool in forecasting skill needs and the scheduling of work.

Many companies are in a skills crunch and are fighting a bidding war for high-tech talent. A recent study by The Information Technology Association of America estimates that 190,000 info-tech jobs stand vacant—half in the information industry. Moreover, U.S. universities produce historically low numbers of computer scientists. The scarcity of digital talent (e.g., adaptable programmers) prompts the escalation of recruiting perks and compensation packages.

Kaufman, writing for two decades on technological change and obsolescence, focused more directly on the engineer, scientist, and computer specialist segment.[5] For many technical professions, radical career change has become a way of life that increasingly requires retraining and occupational mobility. New and altered ways of working are arising in part due to the obsolescence of knowledge and skills. Ironically, the technologists contribute to the technological change and become vulnerable to the consequence of obsolescence, as London reaffirmed.[6] In the 1970s, Kaufman argued that the job tasks (i.e., the work itself) coupled with the organizational climate (perceived or real) were the major causes of employees not continually updating the prerequisite knowledge and skills associated with altered job demands or career redirection. Since restructuring will likely continue unabated, the 1995 Kaufman guidelines to retraining and redeployment should be helpful—and prophetic.

Allocation of Authority in Work Organizations

How is authority (i.e., control) best distributed in the information age? The traditional premise underlying the management of employees has been that efficiency can be achieved more readily by imposing control over subordinate behavior. Hence, hierarchical structures remain prevalent. A counterview by Harvard professor Hackman, for more than a decade, espouses the general principle, with substantial evidence, that employers must elicit the commitment of their people if they are to achieve a competitive advantage in contemporary markets.[7] Recall the earlier point that employee commitment makes the short list of current management challenges in the 1990s.

The prevalence of information technology may be at the heart of this vexing policy and practice issue on who has power. Increasingly, we observe shared responsibilities and dramatic reconfiguring of job tasks and who gets credit and compensation. Thus, we see that the potential for change is the transfer from a control model to a commitment model that honors work motivation. Ironically, control-oriented management models can create outcomes that actually subvert the interest of both organizations and the people working in them. We can envision four types of performing units—from manager-led to clusters of true self-governance, a continuum reflecting increasing amounts of shared authority. Already evident are redefinitions of the managerial role, with a predictable imbalance among the major functions of decision-making and planning, staffing and activating, organizing and controlling, and the need for understanding the sociotechnical systems approach to change, group dynamics, work stress, privacy versus management rights, health risks and disability, labor law—and communication principles.

Continued attention should be given to the relevance of the commitment model in the information revolution that is well underway in causing workplace changes.

Reward Systems and the Compensation Issue

With greater certainty, a consensus is emerging that job-focused pay plans, compensating millions today, are unable to provide the flexibility needed for the prevailing competitive environment.[8] Knowledge workers are at the forefront of this testy labor–management issue, and the skilled elite may predictably flex their muscle into the next century. The traditional job evaluation procedures, including hybrids of the factor comparison and point system, attempt internal equity or fairness. Typically, salary surveys of market rates determine external equity. Human resource (HR) managers then face a balancing act when deciding the rate of compensation for an individual or a work group.

Information technology could contribute to constraints on managerial flexibility in effective utilization of the workforce. For example, compensable factors such as the significant know-how and more abstract but essential problem-solving behaviors may receive a low evaluation. Also, specific job performance is routinely emphasized rather than focus on work outside the incumbent's job classification, which a system perspective would encourage. That traditional "reward" could be counterproductive!

If reduced promotion opportunities occur through the de-layering of organization structures and stiff foreign competition, the literature argues for greater focus on individuals, not the job. In this way, employees are able to increase their compensation as they acquire a broader range of employer-relevant skills associated with company objectives.[9] Managerial flexibility is assumed, so goes the rationale. Lawler wrote extensively on the design of effective reward systems—matched to the

TABLE 4.1.   **Matching Reward Systems to Management Style**

Reward System	Traditional Leadership	Participative Leadership
Fringe benefits	Vary according to organizational level	Cafeteria—same for all levels
Promotion	All decisions made by top management	Open posting for all jobs; peer group involvement in decision process
Status symbols	A great many, carefully allocated on the basis of job position	Few present, low emphasis on organization level
Pay type	Hourly and salary	All salary
Base rate	Based on job performed; high enough to attract job applicants	Based on skills; high enough to provide security and attract applicants
Incentive plan	Piece-rate	Group and organizationwide bonus, lump-sum increase
Communication policy	Very restricted distribution of information	Individual rates, salary survey data, all other information made public
Decision-making locus	Top management	Close to location of person whose pay is being set

most appropriate management style. Note in Table 4.1 the consequences that he envisions when the "traditional" and "participative" styles of leadership are compared.

Personal Injury and Work Stress Among Employees

Stress on the job is an enormous issue worldwide. The rise in reported disorders and worker's compensation claims is a current concern among HR managers. The personal injury symptoms have been given labels, such as repetitive stress injury and carpal tunnel syndrome. Have these phenomena become excessive, and, to what extent is information technology a determining factor in some cases of health impairment?[10] Work determinism questions of this nature are controversial, other than acknowledging the fact that the known occurrences can be costly. As just one illustration, a recent precedent-setting repetitive stress injury case resulted in a keyboard maker being ordered to pay large user claims. Fortunately, ergonomic researchers are helping manufacturers steadily improve the person–machine interface as a partial remedy (e.g., screen brightness, color, resolution; workstation furniture). The legislative relaxation of ergonomic standards in the 1980s may have lessened management concern. However, undue psychological damage (viz. fatigue, tension, or high blood pressure) has been, and will continue to be linked to experienced stress, at least by some grieving claimants.[11]

Work stress and strain, which represent the consequences, are current topics in mental heath research, due to the human cost and financial burden on employers and insurance firms. Stress, a physical or emotional reaction to potentially threatening aspects of one's environment, differs among individuals and is pervasive in the work environment.

Has information technology significantly reduced or exacerbated stress phenomena? Why? It is difficult to find jobs without some degree of stress, but surely the work role makes a difference. From the occupational stress literature, consider the low-stress forklift operator or pharmacist in comparison with the highly stressed role of a surgeon, law enforcement officer, or mayor. Clearly, a person's choice of occupation or profession and the person–organization "fit" are contributing factors.[12] Although some stress may be necessary for psychological growth, creative activities, and the acquisition of new skills, highly tense and prolonged situations invariably have dysfunctional consequences.

Under the aegis of workplace change, several promising stress-reduction strategies are suggested in the literature:

Individual Strategies	Organizational Strategies
• Development of greater self-awareness	• Skills training
• Positive perception and interpretation	• Employee selection and placement
• Physical exercise	• Improved communication
• Finding a personal or unique solution	• Increased participation
• Leaving a job or organization	• Training for personal control

A general feeling of exhaustion (known as *burnout*) is apparently widespread in the office, in the plant, and among managers, engineers, researchers, and teachers, not just air traffic controllers and firefighters.

Career Development as an Ongoing Activity

The computer revolution has spawned a movement referred to as the *technization* of the workforce. These labor-saving devices now require almost a million "techies" in the Internet industry, and competitive pressure is pushing all kinds of businesses to get more efficient. Developers and caretakers of the computer and telecommunications networks represent the "worker elite" with varying levels of formal education and credentials.[13] Competence defines an employee's value rather than a place in an organization's hierarchial pecking order.

In this era of epochal change, individual learning will be a continuous endeavor—in various modes, even on the home TV and in the car. Some corporations are already pressing for employee self-management as a means of upgrading the skill levels demanded for a competitive advantage. Several observers have anticipated this trend when writing about self-regulation. An O'Reilly article in *Fortune* on the new deal in employee–employer "informal contracts" is must reading. "You are responsible for your employability" is the clear message.

Numerous new age implications are evident throughout the available projections, including the more diverse workforce, the shift from goods-producing to service–oriented employment, and added governmental intervention (e.g., deregulation, affirmative action, disability, and pay legislation). We can be astounded to think of the societal impact relating to these interrelated events. Only indirect mention is made of emerging job opportunities resulting from information technology.[14] A concerted public education effort would be helpful to all concerned (e.g., vocational counselors in high schools, colleges, and the private sector as well as parents and the adolescent segment).

Work Groups Are Now in Vogue

Team configurations and decision processes represent a current *zeitgeist* in business and industry. Quality circles, cross-functional teams, customer service teams, autonomous work groups, and even virtual, electronically linked groups decide and act. Although a huge literature exists on small-group research, no generally accepted model of team effectiveness prevails, especially with emphasis on the new age of information technology. In the 1990s, considerable research writing is underway in laboratories and in field evaluations.[15] However, summary recommendations for HR practitioners are just arriving.

One HR consulting firm in Dallas offers a useful 30-page set of practical principles entitled, "Team Reconstruction: Build A High Performance Work Group During Change." This primer sets the stage for handling the relentless pressure of change, shortening the high-risk transition period, and protecting productivity, quality, and profitability—going beyond conventional team-building techniques. It reads well, but no literature base is mentioned and no documentation of the information technology impact is offered.

A recent book is more cognizant of the impact of technological change, using the title, *Team Effectiveness and Decision Making in Organizations*,[16] as is the case for current writings by practitioners Howard and

London who are trained in psychology. The latter two book authors are former AT&T managers who chose a range of colleagues closely identified with the technological imperative. The Hackman publications[17] also deserve monitoring because the author addressed a host of issues beyond the classic work motivation model (viz. work redesign, group productivity, and member satisfaction).

It is clear that teams represent a predictable trend—the configuration and degree of authority still under trial. Many consultants are assisting in the experimentation with work groups that vary in degree of management-shared authority. Although numerous questions remain, the validation process has picked up recently—an encouraging sign.

THE BRAVE NEW WORLD OF INFORMATION TECHNOLOGY

Information technology is influencing dramatically the way individuals live and work. As the continuing wave of computer technology works its way into even more widespread practice, the real challenge is not technical change, but the human adaptation (i.e., prudent use) that accompanies technical innovations.[18]

Futurists speculate about coming events and often shock us with the mention of several dire consequences. However, long delays are usually experienced after breakthroughs occur before open debate is directed toward the observable impact on people. Depending on one's perspective, consequences—especially negative symptoms and troubling trends—prompt concern and diligent search for identifiable causes and remedies. Examples abound in the history of mankind (e.g., the industrial revolution, medical science).

In the present context of faster, smaller, and cheaper computers linked in far-ranging network systems, the impact of information technology is illlustrated by the two young professors at The University of Chicago who got their prophecies published 40 years ago in the *Harvard Business Review*. Their summary projections for organizational structure and worker behavior included a whole new set of options for the 21st century. For example:

- Managers will not just react to technology; they will use it to shape their organization.
- The structure, the process, and the people will change.
- Leadership will be shared or rotated among team members.

In 1988, the editors encouraged their reinforcement of the original ideas due in part to the visible and radical changes in technology and organizational restructuring and the unbelievable accuracy of the behavioral consequences (a thinning of middle management in the large corporations; skilled technicians taking on a bigger role; problems of generalized skill obsolence; data security, integrity, and ownership issues—to name a few examples).

The caution in thinking about the rapid advances in the brave new workplace is to look at not only the human side, but also the technical and social implications. Gradually, acknowledging resistance to change as a barrier to progress, we can be certain that changes in information technology[20] will be followed by a corresponding alteration in the structures and ways of *doing work*.

NOTES AND REFERENCES

[1] A. Carnevale, L. Gainer, & E. Scholz, *Training the Technical Work Force* (San Francisco, Jossey-Bass, 1991). J. P. Craiger, "Technology, organizations and work," *The Industrial Organizational Psychologist*, 34, 1997, pp. 89–96. R. M. White, Technology, Jobs and Society: The New Challenges of Change (Concept paper/speech, personal communication, 1996).

[2] H. Leavitt & T. Whisler, "Management in the 1980s," *Harvard Business Review*, December 1958, pp. 41–48.

[3] R. Steers & S. Black, Organizational Behavior (New York, HarperCollins, 1994).

[4] C.R. Greer, *Strategy and Human Resources: A General Managerial Perspective* (Englewood Cliffs, NJ: Prentice-Hall, 1995). D. Tapscott & A. Caston, *Paradigm Shift: The New Promise of Information Technology* (New York, McGraw-Hill,1993).

[5] H.G. Kaufman, "Salvaging Displaced Employees," in M. London (Ed.), *Employees, Careers and Job Creation* (San Francisco, Jossey-Bass, 1995), pp. 105–120.

[6] M. London, *Employees, Careers and Job Creation: Developing Growth-Oriented Human Resource Strategies and Programs* (San Francisco, Jossey-Bass, 1995).

[7] R. J. Hackman, "The Psychology of Self-Management in Organizations," in M. S. Pallak & R. O. Rerloff (Ed.), *Psychology and Work: Productivity, Change, and Employment* (Washington, DC, American Psychological Association, 1986), pp. 85–136.

[8] E. E. Lawler, S. A. Mohrman, & G. E. Ledford, *Creating High Performance Organizations* (San Francisco, Jossey-Bass, 1995).

[9] E. E. Lawler, *The Design of Effective Reward Systems* (Technical report, Los Angeles, University of Southern California, 1983).

[10] E. Dionne, "Carpal Tunnel Syndrome. Part I—The Problem," *National Safety News*, 1984, pp. 35–36. R. Steers & S. Black, *Organizational Behavior* (New

York, Harper-Collins, 1994). J. I. Savage, "Study refires VDT safety debate: Shows link between heavy use and miscarriages," *Computer World*, 1988, pp. 1–2.

[11] A. Farnham, "Who Beats Stress Best—and How?," *Fortune*, October 1991, pp. 71–86.

[12] D. Hall, *Career Development in Organization* (San Francisco, Jossey-Bass, 1988). K. Barnes, "Tips for managing telecommuters," *HR Focus*, 1994, pp. 9–10.

[13] L. S. Richman, "Work Elite," *Fortune*, August 1994, pp. 56–63.

[14] 14. K. Shelly, "More Job Openings—Even More New Entrants: The Outlook for College Graduates," *Occupational Outlook Quarterly*, 38, 1994, pp. 5–9. H. Fullerton, "New Labor Force Projections Spanning 1988 to 2000," *Monthly Labor Review*, 23, 1989, pp. 39–51.

[15] S. Straus & J. McGrath, "Does the Medium Matter? The Interaction of Task Type and Technology on Group Performance and Member Reactions," *Journal of Applied Psychology*, 79, 1994, pp. 87–97.

[16] R. A. Guzzo & E. Salas, *Team Effectiveness and Decision Making in Organizations* (San Francisco, Jossey-Bass, 1995).

[17] J. Hackman, "The design of work teams," in J. Lorsch (Ed.), *Handbook of Organizational Behavior* (Englewood Cliffs, NJ, Prentice-Hall, 1987).

[18] A. Howard, The Changing Nature of Work (San Francisco, Jossey-Bass, 1995). M. London, *Employees, Careers and Job Creation: Developing Growth-Oriented Human Resource Strategies and Programs* (San Francisco, Jossey-Bass, 1995). D. Nelson & M. Kletke, "Individual Adjustment During Technological Innovation: A Research Framework," *Behavior and Information Technology*, 9, 1990, pp. 257–271.

[19] L. Applegate, J. Cash, & D. Mills, "Information Technology and Tomorrow's Manager," *Harvard Business Review*, 66, 1988, pp. 128–136.

[20] The author and his students are compiling and categorizing a set of work-related implications. Readers are invited to share their input and to receive the available draft material. Facsimile contact is (404) 894-8905 or by mail to the campus in Atlanta 30332–0170. School of Psychology, Georgia Tech, Atlanta, GA 30332–0170. Grateful appreciation is expressed to numerous colleagues and to Phyllis Gregory for administrative assistance.

chapter 5

Office Productivity: The Impacts of Staffing, Intellectual Specialization, and Technology

Peter G. Sassone
School of Economics
Georgia Tech

INTRODUCTION

I n 1985, we began a series of (what has become) 20 office productivity studies in five major U.S. corporations. The purpose of the initial studies was to perform cost-benefit analyses of computer-based information systems. However, after the first several studies were completed, it became apparent that the data collection and analysis techniques that we had developed were yielding important productivity insights beyond the cost justification of office computer systems. In our data, we were finding a very clear, and largely unrecognized, productivity problem: a lack of intellectual specialization by white-collar workers. That is, we found that managers and professionals were devoting a very substantial amount of work time to tasks that could be done by lower paid employees. We found correspondingly serious staffing imbalances in those offices studied. That is, given the intellectual content of the entire spectrum of work performed in an office, that same work could always (in our sample of 20 departments) be performed by a lower cost mix of managers, professionals, and support staff. On average, we found potential payroll savings of at least 15% in the typical office. To put this in

TABLE 5.1. Companies Studied (Comparisons Based on 1990 Data)

Company	Industry	Sales or Revenue (US$ Billions)	Assets (US$ Billions)	Employees
Company 1	Manufacturing	> 50	> 100	> 500 000
Company 2	Consumer products	5–10	> 10	10,000–25,000
Company 3	Financial services	15–25	> 50	25,000–50,000
Company 4	Commercial banking	Not applicable	> 25	10,000–25,000
Company 5	Electric utility	5–10	15-25	25,000–50,000

TABLE 5.2.   Departments Studied

Company	Type of Department	No. of Offices	No. of Locations	No. of Employees
Company 1	Engineering	1	1	476
Company 1	Marketing	1	1	52
Company 1	Accounting	2	2	119
Company 2	Legal	1	1	5
Company 2	Marketing	1	1	104
Company 3	Underwriting	1	1	76
Company 3	Underwriting	1	1	31
Company 3	Underwriting	1	1	67
Company 3	Sales offices	32	32	214
Company 4	Lending offices	11	11	73
Company 4	Corporate banking	1	1	52
Company 4	Corporate banking	1	1	44
Company 4	Corporate banking	1	1	51
Company 4	Cash management	1	1	21
Company 4	International banking	3	1	20
Company 4	International banking	2	1	14
Company 4	Branch banking	16	16	73
Company 4	Branch banking	13	13	72
Company 4	Systems development	1	1	98
Company 5	Treasury	4	1	57
Total	20	95	89	1719

perspective, in many companies an annual savings of 15% of white-collar payroll costs would more than double annual corporate net earnings.

The purpose of this chapter is to report our findings, to describe a new office productivity modeling and measurement technique that can be used to identify and overcome the problems of intellectual nonspecialization, to explore why intellectual nonspecialization occurs, to explore the relation between office technology and nonspecialization, and to present some implications of this work for corporate management.

STUDY METHODOLOGY

Between 1985 and 1994, we studied white-collar work in 20 departments of five major U.S. corporations. Each of these departments represented a separate case study. In total, over 1,700 employees in 95 distinct offices in 89 locations throughout the United States were involved in these studies. Table 5.1 describes the five companies. The names of these companies are withheld in order to honor confidentiality agreements. Table 5.2 describes the 20 departments that we studied.

In each case study, a closed-ended time logging instrument, or diary, was developed to capture employee time by the defined tasks and activities. This instrument was tested, revised, and refined to eliminate any ambiguities, omissions, or other problems. The diaries were broadly similar in all studies, but we developed unique versions specific to each organization studied. In fact, in most cases, we developed versions unique to each level of worker in the organization (e.g., omitting management tasks in secretaries' diaries).

This study is novel in several important respects. First, because it is based on a new conceptual model of the office (which focuses on the intellectual content of office work), we were able to collect detailed work content data that are interorganizationally comparable. This has been a major stumbling block in previous work. Second, by focusing on entire organizational units rather than on isolated individuals, we were able to develop important conclusions about the total volume of work of different intellectual content, the efficiency with which organizations operate, and opportunities for significantly improving office productivity. Third, the magnitude of this study (over 1,700 individuals in 20 organizations) appears to be significantly greater than that of the previous studies of which we are aware.

RESULTS

We use the term *intellectual specialization* to characterize how a manager or professional spends his or her day. Loosely, a manager who spends much of the day doing management-level work (work that cannot be delegated downward to nonmanagers) is intellectually specialized. A senior professional, say an experienced engineer or financial analyst, who spends much of the day doing work that could be done by lesser skilled and lesser paid employees, is intellectually nonspecialized. We found intellectual nonspecialization to be the dominant characteristic of most organizations.

A very useful concept is the *work profile matrix*. The matrix shows the office hierarchy down the left side, and across the top are the categories indicating the intellectual content of the work. The office hierarchy is often managers, senior professionals, junior professionals, technical support workers, and administrative support workers. A more or less detailed stratification can also be used, however. The work categories are defined to correspond to the positions in the hierarchy. So, in this example, all tasks in the office would be uniquely classified as manage-

TABLE 5.3. Mean Work Profile Matrix (*n* = 1,719)

Position in the Office Hierarchy	No.	Management Work (%)	Senior Professional Work (%)	Junior Professional Work (%)	Technical Support Work (%)	Administrative Support Work (%)	Nonproductive work (%)	Sum (%)
Managers	197	29.91	28.91	8.97	3.02	14.46	14.73	100
Senior professionals	550	3.96	41.52	18.07	5.40	18.67	12.38	100
Junior professionals	336	1.52	7.36	51.78	4.72	18.16	16.45	100
Technical support	311	0.08	0.23	5.52	68.44	11.02	14.70	100
Administrative suppport	325	0.00	0.00	0.77	6.57	81.67	10.99	100
Total	1,719	5.07	18.29	18.28	16.74	27.98	13.63	100

ment-level work, senior professional-level work, junior professional-level work, technical support-level work, administrative support-level work, or nonproductive work. The final category (nonproductive work) is always included, regardless of the stratification used. In general, tasks are assigned to an intellectual content category based on the lowest level in the hierarchy to which the task may reasonably be delegated. The work profile matrix, then, is actually an abstract model of an office. It can be used to represent a single office or an aggregation of offices.

The aggregated (mean) work profile matrix for our set of offices is shown in Table 5.3. The major finding is the significant lack of intellectual specialization among managers and professionals. It is interesting to note the clear pattern of intellectual specialization, as measured by the main diagonal of Table 5.3. Intellectual specialization uniformly decreases as job levels increase. That is, managers spend the least time (29.91%) in work at their position level, and at the other end of the diagonal, administrative support workers spend the most time (81.67%) in work at their level. Senior professionals, junior professionals, and technical support workers fall neatly between these extremes. This pattern is so pronounced in most of the individual cases as well as in the aggregated data that it might well be called the "law of diminishing specialization of office work."

The bottom row of Table 5.3 shows the overall distribution of work by its intellectual content. For our sample of 20 departments, about 5% of the work is at management level. Senior- and junior-level professional work each account for about 28% of the total. The sum of technical and administrative support work is about 45% of the total. About 14% of the total is nonproductive work By showing the fundamental structure of an organization's work, the summary row of a work profile matrix is an extremely useful set of statistics. In the next section, we show how these statistics are used to analyze and optimize an organization's staffing structure.

The managers in our study are, of course, the managers of the functional areas listed in Table 5.2. These managers are all either first-line managers or middle managers (in some larger departments that we studied, there were two or three layers of management). However, the managers in our studies would not be considered senior, executive, or corporate management. This distinction is critical. We did not ask senior managers to complete time logs, but we did interview senior managers as part of most case studies. The clear indication from these interviews is that senior managers are more intellectually specialized than lower level managers. That is, they do not perform much work that could be delegated to lower level workers. In most cases, the reason is clear. Senior managers, in general, have adequate staff support. A senior manager usually has more than adequate secretarial support, he or she has priority in marshaling technical support when he or she needs it, and his or her responsibilities usually do not include doing functional professional work. Of course, the position also enables him or her to delegate work more easily than subordinate managers can. Thus, the law of diminishing specialization seems to apply within functional departments, but not at the corporate management level.

Why do managers and professionals spend substantial portions of their time doing work that is more appropriately done by lesser paid employees? The easy (and almost tautological) answer is that organizations are top heavy: There are relatively more managers and professionals, and relatively fewer support staff, than are needed to perform the organization's work. Consequently, some of the support work must be performed by managers and professionals.

Why has this staffing imbalance occurred, and why does it apparently persist? Even though this is an economic issue, economic theory provides little insight in addressing this puzzle. This is because conventional economic theory assumes that firms are efficient resource allocators—that firms know how to determine the least costly mix of inputs (different types of labor, in this case), that they do make such determinations, and that they act accordingly.[1] Thus, economic theory dismisses or at least skirts the problem of firms misallocating resources on a continuing basis.

Based on our observations and our discussions with managers, we can proffer several hypotheses to account for this phenomenon. First, there is the tendency of firms to manage staffing by head count, rather than by payroll. In growing organizations, managers periodically make their case to their superiors for increased head count. Given permission to expand their staff by a given number of employees, the tendency among department managers is to hire additional managers and professionals rather than additional support staff.

Similarly, when business conditions force reductions in staff, those cuts are often planned and executed in terms of head count. The same reasoning leads to management and professional-level workers keeping their jobs and support workers being released. As a company experiences periodic business cycles, this tendency (of hiring managers and professionals on the upswing, and releasing support workers on the downswing) creates and sustains a top-heavy organizational structure. The tendency is reinforced by the recognition among the department managers that their own compensation and the prestige of their departments are both more likely to be enhanced by having relatively more, rather than relatively fewer, managers and professionals in their organizations.

Another cause of top-heavy staffing appears to be office information systems. Compared with traditional expenditures on office capital equipment (typewriters, file cabinets, and desks), office computer systems are a very significant budget item. Many firms decide to pay for their office information systems by reducing their support staff. The reasoning is simply that computer systems can absorb and eliminate some work, and can increase the efficiency with which some of the remaining works gets done. Thus, fewer support workers are needed. The problem has been that many office computer systems have not delivered on this promise. For numerous reasons, these systems have not yet appreciably improved overall office productivity. Thus, with a diminished support staff, the managers and professionals are forced to perform additional support work. Paradoxically, although office computer systems can unmistakably increase productivity in a limited set of office activities (e.g., typing, filing, creating and distributing forms, spreadsheet analyses, graphics), their indirect and unintended effect on staffing may cause overall organizational productivity to decline. This point is discussed further later.

Another contributor to the problem is the combination of stagnant growth and traditional personnel policy. As concerns about competitiveness have proliferated, companies have attempted to control personnel costs by not hiring additional white-collar workers, and not replacing many who leave. However, routine pay raises and career track promotions move some professional-level workers into management-level positions, and at least a few support-level workers into professional-level positions. As new duties and responsibilities are defined for these new professionals and managers, who must now draw on a diminished support staff, the effect is to create or exacerbate a top-heavy organizational structure.

The final, and perhaps the most conspicuous, cause of top-heavy organizations is the efficiency drive. As companies strive to cut costs, office support workers are often released in greater proportions than managers and professionals. Numerous rationales are invoked to support this strategy. One line of thinking is that the volume of needed office support will somehow diminish as the support staff diminishes. Another line of thinking is that support work is less important and less necessary than management and professional work, and that the organization can simply get along with less of it. Another rationale is that managers and professionals, representing substantial investments in training, have high replacement costs, whereas support workers represent little investment and are easily replaced. The net effect, regardless of the rationale, is top-heavy staffing and diminished intellectual specialization.

TABLE 5.4. A Typical Department

Position in the Office Hierarchy	No.	Management Work (%)	Senior Professional Work (%)	Junior Professional Work (%)	Technical Support Work (%)	Administrative Work (%)	Nonproductive work (%)	Sum (%)	Hours Per Week	Weeks Per Year	Annual Loaded Salary (US$)
Managers	11	26.88	27.18	14.29	2.39	16.36	12.90	100	40	46	75,000
Senior professionals	28	3.23	42.01	18.13	5.26	19.39	11.98	100	40	46	60,000
Junior professionals	16	1.51	6.79	55.12	4.27	18.28	14.02	100	40	46	45,000
Technical support	18	0.08	0.23	5.52	68.44	11.02	14.70	100	40	46	35,000
Administrative support	18	0.00	0.00	0.82	4.14	84.57	10.46	100	40	46	25,000
Total	91	165[a]	635[a]	664[a]	619[a]	1,094[a]	462[a]		3,640		4.305 million

Note: [a]In hours per week.

95

TABLE 5.5. Restructured Work Profile

Position in the Office Hierarchy	No.	Management Work (%)	Senior Professional Work (%)	Junior Professional Work (%)	Technical Support Work (%)	Administrative Work (%)	Nonproductive work (%)	Sum (%)	Hours Per Week	Weeks Per Year	Annual Loaded Salary (US$)
Managers		50	25	10	5	5	5	100	40	46	75,000
Senior professionals		5	60	20	5	5	5	100	40	46	60,000
Junior professionals		0	5	70	10	10	5	100	40	46	45,000
Technical support		0	0	5	80	10	5	100	40	46	35,000
Administrative support		0	0	0	5	90	5	100	40	46	25,000
Total	165	635	664	619	1,094						

Top-heavy staffing can persist in an organization because, until now, there has not been a statistically based methodology to confirm its presence, or to measure its extent, or to determine the changes that are needed. The next section describes and illustrates the methodology for analyzing and optimizing staffing structure.

ANALYSIS

What are the costs of this lack of intellectual specialization in white-collar work? Although the data reported here are too narrow to draw sweeping conclusions, some insight into the magnitude of costs (and potential benefits) can be gained by looking at a typical department. Our typical department (represented in Table 5.4) is staffed very nearly as the average of the 20 departments we studied, and the work profile matrix is also near the mean matrix reported in Table 5.3. The hours worked per week, weeks worked per year (52 weeks less holidays less vacation less sick days less training days), and loaded annual salaries are representative of our data, although they are not the actual values for any specific case.

Suppose that the work and the jobs in our typical department could be restructured to increase intellectual specialization. That is, suppose managers could spend, say, 50% (instead of 26.88%) of their time in management type work. Suppose that other workers could also increase their intellectual specialization. And suppose that (through improvements in processes, procedures, and technology) nonproductive time could be reduced to only 5% for all workers.[2] The target work profiles are shown in Table 5.5. These profiles, although not reflecting the exact time allocation for any specific real organization that we are aware of, are a stylized version of the more intellectually specialized departments in our database (the top quartile). In other words, based on our observations of actual departments, the work profiles in Table 5.5 are attainable. Let us now examine the financial implications of increased intellectual specialization.

In order to analyze these potential changes, let us explicitly recognize the variables and the constants in our analysis. The constants are the total number of hours of each type of work that must be performed each week. We assume that the totals given at the bottom of Table 5.5 (i.e., 165 hours per week of management work, 635 hours per week of senior professional work, etc.) represent fixed requirements.[3] We assume that the numbers of employees in each category are variable. That is, because we are changing the work profiles of employees, the optimal number of each type of worker is likely to be different from the baseline numbers of staff.

In order to determine the optimum number of employees at each level, we can formulate and solve the problem using linear programming. Our objective is to find that number of each type of employee that minimizes the total departmental payroll, and at the same time accomplishes the required work.

Let M represent the number of managers, S the number of senior professionals, and F, T, and A the numbers of junior professionals, technical support, and administrative support people, respectively. We want to minimize:

$$\text{Payroll} = 75{,}000M + 60{,}000S + 45{,}000F + 35{,}000T + 25{,}000A \quad (1)$$

Subject to the constraints:

$$20M + 2S + 0F + 0I + 0A \geq 165 \quad (2)$$

$$10M + 24S + 2F + 0I + 0A \geq 635 \quad (3)$$

$$4M + 8S + 28F + 2I + 0A \geq 664 \quad (4)$$

$$2M + 2S + 4F + 32I + 2A \geq 619 \quad (5)$$

$$2M + 2S + 4F + 4I + 36A \geq 1{,}094 \quad (6)$$

$$M, S, F, I, A \geq 0 \quad (7)$$

Equation 1 is simply the expression for calculating the department's payroll. Inequalities 2 to 6 state that the numbers of managers, senior professionals, and so on must be such that, if they spend their time according to the work profile in Table 5.5, the necessary weekly hours of management-level work (165 hours), senior professional-level work (635 hours), and so on will be accomplished. Inequality 7 simply states that the solution values of the variables must be non-negative.

The solution to this linear programming problem is: $M = 5.982$, $S = 22.685$, $F = 15.376$, $T = 14.035$, and $A = 25.528$. The solution values are not integers, but in practice these numbers would be rounded up or down to whole persons. However, for the illustrative purposes of some subsequent calculations, we simply use the fractional values.

The optimized staffing plan indicates that the total number of required employees is 83.6 (vs. 91 originally). The total payroll is now US$3,631,000 (vs. US$4,305,000 originally). The savings, US$674,000 annually, represent 15.7% of the original payroll. In other words, by trimming nonproductive time, by redefining jobs to increase intellectual specialization, and by optimizing the staffing mix, our typical department could save 15.7% of its total labor costs and still continue to get the same amount of work accomplished. Another way to look at this result is that there is US$674,000 divided by 91, or about US$7,400, of potential annual (not simply one-time) savings per white-collar employee in a typical department. For most firms, annual savings of that magnitude (if realized across most white-collar departments) would represent a very substantial increase in annual profits—more than doubling profits in many cases.

What if the productivity goal in this hypothetical department were to increase output while holding costs constant, rather than to decrease costs while holding output constant? In this case, we could simply scale the previous solution up to the initial level of the payroll. That is, we would scale up M, S, F, T, and A by 18.6% so that the payroll reaches US$4,305,000. The solution in this case would be $M = 7.092$, $S = 26.896$, $F = 18.230$, $T = 16,640$, and $A = 30.266$. In other words, by trimming nonproductive time, by redefining jobs to increase intellectual specialization, and by optimizing the staffing mix, our typical department could increase output (or at least increase all levels of work) by 18.6% without increasing payroll costs.

A NEW MODEL OF THE OFFICE

What factors account for an office's work profile, how does that work profile change as the staffing changes, and how are output, productivity, and work profiles affected by technology? In this section, we develop a simple model of an office that answers these questions.

Let us adopt the following assumptions. First, assume that there are three types of employees in the office: managers, professionals, and support workers. Assume that they number 4, 20, and 12, respectively. Second, assume that each hour of management or professional work generates the need for 2 hours of support work. The ratio of required hours of support work to the sum of management and professional work hours is called the *support ratio* (assumed to be 2.00 for this example). Third, assume that managers devote an average of 30% of their time to management-level tasks, that 15% of their time is absorbed by nonproductive activities, and that their remaining time is split between those two work categories. Fourth, assume that everyone works a 40-hour week, and that professionals and support workers lose an average of 15% and 10% of their time, respectively, to nonproductive activities.

TABLE 5.6. Example Work Profile Matrix

Position in the Hierarchy	No.	Management Work (%)	Professional Work (%)	Support Work (%)	Nonproductive work (%)	Hours Per Week	Loaded Salary (US$)
Managers	4	30	a	b	15	40	100,000
Professionals	20	0	c	d	15	40	75,000
Support workers	12	0	0	90	10	40	30,000
Total	36	48 hours per week	$P = 160a\% + 800c\%$	$S = 160b\% + 800d\% + 432$	192 hours per week	1,440	2,260,000

Any or all of these assumptions could be modified without materially altering the model. As they stand, they simplify our example while preserving the basic ideas of the model. The work profile matrix can be initially represented as in Table 5.6.

Notice that the time allocated by managers and professionals to professional and support-level work is represented by the variables $a\%$, $b\%$, $c\%$, and $d\%$. Note also that in the last row of the table, we have defined P as the total number of hours of professional work performed in the office per week, and S as the total number of hours of support work. Because there are four managers and 20 professionals, each of whom works 40 hours per week, the weekly total number of hours of professional level work is $(4 \times 40 \times a\%) + (20 \times 40 \times c\%)$, or $P = 160a\% + 800c\%$. Similarly, $S = (4 \times 40 \times b\%) + (20 \times 40 \times d\%) + (12 \times 40 \times 90\%)$, or $S = 160b\% + 800d\% + 432$.

In what follows, we develop a new model of the office based on the concepts of the supply and demand for support work. Using this model, we show that the variables ($a\%$, $b\%$, $c\%$, $d\%$, P, and S) have unique equilibrium values determined by the intersection of our supply and demand functions.

Because all work hours must add up to 1,440 for this office, the supply of support work, denoted as supply(S), is simply the hours not devoted to management, professional, or nonproductive work. That is,

$$\text{supply}(S) = 1440 - 48 - P - 192 \qquad (8)$$

The demand for support work, written demand(S), is determined by the second assumption: that each hour of management work (48), and each hour of professional work (P), creates a demand for 2 hours of support work. That is,

$$\text{demand}(S) = 2(48 + P) \qquad (9)$$

The equilibrium condition is, of course, that the supply of support work must equal the demand for support work, or

$$\text{supply}(S) = \text{demand}(S) \qquad (10)$$

or, substituting from Equations 8 and 9:

$$1440 - 48 - P - 192 = 2(48 + P) \qquad (11)$$

TABLE 5.7. Equilibrium Work Profile Matrix

Position in the Hierarchy	No.	Management Work (%)	Professional Work (%)	Support Work (%)	Nonproductive work (%)	Hours Per Week	Loaded Salary (US$)
Managers	4	30	26.35	28.65	15	40	100,000
Professionals	20	0	40.73	44.27	15	40	75,000
Support workers	12	0	0	90	10	40	30,000
Total	36	48 hours per week	P = 368 hours per week	S = 832 hours per week	192 hours per week	1,440	2,260,000

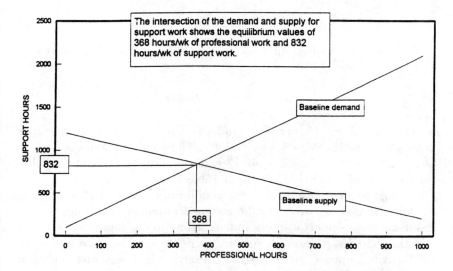

FIGURE 5.1.   Demand and Supply of Support Hours (Baseline Case)

The solution to this equation is $P = 368$ hours per week. Substituting this value into either the supply or demand equation yields $S = 832$ hours per week.

Note that both the supply of support work and the demand for support work are functions of P, the amount of professional work.[4] The more professional work done, the more support work must be done. However, the more professional work done, the less time there is available (to managers and professionals) to do support work. Thus, the demand for support work is an increasing function of the amount of professional work and the supply of support work is a decreasing function of the amount of professional work. These functions and the resulting equilibrium are graphically illustrated in Figure 5.1.

Once the equilibrium values of P and S are determined within the model, the equilibrium values of the work profile variables, a, b, c, and d can also be determined.

Because each row of the work profile matrix must sum to unity, we have

$$30\% + a\% + b\% + 15\% = 100\% \tag{12}$$

$$0\% + c\% + d\% + 15\% = 100\% \tag{13}$$

According to the third assumption, managers and professionals split their total professional and support time the same way, or

$$a/(a + b) = c/(c + d). \tag{14}$$

We know the equilibrium value of P is 368, so from the last row of Table 5.6, we have

$$368 = 160a\% + 800c\%. \tag{15}$$

Statements 12 to 15 are four independent equations in the four unknown variables $a\%$, $b\%$, $c\%$, and $d\%$. The solution values are $a\% = 26.35\%$, $b\% = 28.65\%$, $c\% = 40.73\%$, and $d\% = 44.27\%$. The equilibrium work profile matrix is shown in Table 5.7.

It is easy to demonstrate that the equilibrium values of P, S, $a\%$, $b\%$, $c\%$, and $d\%$ vary according to the assumed numbers of managers, professionals, and support workers and according to the support ratio.

In the following section, we use this model to shed light on why office productivity appears to be stagnant, even as business investment in office information technology has skyrocketed.

TECHNOLOGY, DOWNSIZING, REENGINEERING, AND PRODUCTIVITY

Over the past decade, U.S. businesses have invested hundreds of billions of dollars in information technology (consider that IBM alone has earned revenues exceeding US$600 billion over the past decade). A significant fraction of that investment involved purchasing, installing, supporting, and upgrading office information systems. At the same time, although there are no widely accepted official statistics, it is generally accepted that average office productivity did not improve markedly (or perhaps at all) during that period. What happened? Why was there so little apparent productivity payoff associated with such massive investment?

We can begin to understand these events by identifying and analyzing several common business scenarios:

1. Some firms, as discussed previously, have attempted to control costs by reducing the number of office support personnel.
2. Some firms have installed office technology to enhance professional workers (e.g., engineering workstations), and simultaneously reduced the number of support personnel.
3. Some firms have installed office technology to enhance support personnel (e.g., PCs for word processing), and simultaneously reduced the number of support personnel.

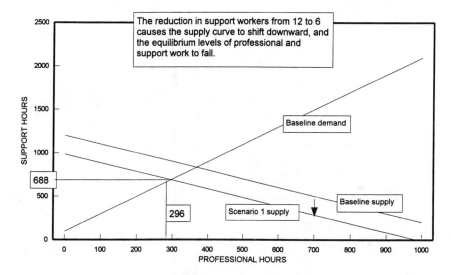

FIGURE 5.2.   Demand and Supply of Support Hours (Scenario 1)

4. Some firms have installed office technology to enhance professional
    workers (e.g., engineering workstations), and have left the number
    of support personnel unchanged.

Each of these scenarios can be analyzed using our model of the supply
and demand for office support work. To make the analysis concrete, let
us continue using the numerical example introduced in the previous
section. Suppose that in each of the first three scenarios, the number of
support workers was reduced from the baseline number of 12 to a new
value of 6. Suppose that in Scenarios 2 and 4, the efficiency of professional work is increased by 25%; and that in Scenario 3, the efficiency of
support work is increased by 25%. Efficiency refers simply to output per
hour. An increase in the efficiency of, say, professional work by 25%
means that 25% more professional work is accomplished per hour
devoted to professional work.

Figure 5.2 shows the effect of decreasing the number of support workers in our example office. The supply (of support work) curve, as
defined previously and depicted in Figure 5.1, shifts downward as
shown. The demand for support work remains unchanged. The new
equilibrium values of P and S, determined by the intersection of the
demand curve and the new supply curve, are 296 hours per week of professional work and 688 hours per week of support work. As expected,
the model shows that a decrease in support workers causes the total

TABLE 5.8. Equilibrium Work Profile Matrix for Scenario 1

Position in the Hierarchy	No.	Management Work (%)	Professional Work (%)	Support Work (%)	Nonproductive work (%)	Hours Per Week	Loaded Salary (US$)
Managers	4	30	21.20	33.80	15	40	100,000
Professionals	20	0	32.76	52.24	15	40	75,000
Support workers	12	0	0	90	10	40	30,000
Total	36	48 hours per week	$P = 296$ hours per week	$S = 688$ hours per week	168 hours per week	1,200	2,080,000

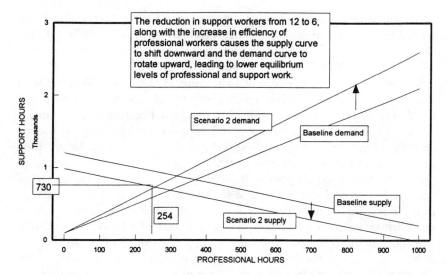

FIGURE 5.3.   Demand and Supply of Support Hours (Scenario 2)

amount of professional work to decline. The reason is clear from Table 5.8, which is the corresponding new equilibrium work profile matrix. With fewer support workers, managers and professionals must increase the amount of time that they devote to support work in order to get the department's work done. The amount of professional work (arguably the best measure of the department's output) declines from 368 hours per week to 296, or a reduction of about 20%. The payroll saving associated with the fewer support workers is about 8%.

Figure 5.3, corresponding to Scenario 2, shows the effect of increasing by 25% the efficiency with which professional work is accomplished (say through information technology), and simultaneously decreasing the number of support workers from 12 to 6 (perhaps to recover the cost of the investment in information technology). Because professional work is done by both managers and professionals, the 25% improvement in efficiency applies to the professional work done by both these groups. As in Figure 5.2, the supply curve shifts downward. Unlike Figure 5.2, the demand curve rotates upward because each hour of professional work now requires 25% more support work. The new equilibrium values of P and S are 253.7 and 730.3 hours per week, respectively. Because of the 25% increase in the efficiency of professional work, the output of professional work would be $253.7 \times 1.25 = 317.1$ hours worth of output. Note that in spite of a significant enhancement in the efficiency of doing professional work, the total output of professional work has still declined by about 14%. The reason, of course, is the unavoidable decrease in intellectual specialization among the professionals, just as in Table 5.8. (In this case, the new equilibrium values of the work profile matrix are $a = 18.17\%$, $b = 36.83\%$, $c = 28.08\%$, and $d = 56.92\%$).

Scenario 3 shows the effect of increasing by 25% the efficiency with which support work is performed, and simultaneously decreasing the number of support workers from 12 to 6. Again, because support work is done by managers, professionals, and support workers, the postulated increase of 25% efficiency applies to the support work done by all three groups. As in the previous figures, the supply curve shifts downward to reflect the truncated support staff. The demand curve rotates downward because the increased efficiency of support hours means that fewer support hours are needed per hour of professional work. The resulting equilibrium values of P and S are 348.9 and 635.1 hours per week, respectively. In this case, the output of professional work declines by about 5%, despite the increased support efficiency of everyone in the department. The new equilibrium values of the work profile matrix are $a = 24.99\%$, $b = 30.01\%$, $c = 38.62\%$, and $d = 46.38\%$.

Finally, Scenario 4 is a case with no postulated decrease in the number of support workers, and with a postulated 25% increase in the efficiency of hours devoted to professional work. It would seem that the output of professional work should increase dramatically in this case. In fact, only a modest increase occurs because the increased demand for support hours (each hour of professional work now requires 25% more support work) is not matched by an increase in the supply of support hours. Therefore, once again, more of managers' and professionals' time must be diverted to performing support work. The supply curve is unchanged, and the demand curve rotates upward. The resulting equilibrium values of P and S are 315.4 and 884.6 hours per week, respectively. Because the efficiency of hours in professional work increased by 25%, professional output would be $315.4 \times 1.25 = 394.3$ hours worth of output. Therefore, professional output increases by about 7%. Again, the reason for the modest increase in output is the unavoidable decrease in intellectual specialization caused by the relative (to support work) increase in the efficiency of professional work. The new equilibrium work profile values are $a = 22.59\%$, $b = 32.41\%$, $c 34.91\%$, and $d = 50.09\%$.

These four cases (Scenarios 1–4) are summarized in the top half of Table 5.9. In that table, all percentage changes are calculated from the base case, which is shown in the first line of the table, and in more detail in Table 5.7.

These four examples—reasonable (even if abstract) representations of the office resource allocation strategies pursued by many organizations

TABLE 5.9. Summary of Office Productivity Impacts Under Various Scenarios

Scenario	Description	Professional Work (Equivalent Hours)	Percentage Change in Professional Work	Support Work (Equivalent Hours)	Percentage Change in Support Work	Payroll (US$ Millions)	Percentage Change in Total Payroll
Base case	See Table 5.	368.00		832.00		2.26	
1	Support workers reduced from 12 to 6.	296.00	-19.57	688.00	-17.31	2.08	-7.96
2	Support workers reduced from 12 to 6. Technology increases efficiency of professionals by 25%.	317.14	-13.82	730.29	-12.23	2.08	-7.96
3	Support workers reduced from 12 to 6. Technology increases efficiency of support workers by 25%.	348.92	-5.18	793.85	-4.59	2.08	-7.76
4	Support workers unchanged. Technology increases efficiency of support workers by 25%.	394.29	+7.14	884.57	+6.32	2.26	0.00
5	Support workers increased to 18.	440.00	+19.57	976.00	+17.31	2.44	+7.96
6	Technology increases efficiency of all office workers by 25%	460.00	+25.00	1040.00	+25.00	2.44	+7.96
7	25% of previously required support work eliminated.	451.20	+22.61	748.80	-10.00	2.26	0.00
8	Support workers increased to 18. Technology increases efficiency of all office workers by 25%. 25% of previously required support work eliminated.	672.00	+82.61	1,098.00	+31.97	2.44	+7.96

during the last decade—shed some light on why office productivity has stagnated in the face of massive investments in information technology. The examples also help to explain the paradox of office technology. On the one hand, the ability of office technology to save office workers' time in specific tasks has been amply demonstrated by vendors and consultants, and even experienced firsthand by a large segment of office workers. Computer-based applications such as word processing, spreadsheets, databases, and graphics can and do save time. There is no longer any serious dispute about that. On the other hand, overall office productivity—however reasonably defined—has not tended to reflect these apparent improvements. Our model and examples demonstrate that extracting overall office productivity improvements from technology depends on more than simply buying and using it. It depends on balancing the impact of technology on support workers and professionals, and on calibrating the office staffing at least to maintain, but preferably to increase, the level of intellectual specialization. Many organizations have invested heavily in technology, but they have not made the essential adjustments in staffing to take advantage of the technology. Indeed, in many instances (Scenarios 2 and 3), firms have made squarely the wrong decisions. They have used technology to decrease, rather than to increase, intellectual specialization.

THE THREE KEYS TO OFFICE PRODUCTIVITY

An effective office productivity strategy involves three elements. We have mentioned two already: recalibrating the staffing mix and using technology to improve the efficiency with which work is accomplished. The third element is, perhaps, the most obvious: using technology or other means simply to eliminate part of the workload.[5] Let us continue to use our example office to illustrate each of these. We analyze the following four scenarios:

5. Suppose our example office increases the number of support workers from 12 to 18.
6. Suppose our example office successfully implements office information technology, which enhances work efficiency by 25% across the board.
7. Suppose our example office finds a way to eliminate 25% of the previously required support work, perhaps through eliminating the preparation of redundant or low-value reports.
8. Finally, as a best case illustration, suppose our example office implements all three of these improvements.

In Scenario 5, an increase in the number of support workers shifts the supply curve upward. The demand for support curve remains unchanged. The new equilibrium time allocation for the office is 440 hours per week of professional work and 976 hours per week of support work. The new equilibrium values of the work profile matrix are $a = 31.51\%$, $b = 23.49\%$, $c = 48.70\%$, and $d\%$. Note that the change in professional work (and presumably output) is from 368 to 440 hours per week, or an increase of nearly 20%. The corresponding increase in the office payroll is US$180,000, or only about 8%. As long as there is the opportunity to use the additional professional hours profitably, this case illustrates the significant productivity opportunity associated with improving the staffing mix.[6]

In Scenario 6, a uniform 25% increase in the efficiency with which management, professional, and support work is accomplished has no effect on the supply of support work, and it causes exactly offsetting changes in the demand curve. The increased efficiency of management and professional work causes the demand for support to shift upward (as each more productive hour of management and professional work requires more support work). However, the increased efficiency of support work causes the demand curve to shift downward (as each hour of professional work requires fewer of the now more productive hours of support work). The net effect in this case is that the upward and down-

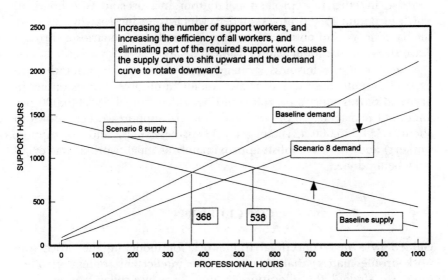

FIGURE 5.4. Demand and Supply of Support Hours (Baseline and Scenario 8 cases)

ward shifts of the demand curve balance each other exactly, and the demand curve remains unchanged. Thus, the equilibrium office time allocation also remains unchanged. However, the output of professional work (and other work as well) increases by 25% in this scenario, due, of course, to the postulated increase in efficiency and to the unchanged number of hours devoted to professional work.

In Scenario 7, the elimination of 25% of the required support work causes the demand curve to rotate downward because fewer hours of support work are now required per hour of professional work. The resulting new equilibrium time allocation is 451.2 hours per week of professional work and 748.8 hours per week of support work. The new work profile matrix values are $a = 32.31\%$, $b = 22.69\%$, $c = 49.94\%$, and $d = 35.06\%$. The amount of professional time (and work) increases by over 22%, whereas the amount of support work decreases by about 10%.

Finally Figure 5.4, illustrating Scenario 8, combines the previous three scenarios as a "best case" example. Here, the firm implements all three prongs of the office productivity strategy. The supply curve shifts upward, efficiency increases across the board, and the demand curve rotates downward. The resulting equilibrium time allocation is 537.6 hours per week of professional work and 878.4 hours per week of support work. The corresponding values of the work profile matrix are $a = 38.50\%$, $b = 16.50\%$, $c = 59.50\%$, and $d = 25.50\%$. Because of the increase in efficiency, professional output increases to 672 hours of worth of output (537.6 hours × 1.25), which is an increase of 83% over the baseline level of output. Note that the results of Scenarios 5 through 8 are shown in the lower half of Table 5.9.

Note that if the business strategy were to cut costs rather than to expand output, these scenarios are equally applicable. For example, in Scenario 8, this office's payroll could be scaled from US$2,440,000 per annum (4 managers, 20 professionals, and 18 support workers) down to about US$1,325,000 (2 managers, 11 professionals, and 10 support workers) and still accomplish approximately as much work as was originally being done.

CONCLUSIONS

Guided by a new conceptual framework for modeling the office (the work profile matrix) that focuses on the intellectual content of office work, we studied the allocation of time by white-collar workers in a series of 20 departmentwide studies within five major U.S. corporations. These studies, conducted between 1985 and 1994, are perhaps the most extensive set of office productivity studies to date. Overall, we collected detailed time log data from over 1,700 individuals in 95 physical offices around the United States.

Our major findings are: (a) there is a widespread and pronounced lack of intellectual specialization among managers and professionals; (b) in a typical office, intellectual specialization tends to decrease as one moves up the hierarchy; (c) the proximate cause of intellectual nonspecialization is top-heavy staffing; and (d) the annual financial cost of this resource misallocation is about 15% of total white-collar payroll costs in a typical case.

Based on our conceptual framework, our empirical findings, our interviews, and discussions with managers, and our related technology cost justification work,[7] we developed a quantitative economic model of office labor resource allocation. The model, which has as its main analytic elements the supply and demand for support labor within the office, explains and predicts how office output and office productivity are affected by the staffing mix, by the intellectual content of the office work, and by office information technology. Among other things, the model helps to explain why massive U.S. corporate investments in office technology have failed to ignite an explosive increase in office productivity.

With the aid of Figure 5.5, let us review the main points of our model of office work. Starting at the right side, office productivity (which can be defined as professional output divided by total office hours, or alternatively as the unit cost of professional output) is determined by the level of intellectual specialization (i.e., the work profile matrix, which shows how much time workers devote to work of differing intellectual content and the resulting total amounts of management, professional, and support work accomplished in the office) and by work efficiency (how much management, professional, and support output is produced by each hour devoted to management, professional, and support work, respectively). Intellectual specialization, in turn, is determined by the staffing structure (how many managers, professionals, and support staff are employed in the office), by the work structure (how much management work must be done and how much support work is required by each hour of professional and management work), and by work efficiency (mentioned earlier). Both the work structure and the work efficiency are affected by the use of information technology (electronic data, text, image, and voice processing). We showed through numerical and graphical examples that in each office there is an "equilibrium" level of intellectual specialization toward which the office will gravitate, that this equilibrium is determined by the supply and demand for support work, that the supply curve is based on the staffing structure, that the demand

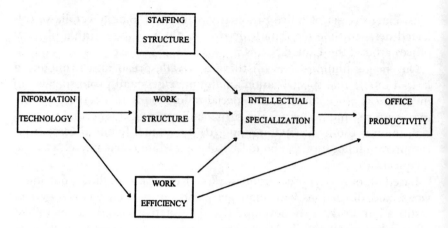

FIGURE 5.5. The Fundamental Elements of Office Productivity

curve is based on the work structure and work efficiency, and that information technology can shift the demand curve up or down (depending on whether the technology enhances professional workers or support workers).

IMPLICATIONS FOR MANAGERS

What implications, useful to managers, can we draw from our empirical results and from our analytic model of the office? Here are several.

- Learn to understand, to measure, and to track the intellectual content of office work, and learn how to staff the office accordingly.
  In every one of the 20 departments that we studied, there was a top-heavy staff. That is, as compared with the most efficient mix of managers, senior- and junior-level professionals, and technical and administrative support workers, every department had more than the desirable number of managers and/or senior professionals, and fewer than the desirable number of support workers. The financial cost of this misallocation of resources is very significant—averaging 15% of the total white-collar payroll. The annual savings associated with correcting this misallocation of resources could double the net earnings of many companies.
- Focus on intellectual specialization.
  Managers must learn and focus on the concept of intellectual specialization, which is the key to productivity in the professional office.

As suggested by Figure 5.5, intellectual specialization is the virtual sine qua non of office productivity. An office simply cannot achieve a high level of productivity unless its managers and professionals are devoting most of their time to professional-level work.

- Recognize that intellectual specialization leads to job enrichment.
Intellectual specialization does not mean task specialization. In achieving intellectual specialization, managers and professionals free themselves from many of the tasks that can be performed by lesser skilled workers. The variety and diversity of the management and professional tasks performed by managers and professionals need not diminish, and might well expand, as they have more time to devote to those activities. Intellectual specialization tends to enrich management and professional jobs, and it tends to reduce the time spent on the tasks that managers and professionals find least enjoyable. Similarly, intellectual specialization in the office can enrich the support jobs as well. As managers and professionals off-load some of the support tasks that they were performing, they increase the diversity and the level of responsibility of the support jobs. We have found (through our interviews of office workers) that, in general, the support tasks performed by managers and professionals are the tasks that support workers would most prefer to do. This is hardly surprising, because managers and professionals, even when circumstances force them to do support tasks, have some discretion in selecting which support tasks they will do and which they will delegate. Of course, they tend to delegate the more dreary tasks and to keep the more interesting ones. In terms of job quality for both professional and support workers, then, intellectual specialization is a win-win strategy.

- Do not use a back office strategy in a professional office.
In formulating office technology strategy, it is critical to distinguish clearly between so-called "back" offices and professional offices. A back office is one whose function and primary work is clerical. Typical back office functions are payroll, accounting, order entry, billing, and claims processing. In a back office, the clerical work is generated externally to the office whereas in a professional office, the support work is generated by the managers and professionals working within (and performing the function of) that office.[8] Unlike the largely successful experience with back office automation during the 1960s and 1970s, the substitution of information technology for support labor in today's professional office is not necessarily a winning strategy. In a professional office, technology is both a substitute and a complement for labor. Depending on which aspect dominates in a particular office, technology may demand more, rather

than fewer, support workers. Unfortunately, the idea that technology is always a substitute for labor still survives in many businesses. The notion is encouraged by technology vendors who can point to past instances of successful back office automation, and who suggest that their current offerings can be similarly cost-justified.

- Develop integrated (rather than piecemeal) office productivity strategy.

Perhaps the primary reason why the past decade's massive investment in office technology has not yielded significant widespread and visible productivity results is that concurrent and short-sighted staffing decisions were inadvertently mitigating the positive effects of the technology. In other words, labor resource allocation decisions and capital resource allocation decisions were unwittingly working at cross purposes. The lesson is that piecemeal office strategies are dangerous. The office is a complex work system where the staffing structure, the work structure, the professional work-enhancing technology, and the support work-enhancing technology all simultaneously affect how the staff members spend their time[9] and how much work gets accomplished. Thus, managers need to develop a holistic vision of office resources and to develop integrated (rather than piecemeal) office productivity strategies.

NOTES AND REFERENCES

[1] For example, see W. Nicholson, *Microeconomic Theory*, 4th Edn (Chicago, The Dryden Press, 1989); E. Silberberg, *The Structure of Economics: A Mathematical Analysis*, 2nd Edn (New York, McGraw-Hill, 1990). For alternative points of view that are consistent with enduring resource misallocation within the film, see H. Leibenstein, "Allocative Efficiency vs 'X-efficiency,'" *American Economic Review*, 1966; H. A. Simon, "Theories of Decision-Making in Economics and Behavioral Science," *American Economic Review*, 1959.

[2] The reduction in nonproductive time is not necessary to our analysis, but because it reflects typical reengineering strategy, we have incorporated it here.

[3] This assumption simplifies our analysis but it can easily be modified. In fact, typically, we might use technology or other means to absorb or eliminate some work, thereby reducing the required hours. Alternatively, we can forecast a growth in business resulting in increased work requirements. The same analytic techniques discussed here can be used under these circumstances.

[4] Our supply and demand functions differ from those normally employed in economic models. Normally, both the supply and the demand for a good or service are functions of the price of that good or service. The supply function is a positive (upward sloping) function of price, and demand is a negative (downward sloping) function of price.

[5] For a discussion of this point, see M. Hammer, "Reengineering Work: Don't Automate, Obliterate," *Harvard Business Review*, July-August 1990, pp. 104-112.

[6] Of course, the change in the staffing mix in this case is not necessarily the optimal change. The concept of the optimal staffing structure and the procedure for determining it is discussed in this chapter. In fact, in this case, a greater number of support workers would provide even greater productivity gains.

[7] P. G. Sassone, "Cost Benefit Analysis for Office Information Systems: A Hedonic Pricing Approach," In R. Taylor (Ed.), *Proceedings of the IEEE First International Conference on Office Automation* (Washington, DC, IEEE Press, 1984); P. G. Sassone, "Cost Benefit Methodology for Office Systems," *ACM Transactions on Office Information Systems* 5, pp. 273-289; P. G. Sassone, "A Survey of Cost-Benefit Methodologies for Information Systems," *Project Appraisal, 3*, 1988, pp. 73-84; P. G. Sassone & A. P. Schwartz, "Corporate Strategy for End User Computing," In J. Goldthwaite (Ed.), *OAC '85 Conference Digest* (Washington, DC, AFIPS Press, 1985); P. G. Sassone & A. P. Schwartz, "Cost Justification of Office Information Systems for Engineering Organizations," In *Proceedings of IEEE Conference on Systems, Man and Cybernetics* (Washington, DC, IEEE Press, 1985); P. G. Sassone & A. P. Schwartz, "Cost Justifying OA," *Datamation*, 15 February 1986, pp. 83-88.

[8] A model of the back office would, therefore, be very different from the model of the professional office that we have discussed in this report. The back office model would look more like a model of a manufacturing assembly line, where parts are shipped in and processed in some way, and then the resulting product is shipped out. In a back office, there is little or no professional-level work, and management work is primarily supervisory.

[9] This is a subtle but critical point: The office's work profile matrix (how people in an office spend their time) is largely determined by staffing, work structure, and technology. It is not determined by the personal preferences of the workers or by management fiat.

chapter 6

The Impact of Groupware: Work Process Automation and Organizational Learning

William M. Riggs
W. Hagood Bellinger
School of Management,
Georgia Tech

David B. Krieger
McKinsey & Company
Atlanta, GA

INTRODUCTION

The impact of groupware is growing, highlighted by the attention attracted by the high-profile maneuverings of corporate giants in the software business (see, e.g., Corcoran[1]). This is part of the phenomenon of *convergence*—the merging of the imaging capability of television, the data storage and processing capacity of computers, and the multichannel, multiparty communication capability of telecommunications. Groupware allows knowledge work to be accomplished by groups who interact via computer network, working from and adding to a common knowledge base.

Economist Paul Romer,[2] a leading proponent of the new growth theory, believed that technology is an integral driver of growth, and that the effort corporations put into discovery and innovation will in the future become more important to competitiveness than effort put into manufacturing. Finding ways to facilitate effective activity directed toward knowledge generation leading to discovery and innovation has therefore become a high priority for organizations.

Japanese scholars Nonaka and Takeuchiu[3] agreed that knowledge creation is a key to robust innovation in companies, and that knowledge is of two types—explicit and tacit. To deal with both types, they said, companies must shape themselves into "hypertext" organizations, with three superimposed structures: a traditional hierarchy to run the day-to-day business and to transmit explicit knowledge, a fluid structure composed of teams that form and reform to generate new ideas and solve problems, and a knowledge structure that includes explicit and tacit knowledge, organized in such a way as to be readily accessible within the organization. This knowledge base would include soft repositories of information such as corporate culture and the accumulated wisdom of older members, as well as hard information contained, for example, in computer databases.

Collaborative use and development of the organization's knowledge base is also of increasing importance. In his best-selling book *The Fifth Discipline*, Senge[4] quoted *Fortune* magazine: "Forget your tired old ideas about leadership. The most successful corporation of the 1990's will be something called a learning organization." He then defined learning organizations as "organizations where people continually expand their capacity to create the results they truly desire, where new and expansive patterns of thinking are nurtured, where collective aspiration is set free, and where people are continually learning how to learn together." Achievement of the learning organization in these terms clearly places a premium on improved means for collaborative work.

It is clear that the ability to build organizational knowledge effectively and to make it readily accessible for collaborative use by innovators and problem solvers is a critical organizational capability. This study begins to address the question of how groupware systems (such as Lotus, Notes, Novell's Groupwise, and Microsoft's promised offering, Exchange) can be optimally implemented to produce mechanisms for developing an organization's knowledge base and keeping it accessible for collaborative use. Following Baecker,[5] we define groupware as "information technology used to help people work together more effectively," or more formally as "the multi-user software supporting CSCW (Computer-Supported Cooperative Work) systems." CSCW is in turn defined as "computer-assisted coordinated activity such as communication and problem solving carried out by a group of collaborating individuals." Lloyd[6] told us, "There is much more to [groupware] than simple e-mail and file sharing....First it enables members of a team to work together—anytime, anywhere; secondly, it increases the richness of the communication between them."

BACKGROUND

Among the anticipated positive consequences of the information revolution is improvement in internal operations of organizations. It can be argued that the long-awaited improvement in productivity will come more quickly now that companies are learning to redesign their work processes[7] to take advantage of the power of computing, especially in networks. The need for such redesign has become increasingly clear. Studies have shown that despite investments in information technology (IT) for the office, productivity gains from IT have been elusive (e.g., Scott-Morton,[8] Sassone[9]). In order to reduce this problem, two kinds of change can occur: Work processes can be adjusted to take advantage of the available technology, and the technology (software in this case) can be modified better to support preferred and productive modes of work. The benefits of these changes should extend to many of the activities of organizations, and should be widely felt as increasing proportions of value-added activities take place in areas other than direct fabrication.[10]

It seems clear that one of the key tools for achieving the hoped-for gains will be the developing array of groupware applications. However, although consultants' case studies of groupware implementations have been appearing for some time, serious research results to guide managers in their efforts at implementation of these tools have only recently begun to appear.[11] A taxonomy of groupware applications is needed to aid in selection of appropriate strategies for implementation: that is, managers need to know what types of applications will provide adoption and acceptance of groupware by the organization so that the organization begins to learn how to use the technology. Then, as the organization begins to adapt to the technology, processes can be designed so that the bigger payoffs in productivity can occur.

In response to this need, we have set out first to identify a simplified, general model of the innovative processes in a company to aid us in identifying and classifying the information flows supporting and associated with these processes. We then use this model to clarify and specify the types of impact of groupware to expect on these information flows, and to guide empirical observation. We then conducted a case study of a Lotus Notes implementation in progress to see if the model is helpful in understanding what is actually happening, and to generate framework for further investigation.

CORPORATE PROCESS REDESIGN AND IT

Facing increasing competitive pressure, most companies have invested heavily in communication and IT to make them more efficient. However, as Scott-Morton[12] reported in MIT's study of companies' use of IT in organizational transformation:

> No impact from information technology is yet visible in the macroeconomic data available. A very few individual firms are demonstrably better off, and there is a larger group of isolated examples of successful exploitation in particular individual functions or business units. However, on average the expected benefits are not yet visible.

This observation raises the question of how IT should be introduced and utilized so that the organization can achieve the benefits the technology offers.

Organizations that extensively utilize knowledge workers have not escaped the competitive drive for efficiency and speed. The widespread use of teams—work teams, self-directed teams, project teams, matrixed teams, remote teams, and so on—has appeared as a response to this need. It is critical for such organizations to learn how to manage the redesign of knowledge work. They must learn how to leverage their intellectual capital through collaboration into new ideas, new discoveries, innovation, organizational learning, and personal growth.

Top managers have traditionally viewed themselves as the designers of the strategy, the architects of the structure, and the managers of the systems that direct and drive their companies. However, Bartlett and Ghoshal[13] found in their study of leading companies that today's environment of complexity and rapid change has eroded the effectiveness of top-level strategy setting.

> The problem is not the CEO but rather the assumption that the CEO *should* be the corporation's chief strategist, assuming full control of setting the company's objectives and determining its priorities. In an environment where the fast changing knowledge and expertise required to make such decisions are usually found on the front lines, this assumption is untenable.

They quoted CEO Andy Grove of Intel: "People formulate strategy with their fingertips. Our most significant strategic decision was made not in response to some clear sighted corporate vision but by the marketing and investment decisions of front-line managers who really knew what was going on." The successful companies note: "The scarcest corporate resources are less often the financial funds that top management controls than the knowledge and expertise of the people on the front lines." Companies are therefore faced with the question of how to tap into the knowledge of the front-line people doing the work and integrate it into organizational learning and corporate strategy. Groupware could be part of the answer.

Many companies today are building closer relationships with their suppliers, distributors, retailers, and customers. They are sharing not just routine information, but also what was once considered proprietary knowledge. This means more than just interconnected technology systems; it means knowledge workers interacting between companies with proprietary knowledge and information. How should these processes be designed and facilitated? Again, groupware would appear to offer help.

Deployment of groupware-based information systems to provide a platform for facilitating these types of interactions is growing rapidly. Lotus Notes is the leading software platform, holding a commanding technological and market advantage.[14] The acquisition of Lotus by IBM serves dramatically to underscore the perceived importance of the Notes application platform for networked computing.

RESEARCH QUESTIONS

This chapter is a beginning effort to understand what factors need to be taken into consideration in understanding the impact of groupware on organizations, and especially on the way work processes optimally change to take advantage of this technological capability. Armed with a clear understanding of the critical factors, companies may avoid the past problem of investing in technology without enjoying the payoff. Our orientation is not toward how technology supports groupware, but rather toward how people interact with and derive value from the technology, and especially toward how companies can improve productive processes through its use. We agree with Lloyd: "Groupware is about people and processes first; technology and systems second."[15]

Questions that we would like to begin answering about groupware information systems include:

- How can groupware best be deployed to improve organizational learning? How can organizations assimilate the knowledge that has been gained from a problem solved by an individual or a work team?
- What are the organizational change issues that are critical in adapting these types of work processes? How should these programs be

introduced? What are the first processes to be implemented? What change factors need to be considered?

- Is productivity improved with use of groupware? Are projects completed faster, or with fewer people? Is there a reduction of average time to complete a project attributable to tightening up of feedback loops, especially the ones that are not plannable? Is redundant work reduced? If shared databases allow people timely and easy access to proven solutions to problems, reinventing the wheel may be avoided.

- Is the quality of work improved? This could be through faster, more timely, or more reliable completion of tasks such as delivery of reports. It might also be some other quality consideration such as making better corrective action decisions due to the availability of more and/or better data on problems.

- What metrics can be employed to identify and capture these changes in work patterns and the associated benefits?

- What is the real payoff for a company? Is there a meaningful way to assess the return?

The first and second of these questions are issues of organizational impact, the third and fourth are productivity and quality issues, and the final two are questions of measurement. To begin to address these questions, we first develop a model that relates the flows of information potentially facilitated by groupware to corporate strategy. We then use this model to aid in interpretation of our case study observations.

THEORETICAL FRAMEWORK

Burgelman[16] proposed a model of dynamic interactions between organizational behavior and a firm's concept of strategy. This model was originally intended to illustrate the nature of innovation and corporate entrepreneurship, but it serves as a base framework that we extend to identify the role of groupware and collaborative work in task completion and innovation.

The model (Figure 6.1) indicates two major forces of organizational behavior acting on an organization's concept of corporate strategy. The first, represented by the lower loop of the model, corresponds to normal strategic action. Examples of this strategic behavior include new product development projects for existing businesses, market development projects for existing products, and improvements to manufacturing process efficiency and quality. Within this loop, the concept of corporate strategy provides a shared frame of reference for the organization, and

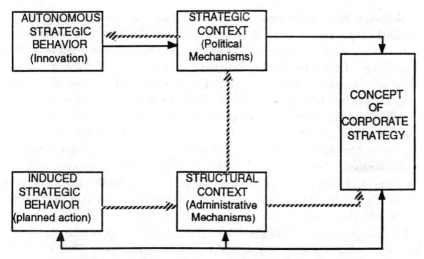

FIGURE 6.1. Model Illustrating the Dynamic Interactions Between a Firm's Strategy and Its Organizational Behavior

provides the basis for corporate objective setting in terms of its business portfolio and resource allocation.

The concept of strategy induces strategic activity in the firm. Induced strategic behavior is activity that fits within the existing categories used in the firm's strategic planning and takes place in relation to its familiar external environments.

The structural context refers to the various administrative management mechanisms that weed out improperly induced behavior and ensures that the operational level functions in a manner consistent with the concept of strategy.

Simultaneously, autonomous strategic behavior refers to the actions of individuals who take it upon themselves to behave in a manner that falls outside the firm's articulated strategy but that they perceive may be beneficial to the firm in the future. Such behavior is represented in the upper loop of the model. In order for the results of such activity to be incorporated into the firm's future strategy, it must be accepted by the organization. The strategic context refers to the political mechanisms through which managers question the new actions, comparing them to the current strategy. If the new approach is deemed beneficial, top management is offered the ability to incorporate the new behavior into a new strategic concept. Innovation within a firm is accomplished through both loops: The induced behavior loop generally results in incremental advances and the autonomous behavior loop in major innovations.

Although this model provides relationships between strategic behavior and corporate strategy, it does not provide links to individual problem solving within the firm. This link, we posit, is the organizational knowledge of the firm, conceptualized by Nonaka and Takeuchi[17] as the third of the superimposed structures of the firm—the knowledge structure. It is constituted from the individual knowledge of the members of the firm and the knowledge embodied in the culture and institutions of the firm—the accepted way of doing things. For our purposes, specifying the interaction between organizational knowledge, problem-solving tasks, strategy, behavior, and innovation allows us to: (a) identify the learning and innovative processes of a firm; (b) provide the framework on which to identify the advantages of groupware; and (c) offer a basis for testing the use of CSCW via empirical studies.

Our model (Figure 6.2) illustrates the interaction between the behaviors within an organization and the task accomplished. This model is centered on the concept of knowledge-based management, which primarily rests on two themes: (a) knowledge is a strategic resource; and (b) IT is the platform that is transforming the economy from the current industrial to an informational base.[18] The postindustrial firm, according

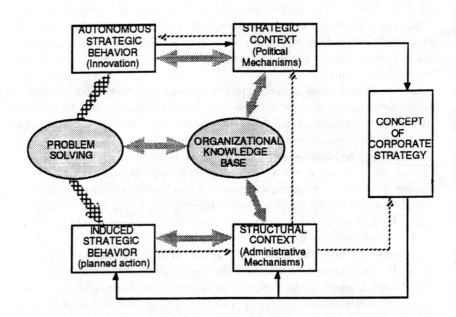

FIGURE 6.2. Model Illustrating the Relationship Between Information Flows in a Firm and Its Strategic Processes.

to Bell,[19] is an enterprise in which "knowledge and information become the strategic and transforming resources." The centrality of knowledge as the key business resource is illustrated in the model, which makes explicit the notion that knowledge serves as the central link between organizational and strategic behavior, innovation and problem-solving task accomplishment. The model thus shows both strategic behavioral relationships and the supporting informational flows.

Knowledge within an organization can be viewed as being of two forms: corporate knowledge and personal knowledge. Corporate knowledge contains past organizational experience, corporate know-how, and other information embedded within the firm in the form of either written records or knowledge individuals share as a result of corporate activity. Personal knowledge consists of information that individuals have gained from activity both outside and within the organization; for example, academic experience and knowledge gained on the job. The organizational knowledge base includes the total span of both personal and corporate knowledge.

This organizational knowledge base directly affects how tasks are accomplished. The means and effectiveness of knowledge accumulation, dissemination, and use clearly can have a profound impact on the goals set by a task team as well as on task accomplishment and task success. For effective organizational learning, the information and experience acquired during task completion must be transmitted back to the organizational knowledge base for future reference.

The information gained from problem-solving task accomplishment influences the strategic and behavioral flows via both individual and organizational learning. This learning comes in the form of personal growth, which the individual may use to become more creative and able to incorporate more of the external environment into his or her thinking, and professional growth, where the individual becomes more valuable to the organization and can offer better informed decisions to management. The information that returns to the knowledge base and the learning that eventually influences the concept of strategy completes the model. The knowledge base directly influences the productivity of accomplishing tasks, but it must also indirectly influence the rate of innovation within the corporation. This occurs when the accomplishment of tasks identifies a void within or opportunity to advance the firm's core business processes and strategies. Through task accomplishment, strategic and operational problem solvers learn about specific needs for innovation activity. Any resulting innovative activity, termed *autonomous strategic behavior* in the model, eventually reenters the strategic process portion of the model via the political mechanism.

From this analysis, there are two basically different types of use to which groupware can be put in an organization. The first category (Type 1) includes workflow automation, project planning, standardized reporting (e.g., travel expenses and monthly activity reports), and the like. These are the applications that will be likely to produce the fastest payoffs in an organization, because they streamline current activities. They are activities that mainly happen inside the boxes in the model. They will not result in either significant organizational change or organizational learning, however. The second category (Type 2) includes activities that add to and draw on the organizational knowledge base, thus contributing to and drawing on organizational learning. Examples of such activity might be solving customer's problems, collaboratively developing business plans, or developing technical solutions for new product development. Such activities will support and drive organizational change—incremental in the case of activity within the existing structural context of the organization, and possibly major and discontinuous in the case of the autonomous or entrepreneurial context. We believe that it is this second type that will produce the truly major benefits of groupware application in organizations, but that they will, in most organizations, be slower to develop, and may not develop at all if the needs and culture of the organization are not aligned toward collaborative work and organizational change. In both Type 1 and Type 2 applications, groupware serves to order knowledge transfer in support of activities—but with very different organizational implications.

In the case study to be reported here, we were seeking evidence for both types of application, with the expectation that we would find mostly Type 1, with (we hoped) some evidence of Type 2. We therefore conducted the case study as a structured observation, with this model in mind and the research questions just outlined as guides.

CASE STUDY

Research Setting and Methodology

This case study of a pilot Lotus Notes implementation was conducted in the spring of 1995 within a product engineering group of a large international company. (We refer to the group as Alpha Group. Its departments, products, and Notes applications have all been disguised.) The study was conducted by a team of four graduate students under the supervision of the authors. The methodology used included interviews averaging about an hour in length with the managers and many of the engineers in the group, and a questionnaire to probe the attitudes and reactions of the users to the program. In addition, a critical survey of the literature on other Notes implementations, telephone interviews with managers in six selected companies of various types that have attempted major Notes implementations, and discussions with technical and sales personnel at Lotus Development were conducted.

Objectives

From the perspective of Alpha Group the objectives defined for the study were:

* Development of measures to evaluate the impact of Notes on the business processes in Alpha Group.
* Benchmarking Alpha Group implementation with other companies that have successfully deployed Notes.
* Analysis of the data gathered from internal user interviews and surveys in order to understand the acceptance and the potential of the Notes implementation.
* Analysis and recommendation of possible methods to facilitate information transfer and to improve team performance.
* Suggestion of future applications of Notes to leverage fully the system's capabilities.

Background

Alpha Group is part of the engineering division of a large international company. The group is responsible for developing and incorporating new technologies for both products and processes. There are at least 60 projects in progress at any given time at Alpha Group. Alpha Group works closely with other divisions in the company, other engineering groups located in foreign countries such as Germany and Japan, marketing, purchasing, distribution, and vendors and suppliers outside the company.

While working on a project, engineers from Alpha Group must often collaborate with people outside the group. Employees of the group work on different projects, and team members change with new projects. Perceived difficulties with communication and information transfer spurred the start of the Notes pilot project within the Alpha Group and its trading partners. The primary purpose of the project was to test the potential of groupware to improve the level of communication and collaboration among the Alpha Group stakeholders. At the time of this study, there was an installed base of approximately 40 users within the group, primarily in Atlanta, but with a few remote users in Japan, South Africa, Germany, the U.K., and at a partner's site in Texas.

For the pilot project, Alpha Group first rolled out Notes applications involving business administration processes, project reporting, and discussion databases. The administrative processes include job approval, travel authorization, and rolling budget submissions, and are designed to streamline the corresponding administrative operations. Alpha Group is building the basis for project management by having employees perform project tracking, milestone reporting, objectives, and personal goals for each project. By having the employees reporting their goals every quarter, the personnel evaluation system has advanced from an annual fuzzy evaluation to a more solid evaluation based on the goals set, the quarterly progress made, and the results achieved in that period. In addition, the following applications are also available: e-mail, bulletin boards, and online information retrieval, including a centralized global contact list for trading partners.

In addition to these applications, Alpha Group currently relies heavily on discussion databases in its effort to realize the potential of collaborative work facilitated by groupware. Discussion databases are categorized by subject of interest or project, and some subgroups have their own databases. The information exchanged is stored in the system and is believed to enhance the company's corporate memory.

Findings

To obtain user feedback on the effects of the Notes implementation, the research team collected relevant data from Alpha Group users. User surveys and interviews were conducted, and system reports were analyzed.

- *Software applications used:* Users ranked word processor and e-mail as the most important tools to do their job. In addition, 35% ranked project management software among their first four choices, but none ranked it as their first choice.
- *Training:* A majority of users felt that the training they received was adequate. However, a significant minority (33%) believed they received insufficient training and that they needed more training on specific Notes applications. Some believed that the type and level of training was not appropriate for their needs. More than half (56%) reported use of books and reference materials to obtain needed user information.
- *Amount of information:* Nearly half of the users reported information overload. This description is commonly used to describe the situation where users need to wade through large amounts of irrelevant

information to find what they need. Not surprisingly, nearly all users reporting information overload believe that the number of applications required should be kept to a minimum.

*   *Quality of information:* Users were asked to evaluate Notes on the quality of information they get and the time spent to utilize it. The answers indicate the following: (a) On average, Notes users agreed that they received information they would not have gotten before, and they felt confident about using its applications. They felt that the quality of work neither improved nor declined with the introduction of Notes. (b) Document management and information searches were reported to be less time consuming with Notes, although other activities, especially monitoring discussion databases, were more time consuming. (c) In general, Notes was judged to be an efficient tool that facilitates teamwork, collaboration, and innovation.

*   *Perceived potential of Notes:* Finally, the users were asked their opinions of Notes potential and to identify the most important requirement for the system to reach its potential. Of the users, 85% agreed with the statement that Notes has high potential to facilitate or improve their work. According to users, the most important requirement for Notes to reach its potential is the development of applications that achieve information transfer without information overload. In addition, the implementation needs to reach a critical number of users, and the dual e-mail problem (there is an e-mail system in place in the corporation that is not presently linked into Notes) must be solved.

Conclusions

The central findings from the on-site study, review, and study of written reports of other Notes implementations, and results of telephone interviews with individuals from selected companies that have attempted major Notes implementations, are summarized in the following.

*   Companies that utilize a pilot project to implement Notes find that they have to achieve a critical mass of users before they see specific improvements. The data from user interviews and surveys indicate that a critical number of users may not have been achieved as yet in the Alpha Group implementation.
*   Research has shown that implementation is much more likely to be successful if it begins with a process change designed specifically for a Notes application.[20] Alpha Group had made few process changes to utilize Notes.

- The company used a proprietary e-mail package for company-wide communications. This e-mail system was not yet linked with Notes and pilot project members had to spend time and effort to check both systems. Any gains from Notes or improved communication seem to have been offset by the overhead placed on users to learn the new system and continue to work with the old.
- The effectiveness of the Notes databases intended to facilitate group work depends on the relevance of the information they contain. According to the user survey results, a majority of users felt they were suffering information overload. Users reported being overwhelmed by an enormous amount of information and communication that was not directly pertinent to their work.
- Alpha Group did not have a common project management system in place and had not yet utilized Notes to develop one. Therefore, setting up metrics to measure improvements in project completion time, manpower used, or other such specifics was not possible.

Despite the difficulties encountered in utilizing Notes, the survey indicated that 85% of the users believed that, Notes has high potential to facilitate and improve their work. This would indicate that, as new users are added, processes are changed for utilization of Notes and the organization learns and understands how to utilize Notes further, Notes does have tremendous potential.

DISCUSSION

In this case study, Alpha Group obtained value added from the application of Notes primarily for Type 1 activities (administrative activities) rather than Type 2 activities (organizational learning). The reports of information overload are related to the attempt to automate processes, resulting in redundant systems, the lack of a focused process to which to apply Notes, and start-up inefficiencies with early use of features with Type 2 potential, such as the discussion databases. Clearly, groupware implementations should be planned to avoid adding additional information functions and work for organization members (such as dual e-mail systems) or the necessity to manually scan newly available data that may not be relevant to the worker.

It is encouraging that users have recognized the opportunity predicted by our model to apply Notes to Type 2 activities, even though little has been achieved in the first phase of implementation. It is to be expected that Type 2 applications will take longer to develop than Type 1, and that measurement of organization learning outcomes must correspondingly be delayed. Future research will study this and attempt to verify the organization learning outcomes predicted by the model.

Evidence in the literature,[21] experience from other reported groupware implementations, and evidence from this study all support the observation that effective implementation and utilization of groupware requires that it be utilized in a major business process of the organization. Ideally, a redesign of a major organization process should be accomplished using groupware as the initial application. This process should be one that is enhanced by the strength of groupware—collaboration and interaction among members of the organization and utilization of the knowledge accumulated in the groupware repository. Such a process will then be enhanced as the organization members interactively build and utilize growing organizational knowledge. By implementing groupware with this type of process, the organization can learn how groupware technology can be utilized and adapted to redesign the organization's jobs, processes, and structures. With this understanding of the ways it can be utilized, other processes can be examined for application and redesign.

Organizational change strategies should be utilized in adapting groupware to the organization, remembering that groupware is a tool for facilitating change and improvement of organizational processes. Some of the strategies that will be effective are organization and process analysis, redesign of work and processes by the individuals in the organization who will be affected, examination of measurements and rewards associated with new processes, and communication to the whole organization of what is being evaluated and changed and why.

Implicit in a groupware implementation is the assumption that collaborative work will be done. If an organization does not collaborate well, the introduction of groupware alone will not change this. In such an organization, the issues preventing effective collaborative work must be dealt with prior to or simultaneously with the implementation if it is to produce the desired gains in productivity. The reward and incentive structure in the organization will have a strong influence on the success of collaborative work applications. Organizations in which individual members get ahead by holding and using special expertise will be less successful than those in which group members feel successful when the group succeeds.

Groupware can serve as a powerful tool for organizational performance improvement if it is implemented in a manner designed to be in accord with these principles. Not only is there an opportunity to improve worker productivity as normally measured (output/person, return on investment), but of greater importance is the potential for improving the effectiveness of organizations by dynamic process improvement and organizational learning.

NOTES AND REFERENCES

[1] E. Corcoran, *Washington Post*, 11 June 1995, p. H1.

[2] P. Romer, interviewed by P. Robinson, reported in *Forbes ASAP*, 5 June 1995, p. 66.

[3] I. Nonaka & H. Takeuchi, *The Knowledge-Creating Company: How Japanese Companies Create the Dynamics of Innovation* (Oxford, Oxford University Press, 1995).

[4] P. Senge, *The Fifth Discipline: The Art and Practice of the Learning Organization* (New York, Doubleday, 1990).

[5] R. M. Baecker, *Readings in Groupware and Computer-Supported Cooperative Work* (San Mateo, CA, Morgan Kauffman, 1993), p. xi.

[6] P. Lloyd, *Groupware in the 21st Century* (Westport, CT, Praeger, 1994), p. xiii.

[7] M. Hammer & J. Champy, *Reengineering the Corporation* (New York, Harper, 1993).

[8] M. Scott-Morton, *The Corporation of the 1990s* (New York, Oxford University Press, 1991).

[9] P. G. Sassone, "Office Productivity: The Impacts of Staffing, Intellectual Specialization and Technology," *Technology Analysis & Strategic Management, 8*, 1996, pp. 247-269.

[10] *Ibid.*

[11] W. J. Orlikowski, "Evolving With Notes: Organizational Change Around Groupware Technology," Working Paper 3823-95, MIT Sloan School of Management (Cambridge, MA, June 1995); W. J. Orlikowski & D. C. Gash, "Technological Frames: Making Sense of Information Technology in Organizations," *ACM Transactions on Information Systems, 12*, 1994, p. 174; K. Okamura, W. Orlikowski, M. Fujimoto, & J. Yates, "Helping CSCW Applications Succeed: The Role of Mediators in the Context of Use," in *Proceedings of the Conference on Computer-Supported Cooperative Work*, Chapel Hill, NC (New York, ACM/SIGCHI & SIGOIS, 1994), p. 55; W. J. Orlikowski, "Learning From Notes: Organizational Issues in Groupware Implementation," in *Proceedings of the Conference on Computer-Supported Cooperative Work*, Toronto (New York, ACM/SIGCHI & SIGOIS, 1992), p. 362.

[12] Scott-Morton, op. cit., Ref. 8.

[13] C. A. Bartlett & S. Ghoshal, "Changing the Role of Top Management: Beyond Strategy to Purpose," *Harvard Business Review*, November-December 1994.

[14] D. Kirkpatrick, "Why Microsoft Won't Stop Lotus Notes," *Fortune*, 12 December 1994, p. 141.

[15] Lloyd, *op. cit.*, Ref 6.

[16]R. Burgleman, "A Model of the Interaction of Strategic Behavior, Corporate Context and the Concept of Strategy," *Academy of Management Review, 8,* 1983, p. 61.

[17]*Op. cit.,* Ref. 3.

[18]W. H. Read, "Managing the Knowledge-Based Organization: Five Principles Every Manager Can Use," *Technology Analysis & Strategic Management, 8,* 1996, pp. 223-232.

[19]D. Bell, *The Coming of the Post-Industrial Society* (New York, Basic Books, 1968).

[20]Orlikowski, *op. cit.,* Ref. 11.

[21]*Ibid.* 3

part III
Implications for Academe

Two domains critically impacted by the Information Revolution are teaching and research. This part of the book investigates implications for the university.

In Chapter 7, a former Georgia Tech Vice President for Interdisciplinary Programs examines the changes in instructional programs and learning environments occasioned by the advent of educational (information) technologies. The span of issues engaged suggests that universities will undergo paradigm shifts.

Chapter 8 examines the research dimension. Electronic information access impacts the conduct of science (teaming at distances) and, in particular, the dissemination of research findings. Electronic teaming and electronic publication will make for drastic individual and institutional changes.

chapter 7

Universities and Information Technologies for Instructional Programs: Issues and Potential Impacts

Gary W. Poehlein
Former Vice President, Interdisciplinary Programs
Georgia Tech

INTRODUCTION

T he past decade has been one of dramatic and rapid change in world structure and in the functional components of society and governments. Global economics and information technologies have been major drivers of these changes that have resulted in political transitions, massive organizational restructuring (downsizing), and altered operational paradigms.

Information technologies, the focus of this chapter, have transformed the entire spectrum of human interactions and changes will continue at an accelerated pace. Information technology impacts in the educational arena are numerous and extremely varied. The fact that, *The Chronicle of Higher Education* has a regular section entitled "Information Technology" reflects the importance of this area in postsecondary education. Wulf,[1] in an article titled "Warning: Information Technology Will Transform the University," suggested that "the time has come to recreate higher education to capitalize on the technology that is here or soon to come." He pointed out that the need for advanced education and life-long learning is increasing but that "a change that will facilitate the flow of the university's essential commodity, information—might provoke a change in the nature of the enterprise."

The theme of the university as an information provider was also discussed by Noam.[2] In contrast to the negative slant of the paper's title—"Electronics and the Dim Future of the University"—Noam indicated that "The question is not whether universities are important to society, to knowledge, or to their members—they are—but rather whether the economic foundation of the present system can be maintained and sustained in the face of the changed flow of information brought about by electronic communications." Noam also pointed out that "people often overestimate the impact of change in the short term, but they also underestimate it in the long term." Thus, it should not be surprising that the dominant mode of instruction in most postsecondary institutions remains a faculty member, with chalk (or magic marker) in hand, lecturing to students for 50-minute periods. Computers are widely used as tools for mathematical calculations and word processing but lectures continue to be the major focus of the formal learning environment.

The new information technologies have the potential for massive transformations in how learning takes place in colleges and universities as well as in other educational enterprises. These transformations will take place; the only questions are how and how fast. Many are projecting dramatic changes in the role of faculty members—from lecturers and communicators to mentors and managers of the learning environment. Such changes were discussed by Schwartz[3] in "The Virtual University," "where, with the help of technology, students have access to the world's best instructors and information sources without having to set foot on campus." A virtual college comprising a 16-credit graduate program entirely via an interactive network at New York University is outlined in a recent article.[4] The National Technological University (NTU) has been offering graduate degrees via distance learning for a number of years and could be called a virtual university. The Open University in the United Kingdom has operated since 1969 and currently has about 200,000 participants.

The purpose of this chapter is to review some of the current issues in postsecondary education and to point out how the new technologies could impact those issues. A second purpose is to examine some of the problems that university and college faculty and administration will need to address in order to adapt to the changes that will characterize the next several decades.

CURRENT ISSUES

A multitude of pressures face postsecondary institutions in the United States and in other countries. Some of the more obvious issues are outlined briefly in the following.

Instructional Mission

Specific missions of postsecondary institutions vary widely among different types of institutions and even among institutions within a single classification, such as, for example, research universities. The gaps between internally developed missions and the expectations of external constituencies have become apparent, with political bodies, students, and parents becoming more concerned about the learning environment and, in particular, how much effort faculty devote to this component of their jobs. Information technologies can have an impact here.

Educational Content

Scholars often cite the accelerating rate of generation of new knowledge, yet the average number of credits required for the first degree in many fields has been reduced in the past 10 to 20 years. The natural response to this situation has been to focus on fundamental concepts, critical thinking, and continuing education. Yet students and their employers want graduates to be able to be productive quickly and to know how to apply their education to real-world problems. Information technologies can have an impact here.

Finances

Budget constraints, tuition increases, and staff reductions have impacted almost all private and public organizations during the past 5 to 10 years. Educational institutions have been impacted significantly and this budget tightening trend is not likely to disappear in the near future. Universities will be expected to do more with less. Students and their parents will expect high return on investments of money and time. Information technologies in the instructional arena can have an impact here.

Retention and Time to Degree

Low retention rates and excessive times to complete degree requirements have surfaced as important issues. Responses have varied from finger pointing to inadequate K-12 (precollege) preparation and poor counseling to proactive programs for remedial work and intensive training efforts to develop successful work habits. Retention and time to degree are clearly related to costs, for both the institutions and students. Information technologies can have an impact here.

Delivery Time, Place, and Duration

Traditional full-time resident students have become a smaller fraction of education consumers. Witness the increasing demand for continuing education products, for specially scheduled degree programs and for just-in-time skills training. The market for materials and programs that address flexibility and specific issues will continue to expand. Information technologies will have an impact here.

Assessment

Institution boards, state governments, and accrediting agencies have become more interested in assessment of institutional effectiveness. In the instructional arena, this will include the normal quantitative measures such as course credit hours, degrees granted, and continuing education units. Retention and time to degree, as mentioned earlier, will also be performance measures, as will job placement statistics and instructional program evolution. The coupling of education and jobs will depend more and more on the abilities of our graduates to enter and thrive in the information age. Information technologies, both taught and utilized in the learning environment, will have an impact here.

Internationalization

The flow and utilization of technology is catalyzing the increasingly global nature of all our institutions. The organizations that recruit our graduates operate in a global environment and the desired skills of professionals often include language and cultural knowledge of other societies. Academic institutions have long been involved in international relationships in research with activities such as student and faculty exchanges and joint research projects. U.S. institutions have a long history of educating students from other countries, especially at the graduate level. In contrast, most U.S. students do not have significant experiences with other cultures and countries. Information technologies can enhance and help to expand international collaborations in both instruction and research.

Competition

The economic magnitude of the education and training enterprise is enormous. The market has been competitive in all segments and the level of this competition will increase. Utilization of information technologies will take competition for education and training dollars to levels beyond past experiences. Impact on regional economic development will be a major part of the total economic machine.

INSTITUTIONAL CHARACTERISTICS AND RESPONSES

The academy has not often been in the forefront of major structural change, especially in the area of instruction. Educational costs have generally increased more rapidly than inflation and more rapidly than costs in other business sectors. Funding for instruction and research has, in the past, been relatively easy to obtain. Hence, motivation for change has been minimal.

Restructuring or reengineering, however, has become a way of life in private commercial organizations and the same pressures are building to change the way education is done. The application of information technologies to the education and training sector will be a significant component of educational change. The important question for individual institutions is not "Will we be part of this change?" but "Will we lead or follow?" The remainder of this chapter focuses on some of the key issues and potential institutional responses, particularly from the perspective of a research university.

Instructional Mission and Learning Environment

Pressures are increasing to elevate the role of teaching in research universities. Historically, most new faculty members have received very little training or mentoring in teaching. Hence, they have continued with the patterns they experienced in their education. The use of information technologies will change this picture in many ways.

First, there will be an increased need for a more widespread understanding of how to design and utilize educational technology. We know that students learn by different methods and at different rates. We also know that learning can be accelerated by doing—that is, by using the material to be learned on something that has real meaning to the student. Teamwork skills are another factor that is being touted as a key to future success.

Creative use of information technologies can help with all these factors. Many changes will be required, however, to derive maximum benefit from the tools that are or will be available. The need for a better understanding of the learning process will require institutional investment in the areas of behavioral science and cognition. This leads to a second, but overlapping, impact on institutional characteristics, namely support staffing.

Faculty will need help with design, production, and utilization of the multitude of new technologies. Changes in the learning environment at most institutions are more likely to be faculty limited than technology limited. Institutions that choose to expand the use of educational technologies significantly will need to alter staffing patterns. The balance between faculty, support staff, and teaching assistants will probably shift away from faculty, especially if economic constraints continue to increase. Some faculty concerns related to planning input and economic impacts were discussed at a recent American Federation of Teachers meeting in Seattle.[5] One conclusion was that "job definition and even job security will be ever harder to defend in the face of technological advance." Staffing shifts to fewer faculty and more support staff will also encounter broad resistance from many fronts because student-faculty ratios are a significant factor in many institutional ranking and accreditation systems. Perhaps some changes in criteria would be appropriate as information technologies are more extensively utilized.

Facilities planning and utilization is a third area that will require some futuristic thinking. The transition from a lecture-dominated learning environment to individual and small group situations will require different facilities. See, for example, the article entitled "Studio Classrooms," which indicates that the Rensselaer Polytechnic Institute is using computers to replace large lectures in introductory courses.[6] Student living areas are increasingly being directly connected to computer and TV cable systems—witness the new dormitories constructed for the 1996 Olympics at Georgia Tech. What kind of facilities will be needed in the academic buildings to implement new learning processes effectively? Will more universities require students to own or rent PCs?[7] Will off-campus students be permitted access to campus information sources via electronic means? Many of these questions are being answered by the rapidly changing environment and external expectations. Georgia Tech, for example, is currently debating the issue of mandatory computers for students but a recent poll has shown that about half of our students already own a PC. Remember the debates about only permitting slide rules in examinations when hand calculators first became available!

The interface of universities with K-12 systems is a fourth area that will be significantly expanded with the aid of information technologies.

Effective collaborations can have a major impact on the quality of K-12 education, especially in the upper grades; on student preparation and selection of colleges and choice of major; and on the important issue of diversity among student populations (see, for example, Blumenstyk[8] and Monaghan[9]).

EDUCATIONAL CONTENT

A recent article entitled "On-line Treasure Hunt" described an interactive system with which students on the Internet can manipulate a robot for uncovering and examining materials in a sandbox at the University of Southern California (USC).[10] The information obtained can be used to solve a puzzle. Each student will have a different experience.

The Eye-Surgery Simulator developed by Michael Sinclair and coworkers at Georgia Tech is another example of an interactive learning device that affords each student an individual experience. In contrast to the USC sandbox, no real eye is involved in the simulator.

These two examples demonstrate the potential of using technology to add realism to the educational process and to provide time and distance flexibility for students. One could consider replacing some expensive laboratory experiences with simulations or combining simple laboratory assignments with simulations of more complex and realistic operations. The quality of learning could be improved and efficiencies achieved by widespread use of learning materials and instructional staffing changes.

Finances and Competition

The potential for improving learning will be a major motivation for increased application of technology in education and training. Economics will also be a major driving force. One only needs to examine some of the competition currently in the marketplace to see the importance of economic issues. *Economics* in the context of this chapter is intended to reflect the total system; that is, income for the provider (short term and long term) and cost to the student in both dollars and time. Some examples of competition include:

- The virtual college, the 16-credit graduate program mentioned earlier, is offered by New York University entirely through an interactive network. Place of learning is a key selling point. Students can learn in their homes or offices.
- The NTU is a successful graduate education organization with a longer history. The *GIT Whistle* (31 July 1995) announced that NTU

courses would be offered via satellite from Georgia Tech to 13 sites statewide. Georgia Tech is one of more than 50 institutions that contribute to NTU offerings.

- Jones International, a cable operation, announced the formation of International University College as a low-cost alternative for graduate education.[11] It intends to contract with faculty from major universities to produce videotape courses. Are the policies of these major universities prepared to deal with the issues associated with this competition?

- J. Michael Orenduff, former Chancellor of the University of Maine System, proposed designating the Education Network of Maine as the system's eighth institution, with accreditation and the ability to award degrees. The pros and cons of this proposal were debated vigorously but clearly expanded impact and economic gains would be possible with such a virtual university.

- More than 40 colleges have joined the Public Broadcasting System's Distance Learning Program—a first nationwide effort to coordinate adult education through television.[12] Associate degrees are to be offered and colleges are expected to license, from PBS, the right to list courses in their catalogs, staff the courses, and collect fees. Staffing and faculty roles with these courses will be different from those with traditional courses. Cost savings and more mentoring of students would both seem to be possible.

- Westcott Communications of Carrollton, Texas, announced a new product for executive training that brings top professors to electronic classrooms (*Dallas Morning News*, 14 August 1995). The university and company participants in this interactive educational venture include Southern Methodist University, the University of North Carolina, Carnegie Mellon, Penn State, the University of Massachusetts (Amherst), Aspen Institute, Eastman Kodak, Disney, Texas Instruments, Johnson & Johnson, Johnson Controls, EDS, Florida Power, Storage Technology Corporation, Land's End, and Digital Equipment. Cost estimates for a single course were quoted as (U.S.)$600 for electronic classrooms versus as much as (U.S.)$5,000 for a residential course at one of the participating universities.

These examples deal mostly with adult education and graduate studies. The potential to reach undergraduates is, however, enormous. The *Chronicle of Higher Education* reported under the title "Double Dippers," that more 4-year college students are taking courses at nearby 2-year colleges.[13] Two reasons are cited: The courses are easier and less expensive. What will happen when such courses become widely available via electronic media? On demand, anytime, anywhere? Transfer credits are readily accepted by most U.S. institutions. Will this be changed to protect turf, quality, and income? Transfer credit has the potential to become a difficult issue for high-tuition institutions. With more student living facilities being connected, it will be possible to take courses from multiple institutions while in residence as a full-time student.

Economics is also a key issue in the retention and time to degree problems. University education, even for traditional students, is not often pursued on a 12-month basis. This is particularly true for students in cooperative education programs. Georgia Tech has begun to offer video-based courses to co-op students on work assignments. The technologies are available to improve the quality and convenience of such offerings. What is the magnitude of the market for such offerings? Can this process be used to increase retention and reduce time to degree? What is the magnitude of the market for co-op students, summer offerings, and part-time students?

Internationalization

Signals on the network, be they photons or electrons, can move to other countries almost as easily as they can move next door. Academic institutions are being asked to prepare graduates for a global marketplace. Clearly, enhanced capability to move massive amounts of information can contribute to globalization in the educational arena. Georgia Tech, for example, operates a branch campus in France. NTU is experimenting with the use of a second satellite to drop its credit and noncredit, long and short courses into Asia. Communication technologies enhance this effort. Cooperative research ventures, data exchanges, and cultural education opportunities will increase significantly as information technologies are more widely applied. Faculty and students will benefit.

CONCLUSIONS

Jacobson, in an article entitled "The Coming Revolution," reported that "this time, campus leaders say, technology will transform academe as never before."[14] The evidence for this revolution is everywhere—look in every issue of *The Chronicle of Higher Education*, the *Education Supplements* of the *London Times*, and on your own campus.

- What?
- How?
- How fast?
- Who will lead?

- Who will follow?
- What will be the impacts?

I hope this chapter causes you to think about these questions and some of the issues discussed.

NOTES AND REFERENCES

[1] W. A. Wulf, "Warning: Information Technology Will Transform the University," *Issues in Science and Technology*, Summer 1995, pp. 46-52.

[2] E. M. Noam, "Electronics and the Dim Future of the University," *Science*, 270, 1995, pp. 247-249.

[3] A. Schwartz, "The Virtual University," *ASEE Prism*, December 1995, pp. 22-26.

[4] R. L. Jacobson, "The Virtual College," *The Chronicle of Higher Education*, 27 January 1995, pp. A21-A25.

[5] P. Monaghan, "Technology and the Unions," *The Chronicle of Higher Education* 10 February 1995, pp. A17-A20.

[6] T. J. DeLoughry, "Studio Classrooms," *The Chronicle of Higher Education*, 31 March 1995, pp. A19-A21.

[7] T. J. DeLoughry, "Mandatory Computers," *The Chronicle of Higher Education*, 15 May 1995, pp. A37-A39.

[8] G. Blumenstyk, "Inner-City Access," *The Chronicle of Higher Education*, 12 May 1995, pp. A23-A25.

[9] P. Monaghan, "Electronic Studying," *The Chronicle of Higher Education*, 19 May 1995, pp. A27-A30.

[10] D. L. Wilson, "On-Line Treasure Hunt," *The Chronicle of Higher Education*, 17 March 1995, pp. A19-A21.

[11] D. L. Wilson, "On-Line," *The Chronicle of Higher Education*, 5 May 1995, p. A37.

[12] D. L. Wilson, "On-Line," *The Chronicle of Higher Education*, 4 August 1995, p. A15.

[13] B. Gose, "Double Dippers," *The Chronicle of Higher Education*, 4 August 1995, pp. A27-A28.

[14] R. L. Jacobson, "The Coming Revolution," *The Chronicle of Higher Education*, 27 April 1994.

chapter 8

Revolutionary Change in the Electronic Publication of Science

Scott Cunningham
NCR Corporation
Atlanta, Georgia

INTRODUCTION

This chapter discusses a number of remarkable changes in science that are leading to widespread electronic publication. The chapter begins by considering the definitions of electronic journals and electronic publication. The next sections consider several fundamental tasks in scientific communication, and outline the telecommunications infrastructure that has grown to support these needs. The shift from a paper and journal system of scientific distribution has a number of significant consequences. The most significant of these impacts are discussed.

Electronic publication of science is driven by social demand, not by the proliferation of new telecommunications technologies. Scientists are choosing to think and interact in new ways. The new information technologies support, not dictate, these new ways to conduct scientific research. Because these technologies are chosen and accepted by scientists, changes in the scientific publication system are likely to continue at a rapid pace. In analyzing the changes in the scientific publication system it is important to begin with a set of definitions. In the next section, a clear definition of an electronic publication is sought.

DEFINING ELECTRONIC JOURNALS AND
ELECTRONIC PUBLICATIONS

Some observers of the science system are arguing that the mainstays of scientific publication will be obsolete within the next decade or two.[1] In this section, I try to define and clarify electronic journals as objects of change so that the consequences of these changes may be better understood.

Defining Science

The most satisfactory explanations of science, and explanations of science as it is conducted online, are pluralist. That is, these explanations acknowledge that there are many ways to approach and attain scientific truth. There are also many ways to apply the results of science. Scientists represent only a fragment of an extended societal network that extracts and utilizes knowledge of science. By widening the audience of scientific fact, and extending the purposes to which published science can be applied, electronic publication both magnifies and diversifies knowledge. In the next two sections, the meaning of electronic publications and electronic journals is explored.

Defining Electronic Publications

There are three important characteristics of an electronic publication. The first characteristic of electronic publication is the great variety of formats in which it may be stored and accessed. The most exciting capacity of these new formats is to include electronic links to other significant or related documents. The second characteristic of an electronic publication is its capacity to be stored in a digital format. Digital formats allow a variety of data forms to be recombined. The final characteristic of an electronic publication is its availability online, via computer networks. Formats such as CD-ROMs are merely transitional forms between paper publication and the new electronic formats.

Defining Electronic Journals

Ringstrom[2] suggested some of the essential characteristics of an electronic journal (or e-journal):

1. An electronic journal must be a periodical, even if irregularly published.

2. It must be available on a computer network, or in a static medium suitable for viewing on a computer network.

3. The electronic journal must be moderated to ensure that its content is suitable for its particular peer group of scientific readers.

Electronic journals must also be properly archived to ensure the durability of their results. Electronic journals are more transitory than other previous forms of publication. Finally, journals must advertise and market their results.[3,4] In the next section, I examine the intellectual and social needs of scientists as they practice a new model of science.

THE SOCIOLOGY OF ELECTRONIC PUBLICATION

In the sections that follow, steps in knowledge production are outlined. These steps are then linked with a set of computer and information technologies that enable scientists to complete tasks crucial to their conduct in science. Finally, an argument is presented that many of these crucial links between technology and conduct developed because of the daily needs of a large number of scientists.

Figure 8.1 outlines this proposed model of scientific activity. Unlike many previous models of scientific activity, this model is not linear. In the conventional and linear model of the conduct of science, there is a direct chain between observation, investigation, and scientific fact. A similar linear model is prevalent in discussing research and development. Pure research, motivated by curiosity, leads to the creation of sci-

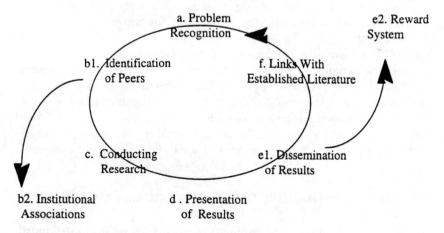

FIGURE 8.1.   A Circular Model of Knowledge Production in Science

ence, new technology, and ultimately economic growth. These models are not entirely satisfactory, and most especially they no longer capture the full complexity of developments in science and technology.

Sociologists of science have noted the trend to increased complexity in the sciences. They have appreciated how science has developed in response to the feedback of social forces and processes. Sociologists of science have also commented on the necessity of creating new methods for understanding scientific activity, methods that involve appreciation of the way science maintains a self-consistent and self-referential set of norms and values.[5,6]

A belief in a nonlinear and self-referential model of scientific activity may perhaps suggest other models than the one outlined here. This model, however, is sufficient to raise some points about the conduct of science and its facilitation with electronic, computer, and telecommunications tools. It should be noted that this model owes much to a model of science proposed by Arrow,[7] who attempted to discern the way that science distributes its resources among teaching, research, and publication.

The model begins with the recognition of a problem (point a). This problem seldom allows a scientist the opportunity of a solution without recourse to previous work in the area and perhaps association with other scientists of complementary abilities (point b). Continued work in a given area sometimes leads from identification of peers (b1) to a lasting institutional association with a given group of scientists (b2). When the necessary intellectual, material, and financial resources are mustered, the conduct of research may begin (c). Once results are achieved, they must be presented in a manner that induces consensus among close peers (d). Once this is achieved, the results may be distributed (e1). If accepted, there are often lasting rewards to a scientist's career (e2). Finally, the work is connected to other relevant issues in the scientific community (f).

All of these activities, (a) through (f), are facilitated by modern information technologies. In particular, the infrastructure of telecommunication helps to close the loop between the problems of science and their application and linkages to problems of society. The additional feedback offered by technology increases complexity and induces a tightly linked and self-referential system. In the next section, the technologies fundamental to support each of these steps of scientific conduct are discussed.

THE TECHNOLOGIES OF ELECTRONIC PUBLICATION

In the following sections a number of technologies are introduced. These technologies are linked by letter to elements of Figure 8.1. More detail is offered in each of these sections as to how the technologies facilitate the conduct of science. A summary is provided at the end of the section that parallels the links in scientific conduct with various enabling information technologies.

Search Engines and Software Agents

Software agents and search engines identify new sources of scientific information for their users. This challenging task is accomplished using a number of different tools. Some search engines have knowledge bases, or specialized software programs, that provide them with domain-specific information to help to clarify user requests. Others use linguistic and statistical data to identify documents and domains that are likely to be relevant. Search engines and software agents play a nascent, but important, role in the conduct of online science. Search engines allow identification of material in an expanding and increasingly specialized body of scientific literature. Finally, agents help to create and synthesize links between bodies of information that may once have been thought unrelated or irrelevant. They therefore encourage the development of interdisciplinary bodies of knowledge.

Software Daemons

Software daemons come in a variety of forms and levels of sophistication. *Daemons* are sets of software routines and instructions for automating network management tasks. These programs aid scientific discussion on the Internet by archiving and retrieving information and by connecting scientists of similar interests. List servers are the primary network tool used for these purposes. They distribute information to those scientists who wish to subscribe.

The scientific information communicated online tends to be regarded as coming in various levels of quality. The highest quality information tends to come via preprint networks that present the results of scientific research that have not yet been made accessible in published form by journals. Electronic journals emulate conventional journals, including the transmission of articles to scientist peers for review. Unlike preprint networks, they forgo the publication of their results in bound volumes. Electronic journals are thought to be likely successors to the current system of paper publication of science. Interest groups come in both moderated and unmoderated formats. Both kinds of electronic format are intended for people of specialized interests to share thoughts and ideas. There are an estimated 15,000 interest and newsgroups on the Internet.[8] Full-text articles are also provided online by some scientific authors who wish to ensure wide dissemination of their research.

High-Speed Data Networks

Perhaps the most fundamental change implied by electronic publication is the use of computer networks by scientists to conduct research. Clearly, computers are likely to be important in areas of scientific research such as computer science and cognitive science. They are also being used as an integral part of particularly data-intensive research fields, such as genetics. High-speed computer networks are also of use where data must be organized or visualized to be understood. Geographic information systems are one example of a primarily visual application in science that is being facilitated by high-performance computer links with satellite sensors. A final area where high-performance computing is central to science is in those many areas of science in which simulations are created and tested. The discipline of fluid dynamics, for instance, creates computer models in place of actual physical experiments.

Collaborative Tools

As was noted earlier, the era of the lone scientist has departed. Modern scientists typically have at least one collaborator; for some scientists, collaborators number in the hundreds. There are a number of ways in which new computing and information technologies are supporting collaboration. Computing tools designed to facilitate scientific collaboration are perhaps one of the foremost examples of these new technologies. The more mundane of the collaborative tools include software applications designed for use in a distributed environment. Other tools, called *groupware*, are designed explicitly to aid in scientific collaboration. Finally, it should be noted that teleconferencing equipment, currently only affordable for corporate executives, may soon play a role in the creation and maintenance of high-profile scientific projects. E-mail, an important tool for maintaining communication among scientists, could easily be regarded as a tool for collaboration. E-mail helps to erase differences in schedule brought about by geographic distance, personal habit, or professional responsibilities.

Transfer Protocols

A basic, but important, communication function is provided by file transfer protocols (FTPs). FTPs offer a structure by which files can be easily portable between machines of different hardware and software. Transfer protocols therefore allow scientists to submit contributions in a digital format suitable for storage and access on computer networks.

Gopher, Kermit, and Fetch are software programs for file transfer that send data between desktop and mainframe computers. TCP is another transfer and computer communications protocol. There are also a variety of different file formats used to allow the information to be easily encoded and ported by various FTPs.

Internet Nodes and Interfaces

The final link of scientific activity to the hardware and software of the Internet is when the scientist links his or her activities to the wider body of scientific literature that is either identified or published online. One of the preferred means of accessing the Internet is rapidly becoming the World Wide Web (WWW). The WWW is a hypertext interface to the Internet. Because the WWW is hypertext based, it is dependent on the creation of links—links between documents, authors, and nodes or places on the Internet. These links are quickly becoming an important source of information in and of themselves. Because the Internet is distributed, and even anarchic in character, the development of linkages between nodes in the Internet allows the development of an emergent and bottom-up structure. There are a number of other interfaces to the Internet, all allowing hypertext and hypermedia interconnections. Two of the most prominent are Netscape and Mosaic. Newer still is Java.

At this point it may be helpful to summarize the steps in scientific research noted here and to comment on the various tools that aid and facilitate scientific activity at each step in the process. The model presented here does not pretend to a fixedness that it does not possess. Both scientific activity and software design change rapidly. The model is merely intended as a vehicle for discussing broad classes of activity.

TABLE 1. A Summary of Scientific Activity and Enabling Technologies

Scientific Activity	Enabling Technology
Problem recognition	Search engines
Peer identification	Software daemons
Research conduct	High-speed networks
Research presentation	Collaborative software
Research dissemination	File transfer protocols
Intellectual linkages	Internet nodes

As can be seen from Table 8.1, there are tools and technologies facilitating all the major steps of scientific conduct. But this may not be conclusive evidence of the pervasiveness of information technology, it does suggest the development of an intimate connection between the needs of scientists and the development of information technology. Some of the key technologies of the information revolution developed not as a result of the commercial markets, but because of the recognition by scientists of an underlying need in science.

It can be seen, therefore, that the Internet developed according to scientific impetus. The tools and techniques used on the Internet parallel scientific needs. The growth of electronic publication on the Internet is therefore more than likely not to be a fad, but the result of fundamental social changes in the conduct of science. In the next section, it is demonstrated that scientific publications on the networks continue to grow at a rapid rate.

TRENDS IN ELECTRONIC PUBLICATION

Trends in Science

There are a number of notable trends in scientific activity. Many of these trends are discussed in Gibbons et al.[9] Scientific activity is increasing in publication output. The volume of scientific writing is growing exponentially and shows no signs of slowing in the short or even medium term. Scientists are becoming increasingly international in their publication trends. Since the mid-1950s, scientific publication with collaborators from two or more nations has been steadily on the rise. Science is becoming more and more specialized in content. Science is diversifying into a larger number of fields and subfields, with, until now, little capacity for scientists from other disciplines to integrate this knowledge into a larger whole. Science is also becoming more interdisciplinary. Knowledge is created and recombined into forms never before seen and anticipated. Even conservative estimates place more than 40% of published articles into two or more traditional disciplines. Interdisciplinarity is becoming a scientific norm.

Science is growing more applied. Scientists are taking a more empirical and data-laden approach to knowledge in most scientific fields. The push toward commercial returns in science funding only furthers these trends. Many of the scientists in this new era take techniques and methods from one problem and apply them to another. The strict boundaries between science and other forms of knowledge are no longer being maintained. This comes partly with the breakdown of the positivist paradigm of science, where science was upheld as an objective and therefore superior form of knowledge. More practically, this comes from scientists taking a more advisory and therefore political role in a number of controversial issues. Collaborative articles are the norm, not the exception, in scientific publication. Most articles have two authors; some articles have authors in the hundreds. Multiauthored articles are likely to increase in the future.

The next section turns to a few basic trends occurring in electronic publication.

Trends in Electronic Publication

In the following section, trends in electronic publication are discussed. Much of this material draws on an electronic publication by Okerson in her directory of e-serials.[10] Electronic publication is not an isolated phenomenon. There were 74 referred e-journals, 440 registered e-journals, and 1,800 high-profile discussion groups in existence in 1995. Electronic publication increases in numbers of publishers and readers every year. The number of refereed journals is doubling every year and the number of e-journals is doubling every year and a half. This rate is consonant with predictions that electronic journals will take over and eventually replace paper-and-print journals within 15 years.

Finally, electronic publication in science covers the spectrum of disciplines. Even disciplines considered "soft science" are widely participating. Areas where one might expect that distaste or unfamiliarity with computers would hinder publication are in fact flourishing in the new media. Once the bastion of the hard scientists of high-energy physics, list servers, newsgroups, and preprint networks have diffused quite evenly across the sciences.

The trend toward electronic publication may be seen as part of a threefold push. First, scientists desire a timely source of scientific information. For many scientists the multiple years it takes to have an article submitted, reviewed, and accepted makes that article already outmoded by the time it appears in print. High-energy physicists are perhaps the prototypical example of scientists searching for a timely source of information. Scientists are also searching for highly accessible sources of information. The discipline of medicine has one of the largest bodies of scientific literature, generating a need for the constant re-creation of classification schemes for identifying sources of information. Scientists and their institutions are also seeking affordable forms of information. The sheer expense and physical setup required to store and archive paper-and-print journals have made many scientific and research libraries look for viable alternatives as a means of storing information. These three pushes—affordability, access, and timelines—are aiding the emergence of the electronic forms of publication.

ISSUES AND IMPACTS OF ELECTRONIC PUBLICATION

In this section, several issues and impacts suggested by the electronic publication of science are discussed. These areas are merely suggestive and cannot be explored in detail in a chapter of this length. Most of the areas warrant detailed research of their own.

The old distinctions between science, journalism, news, and editorials are not likely to be maintained. High-quality science will still be conducted, but it is likely that it will not be sharply distinguishable from the other forms of electronic publication resident in the Internet. The current system of newsgroups that places scientific newsgroups alongside news, hobbies, political, cultural, and lifestyle interests only seems to encourage the mental image of science as one form of knowledge among many.

Peer review may not be as influential as it once was in scientific publishing. With more industrial scientists publishing, the motivation for the communication of results in science has been subtly changed. The need for certification of content will remain, but the older processes of review may be supplanted. In their place we might expect to see more interactive and responsive means of review, with peer commentary and evaluation to be appended directly to the article in question. In addition, we may expect to see certain informatic measures being used as a distributed means of assessing content quality. Admittedly this is a contentious point even among bibliometricians and research evaluators.

The trend toward collaboration may eventually lead to the creation of publication syndicates. The original contributor of a scientific idea or discovery may be quickly wrapped in commentary, extensions, and addenda by a host of other participating scientists. With single-authored papers soon to become the exception in science, an increasing number of scientists will choose to publish in large groups and syndicates. There seems to be a growing trend to acknowledge the extended network of scientists, assistants, and administrators that helped to produce scientific results.

A wider spectrum of society is likely to participate in the conduct and discussion of science online. This is due in part to the blurring of distinctions between science and other forms of knowledge. It also results from the increasing numbers of scientists, technologists, and degreed people in the information society. As noted by many authors, there is a large class of occupations devoted to the creation, collection, and manipulation of information and data in all their forms. These classes of jobs are also increasing. There is also political and economic mileage to be had in influencing and observing scientific discussion. In a more speculative note, the physicist and science fiction writer Brin[11] suggested that scientific authors and scientific participants will have "credibility ratings" by which their comments may be weighted and judged. Presumably their credibility ratings will be based on many of the same things scientific credibility is based on today: education, experience, and previous scientific publication. It is true that today some interest groups provide screens by which the contributions of ill-mannered or ill-informed participants may be ignored.

CONCLUSIONS

This chapter has attempted to give a broad overview of the social, political, and technological trends related to the electronic publication of science. We have given evidence that electronic publication is increasing at an extremely rapid pace, one that is more than capable of making most paper-and-print journals obsolete within 15 years. Another issue entirely is whether these changes are desirable.

There is reason in this to be optimistic. The new media are seen as allowing broader participation in scientific discussion, affording more timely and relevant information, and allowing greater customization of scientific outputs and displays. Feyerabend,[12] for example, welcomed a more pluralist vision of science that supports multiple perspectives and allows established knowledge to be freely questioned. That this new system of scientific production presents challenges of a fundamental nature, and requires a careful governance during in nascent years, is certain.

NOTES AND REFERENCES

[1]A. M. Odlyzko, "Tragic Loss or Good Riddance? The Impending Demise of Traditional Scholarly Journals," gopher.bubl.bath.ac.uk:7070/00/BUBL_Main_Menu/S/SA5/SA572, 1993.

[2]V. Ringstrom, "Electronic Journals in the National Library," In 4th Nordic SSN/Union Catalogue Meeting, 8-9 September 1994, Helsinki.

[3]J. Franks, "What Is an Electronic Journal?" gopher.bubl.bath.ac.uk:7070/00/BUBLAA_Main_Menu/S/SA3, 1993.

[4]Ringstrom, op. cit., Ref. 2.

[5]R. K. Merton, Social Theory and Social Structure (New York, Free Press, 1949).

[6]S. Woolgar, *Knowledge and Reflexivity: New Frontiers in the Sociology of Knowledge* (London, Sage, 1988).

[7]K. Arrow, "A Model of Scientific Participation," Speech given at the Science Policy Research Unit, University of Sussex, England, 1995.

[8]Ringstrom, *op. cit.*, Ref. 2.

[9]M. Gibbons et al., *The New Production of Knowledge* (London, Sage, 1994).

[10]A. Okerson, "The Electronic Journal: What, Whence and When?," *The Public-Access Computer Systems Review*, 2, 1991, pp. 5-24.

[11]D. Brin, *Earth* (New York, Bantam Books, 1992).

[12]P. K. Feyerabend, *Against Method: Outline of an Anarchistic Theory of Knowledge* (New York, Verso, 1978).

part IV
Implications for Political Affairs

The three chapters that comprise this part of the book offer perspectives on democracy and information technology, international affairs and information technology, and the impact of information technology on modern warfare. The conclusion is inescapable: Advanced information technology is a powerful agent of change in domestic and international politics.

Chapter 9 conveys the potential for dramatic change in political processes. Two public policy scholars wonder how ready information access will impact participatory democracy. They take the case of environmental risk to examine ties between information and political action. An empirical study of what information is available on the World Wide Web, and how that is changing, leads to immediate and long-term policy implications with global overtones.

In Chapter 10, a political scientist then shows how new information technologies are coming to impact the major international actors and even reshape the international system. He assesses the impacts of seven emerging information technologies and the attendant information flows on states, nongovernmental organizations, and multinational corporations.

As information becomes a high-leverage competitive element, "information warfare" can break out. The author of chapter 11, a specialist in the area, frames information warfare in terms of five essential elements. He shows how each of these elements can play a significant role.

chapter 9

Citizenship on the Net:
The Case of Environmentalism

Ann Bostrom
Gordon Kingsley
School of Public Policy
Georgia Tech

INTRODUCTION

[I]f we think [the people] not enlightened enough to exercise their control with a wholesome discretion, the remedy is not to take it from them, but to inform their discretion.[1]

There's an opportunity to improve politics and democracy whenever you have an advance in communications technology. The Internet is a tool that lets you find information in a much better way than anything else. Historically, most tools of communication were either broadcast—which meant your material had to appeal to millions and millions of people—or personal and able to address only a very small audience. But the Internet provides a single individual with access to virtually unlimited information on any given topic.[2]

T he art of informing discretion has traveled a spectacular technological trajectory through print, audio, audiovisual, and now digital media. In each succeeding generation, the richness of the information transferred through the technology has grown dramatically. From Franklin D. Roosevelt's fireside chats, to Bill Clinton's electronic town meetings, citizens have been given an increasingly intimate and detailed perspective of leaders, politics, and policy. As the amount of information has grown, so too have the ranks of handlers, pollsters, "spin doctors," and other types of managers of the information flow, representing the varied interests of incumbents, opposition, and interested groups. Never before have information providers been able to target their audience so accurately; nor have citizens had as great an opportunity to tailor the content of information that they receive.

At each stage of development, pundits have pondered the impact of information technologies on democracy and the public's ability to participate.[3] This chapter is but a continuation of this tradition. However, our technological circumstance is, perhaps, unique. Now we stand poised on the brink of an era in which the relatively voyeuristic media of the recent past are subsumed by technologies of instant feedback. For example, elected officials have appeared as guests on such forums as America Online's Live Center Stage, which are interactive "chat" sessions. Technology has also enabled enhanced vote-collection systems, and is on the road to enhancing access to information under the Freedom of Information Act, through the recently passed Government Printing Office Electronic Information Access Enhancement Act.[4] Similarly, government agencies are experimenting with providing information to the public through kiosks that are similar to automatic teller machines.[5] These advances, some familiar to all, others only yet promised, barely skim the surface of the potential for information technology to influence how our version of democracy functions.

Perhaps the most developed of the new interactive technologies is the World Wide Web (hereafter referred to as the Web). One of the most highly touted attributes of the Web is that it provides uniform access to information and informational exchanges. As stated by Lent: "Access to government on-line services and information has been greatly democratized in the last few years. More services are being provided to more people than ever before."[6] The potential of the Web as a tool for democracy has been recognized and advocated through several groups sponsoring web sites.[7] Much of this stems from what Demchak and Friis described as the immediacy of access that the Web allows between stakeholders and public agencies.[8]

The federal government's interest in information technologies, in general, and the Web, in particular, is long-standing. Although the total amount of federal information technology spending is unknown,[9] the Office of Management and Budget has reported that executive branch agencies plan to obligate about $26.5 billion in information technology-related funds in fiscal year 1996, in addition to billions of dollars in unreported spending. Whereas defense obligations have declined, information technology-related obligations have increased by about $4 billion since fiscal year 1991.[10] With regard to the Web, the federal government funded the early development of the Internet through defense research and development projects. Only recently (April 1, 1995) in the United States has nominal ownership of the connecting pathways in the Internet been turned completely over to the private sector. Prior to that time the Web was essentially a government-financed public good.

However, there is a flip side to this growing interest. It is easy to become frustrated with meaningless automated responses sent from congressional and presidential E-mail accounts, or by the numerous dead ends and logjams on the Web. Similarly, reviewers of electronic publishing become skeptical when they see that most publishers are using the Web simply to supplement their primary outlets without regards to the peer review standards employed by printed journals. Nor is it clear that government agencies will welcome, or even allow, the potential for access to ongoing operations. In fact, there is some evidence that a more limited use of the Web may emerge among government agencies.[11] Even when—or if—these problems are solved, there is the more fundamental problem of access: Those who do not have the resources have no access at all to the Internet or the Web.[12] So although government agencies are, in general, getting online,[13] it is questionable that this will produce a government that is more accessible and more participative.

In this study, we review the Web's contents in an effort to understand the extent to which information technology is being used to further public participation in government and, more generally, in public policy. Our research focuses on web sites that share an interest in environmental policy. This case was selected for several reasons: (a) it is an area that captured the attention of the public in the 1996 presidential election; (b) there are numerous interest groups on all sides of environmental issues that have active political agendas and the technical savvy to make use of the Web; and (c) the government agencies involved in environmental affairs, at both the federal and state levels, have specific mandates for seeking community advice and public comment in many phases of operation.

The growth of the Web as a venue for environmental policy was tracked over time in two snapshots: one taken in September 1995, prior to the beginning of the national election campaign season, and the other in January 1997, around the presidential inauguration. The search strategies were intentionally constrained to those a novice accessing the Web might employ. Our goal was not to accurately assess the range and content of information available through the Web dealing with environmental policy. Rather, the objective was to assess what an average citizen with limited knowledge of "browsing" and "surfing" might experience. However, the search was not constrained by the types of web sites reviewed. Our goal was to analyze the full range of information flows regardless of the institutional source. Here again our desire was to emulate the experience of an average citizen attempting to get information over the Web concerning environmental policy.

The results illustrate both the character of current information technology implementation and the nature of the Web. This, in turn, introduces several fundamental policy questions about the role of information and information technology in a participative democracy. The chapter concludes with suggestions for citizens who wish to be informed and participate, policy recommendations for governments, and an agenda for future research.

ENVIRONMENTAL COMMUNICATION MODELS AND PARTICIPATORY DEMOCRACY

One of the central tasks of the environmental policy community[14] is assessing and communicating the risks associated with pollution. Communication models have been developed to assess the effectiveness of efforts to accurately and adequately convey the level of environmental risk to citizens. Public agencies and interest groups who focus on environmental policy have made significant investments in understanding the application of risk communication models. Because this model is familiar in the environmental policy community and addresses core policy issues it serves as a useful framework for the analysis in this study.

Three kinds of goals can be adopted for risk communications: advocacy, education, and decision-making partnership.[15] An advocacy goal would be to enforce or encourage a behavior or belief. It can be argued that in so doing one is attempting to persuade the public to follow expert advice. In education, the goal is to inform the public. This subsumes a category of education that could be called *decision support*, in which the goal is to give individuals enough information to enable them to make their own decisions effectively (according to their own values). The third kind of goal is to establish or foster a decision-making partnership. This requires that the public be involved actively in risk management and decision making, including structuring the problem and selecting management options. With regard to environmental policy, the first two have been more commonly adopted than the third.

Each of these goals implies different patterns of information exchange. In advocacy, or persuasion, one-way communication is most likely: The expert or regulator tells the nonexpert individual or organization what to do. In education, one-way communication is also often presumed. Research on learning has shown that students' prior beliefs influence their learning,[16,17,18] as does the extent to which they explain themselves and question the learning materials.[19] It follows that effective education requires exchange between educators and students (or regulators and others), and that this exchange not be perfunctory, but entail some learning by the educator. Decision-making partnerships require not only two-way exchanges, but some sharing of authority and responsibility, which means some equalization of how information is exchanged. Although each of these patterns is a distinctive form of exchange, the patterns also share three common components of a risk communication model: (a) the parties communicating, (b) the information they are exchanging, and (c) how they are exchanging the information (i.e., the process). In the following, we examine each of these elements in turn.

With regard to environmental issues, the parties (i.e., stakeholders) can be individuals, community groups, government agencies, or governments. In this light, the Web is simply a forum through which the variety of participants pursue their communication objectives. Research on environmental risk communication also divides readily into that which considers individuals,[20,21] communication and conflicts between individuals and organizations,[22,23] organizational research,[24] and research on governments.[25] An important underlying theme in this body of research is that the content of what is communicated, and to whom, are inseparable and essential characteristics of a communication pathway.

This relatively simple model becomes quite complex when multiple actors are involved. Within the federal government alone there is the potential for significant variance. Examples of one-way environmental risk communications from agencies and organizations to individuals abound: radon ads by the U.S. Environmental Protection Agency (EPA) and the Ad Council; ads by environmental organizations trying to prevent clear-cutting of forests; or radio spots promoting electricity conservation. However, the potential for two-way communication is often embedded in statute. For example, government agencies in the United States are required not only to disseminate information (e.g., the Risk Communication Act), but to listen to public responses as well, in at least some limited sense, through public commentary, Science Advisory Boards, and Citizen Advisory Panels.[26] To what extent these communications are equal exchanges has been little analyzed, let alone the extent to which they might be considered decision-making partnerships.

Similarly, complexity is added when there are conflicts about environmental risk among interested parties. Such conflicts about risk are often fanned by accusations of withholding information. The most notable examples of conflict have been associated with superfund sites such as Woburn Massachusetts, Industrial Excess Landfill in Ohio, and the Hanford installation, where there have been accusations by individuals and community groups that commercial organizations or government agencies are withholding or suppressing information about their own activities. Such conflicts are exacerbated when organizations or agencies ignore individuals' or community organizations' complaints.[27] They also serve to illustrate that the communication interests of public agencies, interest groups, and individual citizens are often quite distinct and lead to radically different postures in the communication exchange.

The literature linking technology and citizen participation suggests three uses for the Web in communication patterns concerning environmental policy. First, public organizations may use the Web as a substitute for organizational structure. This is an extension of Perrow's hypothesis that new technologies will be used as a means to avoid structural changes to standard operating procedures, decision flows, or redesigning core operations.[28] Perrow argued that an organization is more likely to embed existing structures in the application of a technology rather than adapting operations in the light of the opportunities the technology entails. In the public sector, the Web can be used as a way to link citizens to government without requiring immediate interaction with government hierarchy.[29] The advantage of such a system is that citizens are not required to meet certain office hours or travel to specific locations to gain a point of entry for interaction. Similarly, if the service is provided through a network of organizations, they can be easily referenced and coordinated through Web technology.

However, the locus of almost all this activity is at the level of service provision, where the technological fixes are being attempted in light of the twin pressures for greater public service and tighter public budgets. The review by Demchak and Friis of government agency use of the Web in the United States and western Europe, also revealed a tendency, particularly in the United States, of managing and controlling interactions with citizens rather than enabling more open forms of dialogue.[30] To the extent that policy issues are presented on the web, the communication is most likely to be in a one-way format.

Second, interest groups are likely to use the communication pathways of the Web as a catalyst for attracting members. Pierce and colleagues argued that the role of interest groups in a post industrial society has evolved from a pluralist model of coalition building to one of providing "policy relevant technical knowledge and information."[31] Affiliation to an interest group is linked to their capacity to organize information flows into a meaningful format. This information will likely address two types of issues: (a) the technical complexity of the policy issues, and (b) the procedural complexity of the decision-making process. Here again, it is expected that the Web would be conducive for one-way transfers of information with limited opportunities for feedback.

Third, an opposite, and in some ways more appealing, possibility is that the attributes of Internet and Web use that differentiate it from older technologies are those that dominate its implementation. Because individuals can access and use the Web with limited or no institutional support, it is argued that two-way communication and participative arrangements (i.e. decision-making partnerships) have a chance to prevail on the Web.[32] Fischer argued that this type of interaction is most likely to emerge, and also most helpful, when it is used as an approach for solving "wicked" policy problems, such as NIMBY (i.e., not-in-my-backyard) issues, where negotiated resolutions are difficult to achieve.[33] However, the impetus for this form of direct democracy is most likely to be generated by local, grass-roots organizations that are born in reaction to a specific environmental event or threat.

Taken in aggregate, it is unlikely that the Web will be used for only one type of communication pattern. The diversity of interests is simply too great and the barriers to entry are simply too low. However, given the participation of large institutional interests, it is also likely that less participative forms of communication will predominate on the Web.

WHAT'S UP ON THE WEB

As a first attempt at evaluating the extent to which new information technologies facilitate public participation in environmental risk management, we have undertaken a survey of the Web, using widely referenced and available search engines. Search engines are software that literally scan the Web, identifying sites relevant to the key words specified by the user. Search engines themselves are under rapid development.[34] In the first search (conducted in September, 1995) the following engines were accessed: Aliweb, Broker Query, Galaxy, Lycos, UUnet, Webcrawler, and Yahoo. A little over a year later there had been significant changes in the search engines available.[35] The following were used in the second search (January 1997): Webcrawler, Lycos and Yahoo were accessed again, and Infoseek, Excite, Magellan, and Alta Vista were new additions.

Studies of citizen participation have noted that frustration in accessing information can lead to nonparticipation. For this reason citizens often use social affiliation as a substitute for assessing the value of information.[36] Consequently, we assumed a rather limited patience in searching the Web. The intent of the survey was to characterize what the naive user of the Web might find in an attempt to communicate with the government, or other interested parties, about environmental risk policy. The survey was implemented using the terms *environment* and *policy* or *environment* and *government*. The search was repeated for each search engine, and the links produced that were (a) above the halfway mark on the engine's scoring system (≥ 50%), and (b) among the first 10 sites reported, were included in the survey.

The survey was conducted in two snapshots before and after the 1996 presidential election. We attempted to conduct the survey carefully in order that it be repeatable, but it became clear that a strategy of frequent data collection for the survey would be a major undertaking requiring significant resources simply because the Web is changing so rapidly. Searches conducted one day and repeated the next produced different results. The searches reported here were conducted between September 1 and September 15, 1995, and January 10 and January 15, 1997.

Web pages can have graphics, text, input forms, and, rarely, sound or video. Pages can include an E-mail address or other address for a point of contact, but input forms are the most active way to elicit input from someone using the Web. Pages can also be organized as indices to more information, can be reports (text), or neither. One of the key features of a page is the nature and number of the hotlinks (embedded Uniform Resource Locators, on which a user can click to jump to another page), which link to other pages at the same site (internal links), or other sites (external links). Most obviously, the page identifies, in some way, who put the page up on the Web, and may also include policy positions advocated by the Web page author. Other attributes—such as the date the page was last updated, the name of the person responsible for the page, and the length of the page—can all be used to describe and evaluate pages on the Web. These provide at least a first-order approximation of the nature of the environmental communication provided—whose page it is, whether it includes graphics or technical information, whether it is one-way, two-way (E-mail address or ftp site mentioned), or interactive (input form included or directly linked), and whether it is organized as an index or a report, or advocates a specific environmental policy position. As a proxy for technical information, we noted whether or not any quantitative information was included on the page (other than telephone numbers, addresses, or other such identifying information). It was also noted when a page could not be accessed.

RESULTS

The characteristics just described are summarized in Tables 9.1, 9.2 and 9.3 for the web pages surveyed. A wide variety of web pages were "hit"

TABLE 9.1. Types of Organizations Authoring Web Sites

	1995		1997	
	# Examined	%	# Examined	%
Environment and policy	40		70	
Government	7	18	19	27
NGO	11	28	13	19
Education	8	20	14	20
Private organization	4	10	8	11
Individual	0	—	3	4
Search engine or index	3	8	4	6
Not accessible	7	18	7	10
Not relevant	N/A	N/A	1	1
Firewall	N/A	N/A	1	1
Environment and government	49		70	
Government	15	31	24	34
NGO	10	20	10	14
Education	5	10	11	16
Private organization	6	12	8	11
Individual	4	8	2	3
Search engine or index	4	8	4	6
Not accessible	5	10	8	11
Not relevant	N/A	N/A	2	3
Firewall	N/A	N/A	1	1
Combined (excluding inaccessible)	77		125	

through our searches. Three general results are noteworthy. First, the overall growth in the Web during the 16 months between searches was astonishing. During the first search (1995), 77 distinct web sites met the criteria of matching our key words at a 50% rate or better, as well as being among the first 10 accessible web sites listed. The major barrier at this time was the 50% match criterion. This means that the population of web sites related to the key words was quite small because fewer than 10 sites were at or above the 50% mark. By the time of the second search (1997) the key criterion for selecting web sites for analysis was whether the site was in the first 10 distinct sites listed by the search engine. Rarely did the match rates among the sites dip below the 80% mark. Consequently, the second search identified 140 web sites for analysis in this study.

Second, the searches rarely turned up the same web pages. This was particularly true when comparing between search engines in the 1995 search. If one were to judge simply from these results, the likelihood of

TABLE 9.2. Web Site Information Content in 1995

1995	Graphics % With	Communications			Report	Policy	Number	Links Internal		External		Organized Index
		1-Way	2-Passive	2-Active				Median	Average	Median	Average	
Combined	82%	39%	38%	16%	26%	23%	17%	7	15	1	11	56%
Policy	87%	48%	41%	10%	23%	23%	7%	7	21	0	5	47%
Government	78%	38%	40%	21%	32%	28%	28%	7	10	1	15	71%

TABLE 9.3. Web Site Information Content in 1997

1997	Graphics % With	Communications			Report	Policy	Number	Links Internal		External		Organized Index
		1-Way	2-Passive	2-Active				Median	Average	Median	Average	
Combined	62%	37%	38%	13%	49%	36%	16%	3	6	0	7	47%
Policy	69%	39%	36%	13%	56%	39%	11%	5	4	0	4	40%
Government	56%	36%	40%	13%	43%	34%	20%	2	6	0	11	54%

Yahoo, Lycos, Aliweb, Webcrawler, and Galaxy producing the same cast of characters is almost nil. Furthermore, even when we compare the different keyword searches (i.e., *environment government* and *environment policy*) within an engine, in most cases we came up with completely different web pages. This pattern was found in both searches, but it was more pronounced in the 1995 search. This is somewhat surprising given that the searches covered such similar terms.

The third general trend is the growth in the presence of government agencies with web sites between 1995 and 1997. Government organizations rarely showed up among the web pages in the first search. However, by 1997, there had been a significant increase in the number of government agencies with web sites. A pattern that remained consistent across searches is that the governmental groups that were most likely to turn up were foreign or federal agencies. However, these federal agencies were not in the majority and were usually the web page of a specific agency (e.g., Office of Environment, Safety and Health Support, http://www.er.doe.gov/production/esh/er8home.html) as opposed to a departmental home page for the EPA or Department of Energy (neither of which turned up in the survey).

Nearly all of the web sites produced by the searches belong to organizations. Only four pages for individuals turned up during the first search, and only five appeared in the second search. The distribution of organizations in the first search heavily favored those outside the public service (49%). Of those, the majority (38% overall, 34 sites) were nongovernmental organizations representing interest groups or universities. The first search produced 25% (22 sites) that represented government organizations, 11% (10 sites) for private organizations, and 8% (7 sites) search indices or engines. In the second search there was a significant increase in the number of web sites from government agencies (from 22 to 43). The other categories remained the same in terms of the overall number of web sites. The one exception to this was the advent of the site with a "firewall" barring entry. This phenomenon was not at all in evidence in the earlier search.

Of the government pages, nearly half were from other countries, including several pages from Australia, Canada, and the United Kingdom, for example: State of Environment Report I & II (Australia); British Columbia Ministry of Environment, Lands & Parks (MELP), Canada; Natural Environment Research Council (UK), Department of the Environment (UK); and a gopher site for a Peru Government Notice. The federal government dominated the remaining government pages. However, none of these pages were from the legislative or the judicial branches of government. The Department of Energy National labs were well represented, including pages from the Lawrence Livermore

National Laboratory, Sandia National Labs, and Oak Ridge National Labs. Also included were a White House Library ftp site and a gopher site for the U.S. Department of State Climate Action Report dated September 1994.

Only one page was from an agency at the state and local levels of government during the first search. This number increased, but only to two, during the second search. This means that the agencies that are most impressionable and accessible to citizen participation (i.e., elements outside the bureaucracy) will not be accessed through this kind of naive search.

Most of the communicating that is going on through the Web is one-way (42%) or passive two-way (41%). Of those sites that were identifiable as U.S. federal government web pages (7), none included active solicitation of input on the accessed page (i.e., active two-way communication), whereas 19% of the other sites accessed included input forms or other active solicitation of interaction. The number of external hotlinks on a page might also be taken as an indication of how open an organization is to the outside. Analysis of variance shows that there are differences by organization type in the number of external hotlinks, with search engines and indices—as expected—and individuals having more than other entities.[37]

Admittedly this is a small sample, but it indicates that organizations are soliciting little in the way of input from citizens on the Web. Rather, they appear to be at a stage in which information about their organization is still being organized for access. The organization of this information is following a distinct pattern. First, organizations provide a page with general information about their organization that is indexed with a variety of internal hotlinks. These may be quite elaborate as was found at the Sierra Club site. However, in most cases it is a simple index of information about the organization and a means to give feedback. Nongovernmental organizations are the most aggressive in seeking feedback—but this appears principally to be a means of generating new members. Once one begins to access these internal links one finds that the information content can be quite minimal. Often one will find a disclaimer that pages are under development somewhere in the text. Also in about half of the cases external hotlinks may be found at the secondary level, as can input forms in many cases.

Perhaps the biggest change in information content over the 16 months between searches was the increase in the number of policy-related reports available over the Web. In 1995, few reports, technical information, calls for political action, policy, or legislation were readily available using a naive searching strategy on the Web. By 1997, the number of sites containing this type of information had almost doubled

(26% to 49%). These reports were of a descriptive nature, containing little in the way of quantitative analysis. The majority of these are evaluations of performance put on the Web by the agency, interest groups, or the author of the report. However, a sizable minority were calls for political action in support of direct democracy. Our conclusion, after reviewing this growth, is that government information is more accessible than ever.[38] However, it is unclear if policymakers are more accessible. Only in one web site did the report actually provide a means for active commentary from the public.

INFORMATION SURFEITS AND DEFICITS

Reports on environmental science and technology must be both accessible, and interpretable to be useful to citizens. As the tables illustrate, it has been only recently that reports have begun to turn up if one "surfs" the web as our survey did. Nevertheless, technical information and reports are available from EPA as well as other federal agencies, through gopher and telnet sites.[39] There are many Wide Area Information Systems (WAIS) that include environmental risk information. The EPA publishes regulations and communications every day, to which one can subscribe over E-mail (e.g., epa-air@dggis.rtpnc.epa.gov for air quality), or reach a number of other ways over the Internet (including the Federal Register Online via GPO Access [wais.access.gpo.gov]). The EPA also maintains a large number of bulletin board systems (BBS) for specific issues, such as the Nonpoint Source Program BBS (telnet to fedworld.gov then gateway to NPS BBS), which is intended for "Federal, State and local agency personnel, university researchers, businesses, and concerned individuals," and "contains lots of information dealing with wetlands in the form of files, bulletins and messages."[40] Another example of Internet services provided by the EPA is the Technology Transfer Network (telnet ttnbbs.rtpnc.epa.gov, E-mail contact person: rorex.h@epamail.epa.gov), which includes 14 bulletin boards about air pollution.

Although we have not examined the ease with which this information can be accessed and used, there is always the possibility that it is user-friendly and fills many of the gaps in information provision that appeared in the survey. From our own experiences, it appears that the EPA's web site has developed substantially over the last year. However, given how little funding in general is available for risk communication evaluation at EPA, judging from past performance,[41] and given that most agencies appear still to be entrenched in web page production, it seems unlikely that these pages have been evaluated for their risk communication properties.

As recent calls for abandoning the Toxic Release Inventory (TRI) illustrate, short-term costs of monitoring the environment may lead to a near-term decrease in availability of information about the environment. Although TRI is widely considered cost-effective and essential for community right to know, and is based on company estimates when data are not available, members of Congress have requested that it no longer be produced. Potentially more significant is that reliable data collection can require expensive monitoring equipment and technical expertise, making it cost-prohibitive in the short term.

POLICY IMPLICATIONS

A distinctive pattern emerges in this analysis regarding the development of the web. The anticipated communication patterns are in evidence, but they appear at different points in time with different levels of strength. At the time of the first search, in 1995, interest groups were already aggressively developing the Web as a means for getting out their message and organizing their sites as information resources in an effort to attract members. Lagging behind, it was not until 1997, during the second search, that government agencies begin to appear in significant numbers. As anticipated, these sites are not designed for dialogue or engagement. Rather, the Web is for information-sharing purposes and aimed toward service provision. The most tentative of the three communication patterns is the interactive form for which the Internet was originally designed. In the 1997 search we saw the first calls for direct democracy as it relates to environmental policy.

However, many key stakeholders remain under-represented on the Web. In particular the legislative and judicial branches of government are silent, as are state and local governments. One-way and passive two-way communication are more prevalent than active two-way communication. Even had the latter prevailed, actually using and responding to the information collected requires significant organizational (staffing) commitment—the capacity for which we did not examine. Thus the Web appears currently to be less of a forum for environmental policy debate and exchanges than a way for the initiate to find out about stakeholding environmental organizations. Although list servers (which distribute E-mail to a list of subscribers) can foster lively debate, that debate can easily get out of hand, making active but useful debate a rarity. Second, given the weaknesses of a naive search strategy (not even Thomas, the Congressional information service, or the EPA's home page showed up), the Web does not appear to be a user-friendly resource for the general population.

As we move toward an electronically sophisticated electorate, access to information technology can determine whose voice is heard. As of 1990, about 16% of U.S. households used personal computers, although use was much higher for those with the highest incomes than for those with the lowest (30% of those households with annual incomes $35,000 and higher, 5% of those with annual incomes under $15,000).[42] This is a large increase over the 3% who owned computers in 1982,[43] but it is still a small proportion of the electorate. Although use of information technology in schools and public libraries has been increasing at prodigious rates,[44] it is not clear that current efforts will suffice. Including usage at work, only about 20% of the population had used a computer in the last week when surveyed in the early 1990s.[45] How information is collected, processed, and distributed influences the course of the nation. Internet books of a year ago are already out of date, as changes in information technology outpace traditional publishing mechanisms.

Policymakers and concerned citizens need evaluations of information handling. Public commentary response procedures may be inadequate, especially when modes of communication are changing; clearance procedures in some agencies leave agency officials handicapped and unable to respond in a timely fashion electronically unless they respond "unofficially." Coordination is necessary for timely production and dissemination of information.

A RESEARCH AGENDA

Integrated information systems could provide much more direct feedback to citizens regarding the state of the environment and the effects of specific risk management activities. With such systems, local environmental problems could be managed locally—with federal and international expert guidance. Unveiled in 1995 by Vice President Al Gore, the Global Learning and Observations to Benefit the Environment (GLOBE) project—an international project to coordinate the work of children, educators, and scientists in monitoring the global environment—is the kind of effort that information technology can enable.

Information technology may be the ultimate tool for developing an informed citizenry, with direct representation.[46] News services can be tailored for individual use even now. Agencies that wish to solicit input from citizens can do so regardless of geographical limitations. Ultimately, we may have nonspatial governments.

Risk-based models are one of many possible approaches to analysis of the effects of information technology on environmental risk management and communication. The analysis presented here is a first step in an attempt to apply a risk framework, but includes only limited examination of content. Such analyses should, ideally, begin with questions such as: What information do people need? How can they get it? What information do they want to share, and who can listen?

Search engines are only one way to access information on the Web. Organized indices, some of which turned up in our searches, are perhaps a better way to explore the Web systematically. As the Web has developed, more and more such indices have become available. Further research on such indices might provide useful information to search engine developers and users, regarding the organization of the Web. Perhaps the most obvious·omission of this study, and an obvious place for further research, was that we did not look at the depth of information at particular sites or the specific substantive content of reports and policy statements that turned up.

As the Web and the use of the Internet become more and more common, there is a risk that other communication modes will be supplanted by these. The nature of this change and how it affects public policy and democratic processes deserve close scrutiny.

NOTES AND REFERENCES

[1] William Ruckelshaus, former administrator of the Environmental Protection Agency (EPA), quoted this famous Thomas Jefferson dictum arguing that the government must accommodate the will of the people in his article: W. Ruckelshaus, "Science, Risk, and Public Policy," *Science*, 221, 1983, pp. 1027–1028.

[2] From an interview with Bill Gates, founder and Chairman of Micrsoft, Inc., entitled "Of Mouse and Man," *George*, February, 1997, pp. 78-81 & 101-102.

[3] For a discussion of this, see J. H. Snider, "Democracy On-line: Tomorrow's Electronic Electorate," *The Futurist*, September-October, 1994, pp. 15–19.

[4] Snider, 1994, op., p. 17

[5] For a discussion on kiosk government see the following: T. Newcombe, "Feds to build national kiosk network," *Government Technology*, May, 1995, pp. 16–17, 48. Also Office of Technology Assessment (OTA), *Electronic Enterprises: Looking to the Future*, OTA, United States Congress (Washington, DC: U.S. Government Printing Office, 1994).

[6] M. Lent, *Government Online*, (New York, HarperCollins, 1995), p. xxiii.

[7] M. J. Macpherson, "*Citizen participation in politics and the new sytems of communication*," at http://www.snafu.de/~mym/CP/sec1.html, 1996.

[8] See C. C. Demchak & C. Friis, "*Webbing" American and European Public Agencies: Modern Advantages of Pre-Modem Structures in Cyberspace*, Paper presented at the National Public Management Research Conference, University of Kansas, Lawrence, October 1995.

[9]General Accounting Office (GAO) *Information Technology Investment: A Government-wide Overview* (Letter Report, 07/31/95, GAO/AIMD-95-208). Because the Office of Management and Budget (OMB) does not collect comprehensive IT budget data on a governmentwide basis; federal agencies do not generally break out IT obligations as separate line items in their budget documents, but they include this information within program or administrative costs.

[10]GAO, 1995, *op cit*. OMB does not require the reporting of some potentially significant types of IT spending.

[11]Demchak & Friis, 1995, *op. cit.*

[12]S. Ratan, "A New Divide Between Haves and Have-Nots?," *Time*, Spring 1995, pp. 25–26.

[13]Lent, 1995, *op. cit.*

[14]In using the term *community*, we are specifically including all the potential sources of information found on the Web from the public, private, and not-for-profit sectors.

[15]National Research Council, *Improving Risk Communication* (Washington , DC, National Academy Press, 1989).

[16]M. T. Chi, "Conceptual change within and across ontological categories: Examples From Learning and Discover in Science," In R. Giere (Ed.), *Cognitive Models of Science: Minnesota Studies in the Philosophy of Science* Minneapolis, University of Minnesota Press, 1992.

[17]M. T. Chi, P. J. Feltovich, & R. Glaser, "Categorization and Representation of Physics Problems by Experts and Novices," *Cognitive Science* 5, 1981, pp. 121–152.

[18]Otero & W. Kintsch, "Failures to Detect Contradictions in a Text: What readers believe versus what they read," *Psychological Science* 3, 229–235.

[19]K. VanLehn, R. M. Jones, M. T. Chi, "A Model of the Self-Explanation Effect," *The Journal of the Learning Sciences*, 2, 1992, p. 1.

[20]For a review, see B. Fischhoff, A. Bostrom, & M. Jacobs-Quadrel, "Risk Perception and Communication," *Annual Review of Public Health.*, 14, 1993, pp.183–203.

[21]A. Bostrom, B. Fischhoff, & M. G. Morgan, "Characterizing Mental Models of Hazardous Processes: A Methodology and an Application to Radon," *Journal of Social Issues*, 48, 4, 1992, pp 85–100; P. Slovic, "Perception of Risk," *Science*, 236, 1987, pp. 280–285; and P. Slovic, B. Fischhoff, & S. Lichtenstein, "Rating the Risks," *Environment*, 21, 1979, pp. 14–20, 36–39.

[22]A review of the use of advisory committees is given by: F. M. Lynn, & G. J. Busenberg, "Citizen Advisory Committees and Environmental Policy: What We Know, What's Left to Discover," *Risk Analysis*, 15, 1995, pp. 147–162.

[23]See also W. K. Hallman & A. Wandersman, "Attribution of responsibility and individual and collective coping with environmental threats," *Journal of Social Issues*, 48, 1992, pp. 101–118.

[24]See, for example, C. Chess & B. J. Hance, "Opening Doors: Making Risk Communication Agency Reality," *Environment*, 31, 1989, pp. 10–15, 38–39; also W. Leiss & C. Chociolko, *Risk and Responsibility* (Montreal, McGill-Queens University Press, 1994).

[25] For example, see the following references: S. Jasanoff, *Risk Management and Political Culture* (New York, Russell Sage, 1989); L. B. Lave, *The Strategy of Social Regulation: Decision Frameworks for Policy* (Washington, DC: Brookings, 1982): C. Chess, "Encouraging Effective Risk Communication in Government: Suggestions for Agency Management," In V. T. Covello, D. B. McCallum, & M. T. Pavlova (Eds.), *Effective Risk Communication: The Role and Responsibility of Government and Nongovernment Organizations* (New York, Plenum, 1989), pp. 359–365.

[26] Lynn & Busenberger, 1995, *op. cit.*

[27] Science Advisory Board, U.S. Environmental Protection Agency. "An SAB Report: Review of EPA's approach to screening for radioactive waste materials at a superfund site in Uniontown, Ohio." Prepared by the ad hoc Industrial Excess Landfill Panel of the Science Advisory Board. Panel Members: Jan Stolwijk (Chair), Ann Bostrom, Norman H. Cutshall, Robert Morrison, Oddvar Nygaard, Mitchell Small, Michael Stein, and Myint Thein. Robert J. Huggett originally served as chair (EPA-SAB-EC-94-010, US EPA SAB, Washington, DC, 1994).

[28] See C. Perrow, *Complex Organizations* (Glenview, IL, Scott, Foresman, 1978).

[29] H. B. Milward & L. O. Snyder, "Electronic Government: Linking Citizens to Public Organizations Through Technology," *Journal of Public Administration Research and Theory*, 6, 1996, pp. 261–276.

[30] Demchak & Friis, 1995, *op. cit.*

[31] See J. C. Pierce, M. A. E. Steger, B. S. Steel, & N. P. Lovrich, *Citizens, Political Communication, and Interest Groups: Environmental Organizations in Canada and the United States* (Westport, CT, Praeger, 1992), p. 6.

[32] Macpherson, 1996, *op. cit.* Also see P. Miller, "CTCNet (Community Technology Centers Network) and the Movement for Democracy," *The CPSR (Computer Professionals for Social Responsibility) Newsletter*, 14, 1996, pp. 5, 21.

[33] See F. Fischer, "Citizen Participation and the Democratization of Policy Expertise: From Theoretical Inquiry to Practical Cases," *Policy Sciences*, 26, 1993, pp. 165–187. Wicked problems are those that have no adequate solutions and only temporary or imperfect resolutions (p. 1972).

[34] Technical discussion of search engines is available through the Lycos hom page, which references several academic papers on the topic.

[35] The search engines used were those readily available through Netscape software.

[36] Pierce et al., 1992, *op. cit.*

[37] $F(5,64)=3.5$, $p<0.0$. Least squares, means, standard errors, and sample sizes are provided from an analysis of variance on the number of external links by organization type: Government 4.1 (8.1), $n = 21$; Individuals 42.3 (18.5) $n = 4$; NGOs 5.5 (8.5) $n = 19$; Private, 5 (13.0) $n = 8$; Search engines and indices, 68.8 (16.5) $n = 5$; University pages, 0.6 (10.24), $n = 13$.

[38] Lent, 1995, *op cit.*

[39] T. H. Hatfield, "Environmental Health Bulletin Board Systems and Databases," *Journal of Environmental Health*, 57, 1994, pp. 30–31.

[40] Lent, 1995, *op cit.* p. 172.

[41] A. Bostrom, C. J. Atman, B. Fischhoff, & M. G. Morgan, "Evaluating Risk Communications: Completing and Correcting Mental Models of Hazardous Processes, Part II," *Risk Analysis*, 14, 1994, pp. 789–798.

[42] U.S. Department of Commerce, Bureau of the Census, *Statistical Abstract of the United States*, Table 1223. Appliances Used by Households, by Region and Family Income: 1990. (Washington, DC, U.S. Energy Information Administration, 1994).

[43] W. G. Meyer, "The Polls—Poll Trends: The Rise of the New Media," *Public Opinion Quarterly*, 58, 1994, pp. 124–146.

[44] U.S. Department of Commerce, Bureau of Labor Statistics, *Statistical Abstract of the United States*, 1994, Section 4.

[45] Meyer, 1994, *op. cit.*

[46] K. Phillips, "Virtual Washington," *Time*, Spring, 1995, pp. 65–68.

chapter 10

The Impacts of Advanced Information and Communication Technologies on International Actors and the International System

Daniel S. Papp
School of International Affairs
Georgia Tech

INTRODUCTION

T wice this century, the coming of age of significant new technologies has coincided with (but not caused) the collapse of an international system. Both times, the emerging technologies played a significant role in shaping the new international system.[1]

The first occurred during World War I when the old European balance of power system collapsed even as the internal combustion engine was widely used for the first time in warfare. Trucks and planes played major roles in ending the "war to end all wars," and they also played large roles in the interwar era of collective security that followed.

The second time was during World War II, which ended with the use of the most destructive weapon ever used in warfare, the atomic bomb. Not coincidentally, nuclear weapons and technologies played a major role in shaping the post-World War II bipolar system.

This phenomenon is now unfolding for the third time this century as advanced information and communication technologies emerge even as the old bipolar international system collapses. Once again, these technologies promise to play a significant role in shaping international actors and the new international system.[2]

THE TECHNOLOGIES AND THEIR EFFECTS

Seven technologies stand out.[3] First is fiber optics, which can carry over a billion bits of information per second. Some experts predict that fiber optic capacity will eventually exceed a trillion bits per second. This is an immense increase over the perhaps 64,000 bits of information per second that copper wire can carry.

Second are computers. Although computers are central to all aspects of the information and communication revolution, computerized switching requires special mention because it has helped to create a global network that connects most of the world's estimated 700 million telephones. Similarly, with modems, any computer attached to a phone line can talk to any other computer attached to a phone line regardless of location.

Third is improved human-computer interaction. Wider availability of easier operating systems and software such as Windows is simplifying human-computer interaction. Simpler interface systems such as voice recognition and handwriting identification are on the horizon. With easier human-computer interfaces, the potential exists for a considerable increase in the number of computer users.

Fourth are digital transmission and digital compression. Digital transmissions use binary digits carried as electrical pulses to represent data and information. Digital signals have numerous advantages over analog signals, which have historically been used for electronic communication. Digital signals are fast, completely accurate, and less subject to attenuation. They are also the language of computers. Digital technology also allows only new information to be sent, thereby increasing how much data can be sent. Some experts estimate that this process, called *digital compression*, will allow up to 100 times more information to be sent over a channel.

Fifth are communications satellites, which have played a major role in global communications since the first was launched in 1964. Today, the entire world is linked via satellite. Satellite communications at first had only a few hundred channels, but thousands are now available. As computer advances, digital technologies, digital compression, and cellular technologies are married with satellites, the global network will become even more interconnected.

Sixth are cellular technologies. In the United States and other developed countries, cellular technologies already have had sizable impacts on the way people live and the way they conduct their affairs. These technologies are becoming available in developing world states as well. The implications of cellular technologies for economic development and political affairs are immense.

Seventh is networking; that is, the ability of communication technologies to talk to each other and to talk to each other faster. The largest network is the Internet, the growth of which has been explosive. In 1988, the Internet had barely 100 networks; by late 1991, perhaps 4,000 networks, approximately two thirds of which were in the United States, and by 1995, approximately 50,000 networks, with 30,000 of them in the United States. Over time, networking will proliferate further, significantly enhancing global connectivity.

Taken together, these seven technologies have the potential to revolutionize the fields of information and communication. Collectively, they most likely will have six major effects on the way international actors and the international system evolve.

Increased Speed

The speed with which messages, data, and information can be sent, transmitted, managed, manipulated, received, and interpreted will increase significantly. This will happen within and between international actors, although at different rates of speed depending on factors that apply within and between actors and groups of actors.

Increased speed will matter more for some information and communication uses than for others. Some international actors will benefit more from faster information and communication than others, but the fundamental verity is that information and communication flows will be faster.

Greater Capacity

The capacity to send, transmit, and receive messages, data, and information will also increase as technologies are improved. Again, increased capacity will become available within and between individual international actors. It will not become available to all international actors at the same time or at the same level of access or sophistication.

Greater information and communication capacity will matter more for some actors than for others, and some will benefit more than others. Here, the point to stress is that for some international actors, for the first time in history, the ability to send, transmit, manage, manipulate, receive, and interpret information and communications may not be constrained by the technologies involved. Many international actors will experience an immense growth in their capacity to send, transmit, manage, manipulate, receive, and interpret information and to communicate.

Enhanced Flexibility

These technologies will also enhance the flexibility of information and communications flows because those needing information and needing to communicate will be able to send, transmit, manage, manipulate, receive, and interpret messages, data, and information from more sites than ever before. Put differently, location dependence of any of the stages of information and communication flows will decrease.

Again, enhanced flexibility will matter more for some actors than for others. Some will benefit more than others, and some will attain enhanced flexibility earlier than others. Regardless, enhanced flexibility in information and communication flows is coming. Its impacts on international actors and the systems they create have the potential to be significant.

Greater Access

The seven technologies discussed will also provide improved access to information and communication. More and more people will be able to send, transmit, manage, manipulate, and receive messages, data, and information than before.

Some observers believe that improved access will lead to the democratization of information and communication flows throughout the world; that is, a decreased ability of a few international actors to dominate information and communication channels. This may be true. However, given that improved access will not occur throughout the world at the same rate of speed, will be organized in different ways depending on the actor, will not benefit all actors equally, and will not have the same impacts on all actors, whether this is accurate remains to be seen.

More Types of Messages

Little more than a century ago, electronic communications was confined to sending electrical pulses that represented letters a few hundred miles along wire cables. Today, voice, data, graphic, and picture messages are sent electronically from one site to another virtually on a global basis.

To the extent that more complex messages such as graphics and pictures more accurately represent reality than pulses and words, the expansion of message type from pulse to voice, data, graphics, and pictures has been an important factor in enhancing what might be termed *global connectivity* as individuals and groups around the world acquire, or believe they acquire, visual and audio information about people, places, and events in formerly remote locations. The potential impact of this new capability on international actors and the international system is immense.

Heightened Demand

Heightened demand is a function of how individuals and other international actors react to capabilities provided by the technologies. Heightened demand will occur unevenly around the world and at different speeds in different international actors as these technologies become readily available. Heightened demand for the capabilities provided by advanced information and communication technologies will have an immense effect on international actors and on the international system they create.

INTERNATIONAL ACTORS AND
THE INTERNATIONAL SYSTEM

Before the impacts of these technologies on international actors and the international system can be assessed, current international actors must be identified and the present international system must be described.[4] I begin with the state.

States

For over 300 years, the state has been the central actor in international affairs. It remains so today. Throughout the centuries of their domination of the international system, the primary purposes of states have been to provide for the security of their population, to provide for the economic well-being of their population, and, for those states that are nation states, to provide a sense of belonging to the dominant nationality within them.

States are geographically bounded entities governed by central authorities that have the ability to make and enforce laws within their boundaries. States are recognized by international law as sovereign entities that determine their own policies and establish their own governmental forms, which often differ significantly from state to state. Most observers place the number of states over 190.

States are similar but not identical to nations or nation states. A nation is a grouping of people who believe themselves linked in some way, shape, or form; it need not be geographically defined. In contrast, nation states are states whose inhabitants consider themselves a nation. A nation state is a geographically defined entity ruled by one government, the population of which considers itself to be in some way, shape, or form related.

International Governmental Organizations

International governmental organizations (IGOs) are organizations created by two or more states to provide services to member states where cooperation offers advantages for all. IGOs operate in politics, economics, and the military; social and cultural undertakings; technology, science, and health; and a host of other areas. There are over 450 IGOs in the world. The most prominent is the United Nations.

IGOs serve several purposes. They act as forums for communication, serve as regulators, provide military security, and distribute goods and services. On occasion, they also provide a supranational political function, as with the European Union. However, many states oppose extending supranational authority to IGOs, fearing that this would undermine national sovereignty.

Multinational Corporations

Multinational corporations (MNCs) are corporations that have headquarters in one country and own and operate subsidiaries in other countries. Although MNCs perform many functions, their primary purpose is to make a profit for their shareholders.

Globally, there are at least 10,000 MNCs that operate at least 90,000 subsidiaries. Many are huge and draw on significant financial and human resources. Many have the ability to transfer their production or other services around the world as more profitable opportunities become available. To take fullest advantage of the opportunities that their size and worldwide operations provide, MNCs often have centralized decision-making structures, enabling them to respond quickly to changing political and economic situations and conditions.

Nongovernmental Organizations, Individuals, and Other Actors

This category includes a multitude of international organizations, including true nongovernmental organizations (NGOs), national liberation movements, and a host of other international actors.

There is no precise definition for NGOs. They operate internationally, have an organizational structure and have specific objectives that may be in any area of human activity. They may or may not have permanent staffs and secretariats. NGOs are their own masters, the creation of the individuals who are their members. Greenpeace, the International Red Cross, and Amnesty International are all NGOs.

National liberation movements also play major roles in international affairs. Some national liberation movements seek to break a part of a country away from the state of which it is a part to establish a separate nation state; others seek to create not a new state, but a new government for an old state; and still others pit colonial peoples struggling for independence against colonial powers fighting to maintain empire. The Basques of Spain, the Sandanistas in Nicaragua before they acquired power, and the Mau Maus in Kenya are examples of each type.

Terrorist movements also play a prominent international role. *Terrorism* denotes the use of violence to achieve a political objective. Terrorism has been and is used by groups of all ideological persuasions, and no region of the world is immune to it. In the Americas, Peru's Shining Path and Uruguay's Tupamoros have been or are widely regarded as terrorist movements.

Transnational religious movements are also prominent actors that have played major international roles for centuries. The Christian Crusades to the Middle East and the Islamic Jihad through northern Africa are two prominent examples. Today, the Catholic Church, Islam, Buddhism, and other religious movements continue to have considerable influence across state boundaries.

Transnational political movements must also be considered. Although it is now defunct, the international communist movement played a significant role in world affairs for much of the 20th century. Many European political parties also maintain close ties across national boundaries. To the extent that Islamic fundamentalism proposes public policies and governmental actions, it is also a transnational political movement.

Finally, the role that individuals play in international affairs cannot be overlooked. Some, such as Jimmy Carter, are prominent because of positions they held in the past. Others, such as Ted Turner, Madonnna, and PelÇ, are significant because of their business, celebrity, or athletic status. Individuals are rarely as influential as major states or MNCs, but they nevertheless are important.

Large numbers of more obscure people who move from state to state also have a significant international impact. Refugees, tourists, businessmen, students, and others who travel internationally may have only a limited international impact on an individual basis, but cumulatively their impact is considerable.

Defining the Present International System

International actors plus their interactions with each other form the international system. Today's international system is in flux. The old bipolar system based on the East-West conflict and to a lesser extent the North-South conflict is no more, brought down by the collapse of the Soviet Union, the resurgence of nationalism, a rediscovery of the importance of economics, and the emergence of global problems such as environmental deterioration.

What will replace the old system remains unclear. Some analysts foresee a multipolar world in which different actors use different parameters of power in different situations to achieve their objectives, with no single actor or parameter of power preeminent. Others see a cooperative, economically oriented, tripolar world built around regional trading blocs centered in the Americas, Europe, and East Asia emerging, and still others predict a cut-throat competitive, economically oriented, tripolar world built around the same regional blocs. A few U.S. observers assert that a unipolar world dominated by U.S. military strength, economic clout, and technical prowess will emerge.

What, then, will the emerging international system be like? Many variables will determine the answer. Here, however, our task is to identify the impacts of only one: advanced information and communication technologies.

THE IMPACTS OF ADVANCED INFORMATION AND COMMUNICATION TECHNOLOGIES ON INTERNATIONAL ACTORS

Advanced information and communication technologies will be absorbed, diffused, and operationalized by different international actors in different ways and at different speeds. This will lead to different types and rates of change in different international actors. Factors that will influence the way and rate in which these advanced technologies will be absorbed, diffused, and operationalized include:

1. Purchase and upkeep cost.
2. Age and utility of in-place technology.
3. An actor's social and cultural receptivity to new technology.
4. Degree of insularity within an actor.
5. Level and reliability of an actor's human, technical, and economic support infrastructures.

6. Level and strength of traditional values and outlooks within an actor.
7. Level of education within an actor.
8. Degree of technical sophistication of users and potential users of advanced information and communication technology within an actor.
9. Levels of concern over sovereignty on the part of states, and over control of decision-making processes on the part of the actors.
10. Many political, social, and economic factors idiosyncratic to each actor and therefore impossible to detail.

How, then, will advanced information and communication technologies shape and form international actors? This shaping and forming process will be complex, but it is worthwhile to speculate on how that process may affect each class of actor.

States

The advent of advanced information and communication technologies challenges the primacy of the state from three directions. First, as regards a state's ability to provide security for its population, the increased importance of information and communication technologies has rendered states vulnerable if information and communication flows are disrupted. Given the reliance of advanced industrial states on electronic transfer of financial data, any disruption of such transfers could raise havoc within a state. Similarly, given the reliance of most governments on electronic communications to maintain contact with their peoples, disruption of communications could significantly degrade a government's ability to maintain control over its people. Indeed, several countries, including the United States, are pursuing "information warfare" research.[5]

This is not the first time that new technologies have raised questions about the ability of states to provide security for their people, so the degree of threat should not be exaggerated. Nevertheless, as advanced information and communication technologies are increasingly applied to the tools of war, the ability of the state to provide security will increasingly be questioned.

Second, because economic activity is increasingly being conducted across international boundaries, the question of whether states are losing their ability to provide economic well-being for their population arises. Indeed, the growth in global trade has been phenomenal, climbing from approximately $270 billion (U.S.) in 1960 to $1.6 trillion (U.S.) in 1975 to $6.8 trillion (U.S.) in 1990.[6] A growing percentage of

this trade was in information and communication flows, and this percentage is likely to increase still further.

This will have an immense impact on states as more and more international actors use advanced information and communication technologies and obtain the ability to act beyond a single state. Thus, the ability
of states to provide for the economic well-being of their population will
be reduced. The capability to do this will increasingly reside with other
types of international actors.

This phenomenon is already occurring. International finance and
banking has been transformed by global electronic fund transfers at a
moment's notice. Other service sector industries are also internationaliz-
ing their capabilities with advanced information and communication
technologies. This leads to the question of whether states are losing
their ability to provide economic well-being for their population. If they
are, why need states exist?

The same question may be asked about nation states' provision of a
sense of belonging to the dominant nationality within them. Even
though nationalism is on the rise, as evidenced by the dissolution of the
Soviet Union, Yugoslavia, and Czechoslovakia, and nationality problems in Belgium, Canada, Ethiopia, India, Malaysia, and elsewhere,
nations have not always needed states to consider themselves nations.
Indeed, the advent of advanced information and communication technologies opens possibilities for peoples of a single nation to be geographically remote from one another but still retain a sense of identity.
Put differently, advanced information and communication technologies
may allow individuals to overcome boundaries of time and distance, rais-
ing questions about whether states remain necessary for nations to have
an identity. Advanced information and communication technologies
thus raise questions about the validity of the third reason states exist.

This does not imply that states may soon disappear. Even so, with
advanced information and communication technologies helping to raise
questions about all three primary reasons that states exist, the transformation that is occurring in today's international system may be more
significant than the collapse of the bipolar international system.

IGOs

As creations of states, IGOs in most respects are hostage to states. The
advent of advanced information and communication technologies will
do little to change this. Nevertheless, because IGOs transcend state
boundaries and often must cope with problems of time and distance,
capabilities provided by advanced information and communication technologies will help to overcome some of the difficulties that IGOs face.

Even so, IGOs will find it as difficult as ever, perhaps more difficult than ever, to acquire supranational authority and capabilities. However, to the extent that advanced information and communication technologies increase the ability of IGOs to perform tasks that states cannot successfully accomplish, these technologies may lead to the migration of more responsibilities from states to IGOs.

MNCs

MNCs are already among the largest users of information and communication technologies, and they will be at the forefront for use of advanced capabilities as they become available. Indeed, a significant percentage of advanced information and communication technologies is being developed by MNCs.

Already, businesses in the service sector transmit tremendous amounts of data throughout the world. Often, geography has little impact on the decision as to where service sector businesses locate their data and information facilities. For example, several U.S. airlines and other reservation services have sited facilities outside the United States because of lower labor costs available there. The ability to transfer funds electronically at a moment's notice throughout the world has also already had an immense impact on international banking and finance. Some observers believe that the world is well on its way to becoming a single banking and financial market.

Advanced information and communication technologies may also accelerate the trend toward regionalization and globalization of business as more and more companies acquire cost-effective access to international communications. On a regional basis, this phenomenon was a factor that strengthened pressures in Europe for political and economic unity. In short, advanced information and communication technologies will allow many more firms to become multinational.

Thus, advanced information and communication technologies will enhance the already significant role that MNCs play in international affairs. Several decades ago, a noted business professor observed that MNCs could place state sovereignty at bay.[7] With the advent of advanced information and communication technologies, that observation has greater potential than ever to become reality.

NGOs, Individuals, and Other International Actors

Because this group of actors is so diverse, advanced information and communication technologies may be expected to have a diverse impact on the international role that these actors play. Nevertheless, some general observations may be made.

Many of these actors have widely scattered memberships. Thus, many may be expected to benefit significantly from the increased speed, greater capacity, enhanced flexibility, and improved access afforded by these technologies. It is therefore reasonable to assume that many NGOs will become increasingly active, better coordinated, and more influential as advanced information and communication technologies become more widely available.

At the same time, many actors in this category are not well off economically. However, this may not necessarily be a significant disadvantage if greater capacity drives down costs of communicating.

One may also expect a proliferation of NGOs and related organizations and a networking of such organizations as a result of the capabilities afforded by advanced information and communication technologies. At least one such NGO, the Association for Progressive Communication, has already formed, linking 20,000 NGOs and individual members in 95 countries via electronic mail and facsimiles.[8] Its membership includes some of the world's most prominent NGOs and related organizations such as Amnesty International, Greenpeace, the Sierra Club, labor unions, and peace organizations.

On the level of individuals, telephones, electronic mail, and facsimiles already link many people. Much of the personal use of these technologies is for social, educational, and business purposes. However, on at least two occasions—following the Tiananmen Square massacre in China in 1989 and during the Soviet coup attempt in 1991—electronic mail and facsimiles provided an important link to the outside world—and vice versa—for individuals in China and the former Soviet Union.[9]

At the same time, the ability of the international media to provide foreign perspectives and outlooks to every major media outlet in the world creates a sense of global connectivity, if not community, that has never before been widespread among masses of the population. It is too much to argue that this connectivity is leading to changed views on the parts of individuals about their role and the role of their countries in the world, but it is not too much to say that the international media are altering the way many view the world. What the consequences of this will be are unclear.

To reiterate, given the diversity of this group of international actors, advanced information and communication technologies will have a diverse impact on the international role that these actors play. Many will enhance their international roles as a result of the increased speed, greater capacity, enhanced flexibility, and improved access afforded by advanced information and communication technologies.

IMPACTS ON THE INTERNATIONAL SYSTEM

The task in this section is to identify the impacts that advanced information and communication technologies may have on the international system itself. Three appear most probable.

The Disruption of Current Power Relationships Between and Among Types of International Actors

For most of the past 300 years, states have dominated the international system. This is changing, driven in part by the advent of advanced information and communication technologies. These technologies will enable other types of international actors to challenge this dominance as never before.

This process has already begun. MNCs already electronically transfer large quantities of funds and information across national borders with little regard for state sovereignty, and NGOs have increased their importance in and impact on international affairs. The role of MNCs and NGOs in international affairs has often expanded at the expense of states and intergovernmental organizations: Witness the NGOs' women's conference outside Beijing and recent NGO efforts to stop French nuclear testing in the Pacific.

This does not imply that the era of dominance of the international system by the state is over; nor does it imply that the role of the state as a class of actor will significantly diminish in the near-term future. It does imply that state sovereignty will be increasingly challenged. It also implies that the analysis of international affairs and the international system cannot be restricted to state actors.

Inevitably, struggles for power and influence will erupt between different types of actors as a result of information and communication technologies. Advanced information and communication technologies will help to make the emerging system more diffuse and ambiguous than past international systems as current power relationships between international actors are disrupted.

Enhanced Globalization and Regionalization

Aron once observed that the international system was like an echo chamber, with events in one part of the world rebounding off each other and eventually impacting events on the other side of the world.[10] Aron's observation was accurate, but it will be even more accurate in the emerging international system. Given the greater connectivity that advanced information and communication technologies will provide, the future international system will in all probability be increasingly globalized.

However, increased globalization is not necessarily inevitable. Advanced information and communication technologies may contribute to the development of a more regionalized world instead. To an extent, this is already occurring with the development of regional trading blocs such as the European Union, the Free Trade Area of the Americas, and the Asia-Pacific Economic Cooperation zone. These blocs are not results of advanced information and communication technologies, but the growth in importance of these blocs and even subregional blocs such as the North American Free Trade Area is abetted by these technologies.

There will be opposition to both globalization and regionalization. This, too, is happening today. Fearful of losing control or influence, some actors are already restraining the use of advanced information and communication technologies. Similarly, jingoistic nationalism or ideological or religious extremism may view advanced information and communication technologies as a danger to the nation, the ideology, or the religion, and act to curtail their use.

There is no doubt that advanced information and communication technologies will provide humankind with tantalizing new capabilities for global connectivity far beyond any past capabilities. These capabilities enhance the probability of enhanced globalization or regionalization, but such a conclusion is by no means inevitable.

Increasingly Skewed Patterns of Distribution of Wealth Between Actors and Within Actors

Not all international actors will adopt, diffuse, or operationalize advanced information and communication technologies at the same rate. Thus, some actors will benefit more than others from these technologies. In all probability, North America, western Europe, and Japan will lead the way. Argentina, Brazil, India, several of the Association of Southeast Asian Nations states, and a few other countries will follow somewhat behind. Most of the rest of the world will lag behind further.

Even within those regions that lag behind the leaders, there will be users of advanced information and communication technologies. Those users will be certain MNCs, NGOs, individuals, and other nonstate and non-IGO international actors. Regardless of their location, they will be at the forefront of benefiting from advanced information and communication technologies. The implications of these different rates of adoption are immense for the international system and for individual actors, especially states.

On the international level, to the extent that advanced information and communication technologies will create new wealth, different rates of adoption, diffusion, and operationalization have the potential to increase already skewed patterns of distribution of wealth that exist between states. Thus, advanced information and communication technologies have the potential to exacerbate the North-South conflict.

At the state level, this could lead to greater tension between wealthy and poor states. Given the empowerment that advanced information and communication technologies will provide other classes of actors, some NGOs, small groups, and individuals could take it on themselves to attempt to redress real and perceived imbalances in the distribution of wealth. They may even choose to use advanced information and communication technologies—information warfare, if one prefers that term—to undertake such action.

Within states, much the same thing could occur. Again to the extent that advanced information and communication technologies will create new wealth, skewed patterns of distribution of wealth will be exacerbated, increasing the potential for strife and conflict within states. Again, NGOs, small groups, and individuals could decide to try to redress real and perceived imbalances in the distribution of wealth within states.

As new wealth accumulates because of advanced information and communication technologies, decisions must therefore be made about how that wealth will be distributed. The stability of the international system and individual actors within the system may rest with how well such decisions are made.

CONCLUSIONS

Clearly, advanced information and communication technologies will help to make the emerging international system more diffuse, and ambiguous than the recently departed bipolar system. How diffuse, ambiguous, and stable the emerging system will be is less clear. Advanced information and communication technologies will provide new capabilities, but how those capabilities are used and for what purposes remains the stuff of human decision.

NOTES AND REFERENCES

[1] For two of the leading studies of the roles that science and technology play in international affairs, see E.B. Skolnikoff, *The Elusive Transformation: Science, Technology, and the Evolution of International Politics* (Princeton, NJ, Princeton

University Press, 1992); and J. - J. Salomon & A. Lebeau, *Mirages of Development: Science and Technology for the Third World* (Boulder, CO, Lynne Rienner Publishers, 1993).

[2] A host of studies examine the roles that information and communication technologies play in international affairs, but few of these studies try to gauge the role that these technologies play in changing the international system. Among the few that make this effort are A. Arno & W. Dissanayake (Eds.), *The News Media in National and International Conflict* (Boulder, CO, Westview Press, 1984); T. Van Dinh, *Communication and Diplomacy in a Changing World* (Norwood, NJ, Ablex Publishing, 1987); and T. L. McPhail, *Electronic Colonialism: The Future of International Broadcasting and Communication* (Beverly Hills, CA, Sage Publications, 1981). For several studies of the role that information and communication technologies have played in human history, see D. Crowley & P. Heyer (Eds.), *Communication in History: Technology, Culture, Society* (New York, Longman, 1991); G.A. Foster, *Communication: From Primitive Tom-toms to Telstar* (New York, Criterion Books, 1965); H. E. Neal, *Communication From Stone Age to Space Age* (New York, Messner, 1974).

[3] For in-depth analyses of these technologies, see the following.

For fiber optics, see L. D. Greene, *Fiber Optic Communications* (Boca Raton, FL, CRC Press, 1993); R. J. Hoss & E. A. Lacy, *Fiber Optics* (Englewood Cliffs, NJ, Prentice Hall, 1993); A. T. Futro & L. D. Hutcheson, *Fiber Network for Voice, Video, and Multimedia Services* (Bellingham, WA, USA SPIE, 1993); G. J. Brown, *Technologies for Optical Fiber Communications* (Bellingham, WA, USA SPIE, 1994); and J. P. Powers, *An Introduction to Fiber Optic Systems* (Pacific Palisades, CA, Aksen Associates, 1993).

For computers, see T. J. Allen & M. S. Scott Morton, *Information Technology and the Cooperation of the 1990s: Research Studies* (New York, Oxford University Press, 1994); M. Laver, *Computers, Communications and Society* (New York, Oxford University Press, 1975); J. E. Johnston, *Connectivity and Networking* (New York, McGraw-Hill, 1994); and IEEE, *International Phoenix Conference on Computers and Communications* (New York, IEEE, various years).

For human-computer interaction, see A. Dix, *Human-Computer Interaction* (New York, Prentice Hall, 1993); M. W. Lansdale & T. C. Ormerod, *Understanding Interfaces: A Handbook of Human-Computer Dialogue* (London, San Diego, Academic Press, 1994); and B. J. Blumenthal, *Human-Computer Interaction* (New York, Springer Verlag, 1994).

For digital transmission and compression, see R. E. Matick, *Transmission Lines for Digital and Communication Networks: An Introduction to Transmission Lines, High-Frequency, and High-Speed Pulse Characteristic* (New York, Institute of Electrical and Electronics Engineers, 1995); A. N. Netravali, *Digital Pictures: Representation, Compression, and Standards* (New York, Plenum Press, 1995); R. J. Clarke, *Digital Compression of Still Images and Video* (New York, Academic Press, 1995); and *IEE Proceedings, E, Computers and Digital Techniques* (New York, Academic Press, 1995); and *IEE Proceedings, E, Computers and Digital Techniques* (Stevenage, Institution of Electrical Engineers, 1980, 1993).

For communication satellites, see G. D. Morgan & W. L. Morgan, *Principles of Communications Satellites* (New York, Wiley, 1993); J. Wood, *Satellite Communica-*

tions Pocket Book (Boston, Newnes, 1994); and G. Marall & M. Bousquet, translated by J. C. C. Nelson, *Satellite Communications System: Systems, Techniques, and Technology* (New York, Wiley, 1993).

For cellular technologies, see R. G. Winch, *Telecommunication, Transmission Systems: Microwave, Fiber Optic, Mobile Cellular Radio, Data, and Digital Multiplexing* (New York, McGraw-Hill, 1993); and United States International Trade Commission, *Global Competitiveness of US Advanced-technology Industries: Cellular Communications* (Washington, DC, US International Trade Commission, 1993).

For networking, see D. E. Comer, *Internetworking with TCP/IP* (Englewood Cliffs, NJ, Prentice Hall, 1991-93); T. Valovic, *Corporate Networks: The Strategic Use of Telecommunications* (Boston, Artech House, 1993); L. M. Harasim, *Global Networks: Computers and International Communication* (Cambridge, MA, MIT Press, 1993); D. E. Comer, *The Internet Book: Everything You Need to Know About Computer Networking and How the Internet Works* (Englewood Cliffs, NJ, Prentice Hall, 1995); F. Werner, *Novell's Complete Encyclopedia of Networking* (San Jose, CA, Novell Press, 1995); R. Tennant, J. Ober & A. G. Lipow, *Crossing the Internet Threshold: An Instructional Handbook* (Berkeley, CA, Library Solutions Press, 1994); and D. P. O'Doherty, *Globalisation, Networking, and Small Firm Innovation* (Boston, Graham & Trotman, 1995).

[4]For a more detailed analysis of international actors and the international system, see D. S. Papp, *Contemporary International Relations*, 4th ed. (New York, Macmillan, 1994).

[5]See, for example, "Onward Cyber Soliders," *Time*, 21 August 1995, pp. 38-44; and G. R. Sullivan & J. M. Dubik, *War in the Information Age* (Carlisle, PA, US Army War College, 1994).

[6]International Monetary Fund, *Direction of Trade Statistics*, various years.

[7]R. Vernon, *Sovereignty at Bay" The Multinational Spread of US Enterprises* (New York, Basic Books, 1971).

[8]H.H. Frederick, *Global Communications and International Relations* (Belmont, CA, Wadsworth Publishing Company, 1993), p. 97.

[9]See, for example, S. Loory & A. Imse, *Seven Days That Shook the World: The Collapse of Soviet Communism* (Atlanta, Turner Publishing, 1991), p. 36.

[10]R. Aron, *Peace and War* (Garden City, Doubleday & Company, 1966), p. 373.

chapter 11

Information Warfare: A Consequence of the Information Revolution

Myron L. Cramer
Research Institute
Georgia Tech

INTRODUCTION

This chapter defines information warfare (IW), provides some historical background and context, and describes its applicability to business. An underlying element of the information age is that information carries more value than in previous periods of history. Information warfare involves achieving and maintaining an information advantage over competitors or adversaries. Because competitive advantages can impact an organization's success or failure, it is important to understand the factors that affect this balance and to understand the framework created by the new technologies and the new paradigms.

BACKGROUND

Military Roots

The terminology of IW has its roots in military operations and many of its elements have been part of military doctrine for many centuries, including terms such as *psychological operations, operations security, tactical deception*, and *electronic warfare*.[1] But although the military drapes IW in the robes of the past, the modern concepts of IW are of recent evolution, born of the changes that have been driven by the new technologies. In current military doctrine, the information space or *infosphere* is considered the fifth battlespace together with land, sea, air, and space. The military considers this infosphere a "place" where primary battles may be fought and has actually issued a Field Manual on Information Operations.[2] Although there may be legal, regulatory, and ethical reasons for a business analogy not to exist, both anecdotal evidence and the results of a recent survey conducted by a Senate subcommittee indicate that the extent and seriousness of cybercrime is more than may be publically appreciated.[3]

New Information Technologies

Much has been written about the information revolution and the societal impact that has been resulting from the increasing role of information and information systems in the endeavors of individuals, businesses, governments, and nongovernmental organizations. This revolution is built on a framework of many individual elements, such as those listed in Table 11.1, which contribute to an aggregate effect that is highly synergistic in its effect on society, and which enables effects such as those described by futurists (e.g., Alvin Toffler[4]) and other researchers.

It is important to recognize that these new developments are only technologies that of themselves are neither good nor bad; they can be used for great benefit, or can lead to disaster if used without consider-

TABLE 11.1. New Information Technologies

Computer-aided design	Fax machines
Paperless manufacturing	Scanners
Groupware	Pen notebooks
Online services	Flash technology
Document management	Advanced fiber optics
Customer service technology	Wireless technology
Point-of-sale terminals	Video-conferencing
Servers	Graphics technology
Networks	Data compression
Databases	Object orientation
Printers	Virtual reality
Voice recognition	Geographic systems
Storage protection	

Note: From *U.S. News & World Report*, "The New Information Technologies," May 2, 1994.

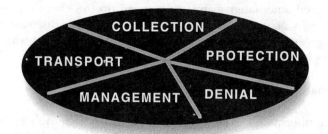

FIGURE 11.1.   Information Warfare Mix

ation for their potential consequences. One key difference comes from an understanding of the commercial perspective of IW.

A BUSINESS PERSPECTIVE

In this discussion, organizations are discussed generally; they can be any commercial business, government entity, or military unit that operates in any competitive or adversarial environment or scenario containing at least one opponent. With the increased value of information comes the need to approach it in new ways. IW has many aspects. To appreciate these it is important to discuss IW from several perspectives that may be thought of as the constituent elements. These are *information collection, protection, denial, management,* and *transport*. Together, these define options, risks, and opportunities; how an organization chooses to implement and prioritize these elements is its IW strategy, which will impact its competitive position. This is illustrated in Figure 11.1.

Information Collection

An organization needs a variety of information to support its operations. These needs include planning its activities, executing its plans, monitoring its progress, and reporting its results. Information collection includes the entry points for information into an organization from both internal and external sources. Issues include quantity (completeness), quality (accuracy), and timeliness of this information. Business examples of collection systems include point of sale (POS) systems, market surveys, government statistics, and internal management data. Military examples of collection systems include tactical radars and other sensors.

The increased reliance on information has resulted in an increasing appetite for data and new collection systems. By example, grocery stores introduced automated scanners to speed up the check out process and improve its accuracy. Then they issued customers discount and check-cashing cards that allowed them to correlate customers with their purchasing habits.

Information Protection

Once information is collected by an organization, the next logical consideration is how to protect it. The vulnerability of the information infrastructure is widely discussed and publicized and is one important aspect of protection. Information protection addresses two types of threats: information compromise and destruction. *Compromise* involves a competitor gaining access to an organization's proprietary data. *Destruction* involves the loss of these data (or loss of access to these data) as the result of mismanagement, accident, or a hostile attack by an adversary.

Information Compromise

An organization's information includes items that may have a high value to a competitor. Examples include future plans, product technical data, customer lists, personnel files, and financial records. This type of data needs to be protected from disclosure to competitors by controlling how, where, by whom, and when it is generated, stored, or accessed. The specific data being protected in these ways are often identified in some distinguishing manner and labeled as proprietary, sensitive, or classified. In some cases, formal control systems are established to encourage the desired behavior among employees. An often overlooked area involves the protection of nonproprietary data of a seemingly harmless nature. These data, when combined with other information available to a competitor may become important. For example the travel schedules of key executives may be a tip-off of pending business activities such as mergers or new customers. Protecting information of this nature is sometimes referred to as *operations security*. An internal organization chart or phone directory can be valuable to an adversary's recruiters in identifying and contacting key staff. These people will bring with them their knowledge of ongoing programs, products, and customer contacts.

Information Destruction

With the increasing use of collection systems have come new opportunities for information attacks by adversaries for either purposes of compromise or destruction. The adversary's purposes in making these attacks may include obtaining competition-sensitive information or hindering (sabotaging) an organization's operations. In the fast-paced and global economy of the information age, organizations may resort to actions and methods that would be considered improper, unethical, or illegal in previous generations. The new information system technologies actually encourage this behavior by lowering the technical threshold to be crossed to a level available to virtually anyone with a personal computer and a telephone. The level of automation is such that intrusions are difficult to detect or trace, tempting the perpetrator with a low likelihood of being caught and large rewards for success.

Information Denial

Information denial includes measures beyond normal protection to specifically target an adversary's collection systems. There are two types of denial: direct attacks on the adversary's information systems, and providing misinformation to its systems to deceive and induce the adversary to take actions that are not to its advantage.

Direct Attacks

For the military, direct attacks include electronic warfare (jamming) of sensors and radio links. In business, analogous forms of direct attack are possible to attack the integrity or availability of a competitor's systems. Through the Internet, all of an organization's networked computers are connected by high-speed links not only to each other, but also to every competitor around the world. Through standard Internet protocols such as the file transfer protocol (FTP), the entire contents of a computer can be copied or replaced within minutes. Integrity attacks include introduction of corruption into data or software so that the targeted competitor will not be using the information or processes it expects. Availability attacks include many methods of interfering with the normal operation of a competitor's networked systems so that they will not be operational when the competitor needs them. Direct attacks on an adversary's computer networks are a highly risky and usually illegal activity. Nevertheless, the current state of the Internet makes attacks difficult to trace and international intrusions difficult to prosecute. Because direct attacks are an element of IW that an adversary may choose to employ as part of its strategy, they must be considered in formulating strategy and in planning protection.[5,6,7,8]

Misinformation

Besides direct attacks, there are safer ways to corrupt an adversary's databases. These rely on providing false information to the targeted competitor's collection systems to induce this organization to make bad decisions based on this faulty information. Consider the "vaporware" example in which a software developer, Company A, gets information about a new product being developed by a competitor, Company B. Although it has no comparable product in development itself, Company A issues a press release describing its own "superior" (but fictional) product. In response to Company A's press announcement, Company B thinks that it has lost its market lead and puts its development efforts elsewhere. Even after Company B brings the real product to market, its lead can be effectively lost when potential customers postpone their purchases waiting for the fictitious product from Company A. This example may have become commonplace in today's software market. The military versions of this type of denial operation include tactical deception and psychological operations (PSYOP). In all of these cases, the true situation is concealed, while evidence is generated and made available of a fictional reality. In the information age, we can expect these practices to become increasingly commonplace. Organizations need to protect themselves from these practices by anticipating them and by controlling the quality of their information sources. They also need to be ready to respond quickly to counter an adversary's misinformation. Company B would have done this in the vaporware example cited by issuing its own press release about the inferiority and immaturity of Company A's imitation product or with money-back guarantees to purchasers of its product.

Information Management

An important element of IW is information management. This is evolving as a new discipline because it involves combinations of computer science and management. The underlying concept is that with the increasing value of information in business, a competitive advantage can result from improved management of this resource. There are many aspects to this element including the selection and introduction of information technologies and the methods for controlling data within information systems. We have seen the transition to distributed computing through increased use of personal computers in business. This has resulted in a decentralization of computing and data resources within organizations and the loss of central control. This creates many issues for corporate data managers, including questions of: Where is the data? Who has it? and Which version is the most current? Other issues include deciding which data to retain (archive) for future reference, and how to store these archived data so that they will be readable by future systems. As an organization's intellectual property exists increasingly in electronic forms, it is harder to manage using traditional methods (such as paper records) that may be more easily misplaced, lost, or discarded. Automated solutions are important elements.

Information Transport

An essential element of IW is information transport. Transport involves moving data from points of collection to points of storage or use. The speed with which this is done affects the timeliness of the data availability and therefore the responsiveness of the organization to situations. Because this responsiveness can be a big factor in the competitive process, the speed and efficiency of an organization's transport capabilities can be an important factor in the organization's survival or failure. An example is an organization's ability to use Internet e-mail to provide time-critical bids or proposals to a customer and thus beat competitors whose express delivery packages may still be en route. Competitive transport systems must be fast, reliable, and controlled. Transport considerations must be viewed within the overall IW perspective, because the same efficiency that facilitates rapid message and data transportation also may be used by a competitor to download proprietary databases in seconds or minutes.

IW STRATEGIES

An IW strategy is an organization's relative mix of efforts among the five elements (information collection, protection, denial, management, and transport); this balance, whether explicitly selected or the result of separate investment and operational decisions, affects the organization's competitive posture. Significant factors include market opportunities, likely competitor actions, and current competitive situation.

POSTURES

Incorporating IW into operational missions involves many choices. These choices are driven by competitiveness consideration. The aggressiveness shown by competitors in collecting information will affect the need for protection and denial. There are many possible postures an organization can take, each of which reflects the results of different attitudes toward the information war. I illustrate these differences by considering five extreme positions in which a single information warfare element is dominant.

- **Defensive.** A heavily defensive posture is characterized by an emphasis on information protection, including significant access-control and limited external system interconnections. This posture might be appropriate for a dominant market leader or an organization that benefits from the status quo. This strategy will have advantages in an environment containing emerging adversaries who are pursuing strategies to attack the leader or to change the current situation.

- **Offensive.** The offensive posture is characterized by an emphasis on information denial, including attacks on the market leader. This posture might be taken by organizations that are dissatisfied by their current standing and that may be desperate to take down their stronger adversaries.

- **Quantity.** The quantity posture is characterized by an emphasis on supreme information transport capability. An organization adopting this posture places its confidence in its ability to move and use massive amounts of information over large well-established infrastructure. It depends on the sheer volume and timeliness of its data to make attacks impractical. This posture will work best when the value of the organization's information is widely distributed and is of low sensitivity.

- **Quality.** The quality posture is characterized by an emphasis on information management. A practitioner of this posture gains its advantage by its ability to manage its information needs better than its competitors. Compared with these competitors, its investments may be more modest, but they are wisely made. It makes better use of less information, and optimizes its use of modest protection. This posture may have advantages in a highly competitive, cost-sensitive market.

- **Sponge.** The sponge posture is characterized by an emphasis on information collection and an insatiable thirst for large amounts of information. Practitioners of this posture may have adopted a follower strategy in which they quickly bring products to market based on the innovations of others. They gain their competitive advantage by saving in research and product development. To avoid being left behind, they must monitor the activities of other more innovative adversaries and survey market responses so that once they decide to follow a given initiative, they can quickly catch up in the marketplace using their previous market presence.

Game Theory

A more scientific treatment of strategy analysis is possible through game theory. In a competitive environment, the optimum strategy may depend on what the competition is doing, as illustrated in Figure 11.2.

Benefit/Cost	Player A		
	Option 1	Option 2	Option 3
Player B — Option 1	0	High	Low
Player B — Option 2	High	0	High
Player B — Option 3	Low	High	0

FIGURE 11.2.   Game Theory Option Matrix.

In this example, Options 1, 2, and 3 are progressively more expensive in terms of capital investment in information system technologies. Each option provides a relative market share benefit over a competitor investing less.

SUMMARY

In this chapter, I examined IW as a consequence of the changes brought about by the information revolution. This consequence positions an organization's information systems as a high-leverage element in the competitive process. To better understand this role, I discussed five perspectives of IW: information collection, protection, denial, management, and transport. From each perspective I examined its role in the competitive process, and discussed concepts for designing a balanced information warfare strategy.

NOTES AND REFERENCES

[1] A. D. Campen, *The First Information War: The Story of Communications, Computers and Intelligence Systems in the Persian Gulf War: An Anthology of Studies of Communications in the Gulf War*, 1992.

[2] Department of the Army, *Information Operations*, FM 100-6 (U.S. Department of the Army, Washington, DC, 1996).

[3] WarRoom Research, *Safeguarding Corporate America and the National Information Infrastructure* (Report for the President's Infrastructure Protection Task Force and the Federal Bureau of Investigation) January 1997.

[4]A. Toffler, *Future Shock* (Random House, New York, 1970).

[5]National Research Council's System Security Committee, *Computers at Risk: Safe Computing in the Information Age: An Unemotional Examination of the Threat and our Vulnerabilities.*

[6]W. Schwartau, *Information Warfare: Chaos on the Electronic Superhighway* (Thunders Mouth Press, 1994).

[7]Toffler, *op. cit.*

[8]U.S. General Accounting Office, *Economic Espionage: The Threat to US Industry,* (GAO/T-OSI-92-6, 1992).

part V
Implications for Information Societies

In the preceding parts of this book, we have seen some of the consequences of, what might be called, "informationalization." However, beyond the realm of introducing information technology as a resource that transforms established practices and processes, there lies a potentially more profound outer ring of indirect and extended consequences. These are much more difficult to identify and pin down. This part explores several consequences that are apt to change the very nature of human life.

We begin with the impact of information technologies on our use of physical space. The topic is addressed by a distinguished architect. In Chapter 12, she proposes that public and private "spaces" are being blurred due to the spread of information. She sees a serious threat to democratic processes in the demise of the "public realm."

Next, in Chapter 13, a specialist in cultural communication explores two guiding myths of the information revolution: She asks whether this revolution really empowers individuals and whether it will augment democratic practices. She does so from a cultural, rather than political, point of view. The amount and nature of information leads to issues such as veracity (e.g., in advertising) and information overload experiences. These translate into overarching issues of information ownership, originality, and human identity.

*In Chapter 14, provocatively titled "*Less Labor, Longer Lives, Time to Share,*" a pair of writers weave in the compounding driver of increasing longevity, keying on how we spend our time. They suggest that alternatives to the traditional job need be devised to meet our human needs.*

The concluding Chapter 15 is both sobering and challenging. The subject is jobs in a rapidly changing technological environment. The authors track the record of technological advance and increasingly global competition. Recent events dramatize that technology-based productivity gains are indeed reducing the need for labor. Increasing social inequality looms.

chapter 12

The Impact of Information Technology on the Relationship Between the Public and the Private Realms

Micha Bandini
College of Architecture
Georgia Tech

INTRODUCTION

Much has been written recently both on the public realm and on information technology (IT), but although some of the material has been presented in scholarly publications, most of it, because of its newness and its genre, can only be found under miscellaneous categories. Moreover, the level of information available is very uneven and often anecdotal, and it addresses different audiences: from those who have a professional interest in this new technology to those who are asked to underpin new developments with their purchasing power.

Within this setting, several discourses consider the impact of the IT revolution on place and space. The first is concerned with the physical quality of our surroundings and their implications; the second focuses on the arguments advocating the shift from physical to virtual spaces for many of our activities; the third discourse tries to open up the question of levels of governance; and the fourth concerns the effects of IT on the relationship between space, place, and time.

CHOICE

Until recently, individuals living in advanced industrialized countries still seemed to be able to choose whether or not they wanted to allow IT to influence their lives. Anyone could decide whether or not to buy what the market offered; that is, a series of independent gadgets that increased the efficiency of previous machines by either ease of operation or by augmenting their functions. Recent known factors have changed this situation. First, costs of production and prices have decreased. Second, ease of operation, added uses, and the number of users has increased. However, third, and perhaps more importantly, this kind of technology has become a. device with political potential and it has become identified with societal progress. It is interesting to note that IT played a prominent role in both the Bill Clinton and the Newt Gingrich political campaigns, each of which used it to their advantage. The IT theme was also prominent in the speeches of all candidates for the 1996 presidential elections. The different connotations of IT and the influence yielded by the myth of IT within the United States cannot be dismissed by anyone reflecting on the hegemonic cultural power exercised by the United States as a leader of what constitutes a desirable lifestyle for Western society.

Even if individuals might not wish to learn IT for their private use, they may no longer have such a choice because the skills associated with this technology are needed in order to work and to interact with financial or community services. This was the case of Robert Post, curator of technology at the Smithsonian Institution's Museum of American History, fellow at the Massachusetts Institute of Technology, and author of *High Performance: The Culture and Technology of Drag Racing*. In his book, he affirmed that those who pursue high-tech development do so mainly because of their love of discovery and the availability of research grants in this field, and not because of societal needs. Until recently, Post was able to refuse to learn about computers, but this is no longer so, as his employers told him to join the e-mail community.[1] Moreover, the possibility of using obsolete technology might not be there for any of us, as the machines that provide that technology might no longer be in production.[2]

Many activities have progressively shifted from human interactions that require people to move from place to place, and very possibly being interested in their physical quality, to a new class of human-machine interaction between people and mechanical devices ubiquitously located and not needing specific spatial requirements, and finally to a whole new way of communicating in which personal interactions have no physical dimension attached to them. We might care to record the psychological adjustments demanded in the case of obtaining financial transactions. They range from the familiar habit of entering the bank building and perhaps chatting while waiting to be served, to the less familiar pattern of accessing by car the fast-cash-dispenser lane, to the increasingly popular choice of ringing the bank teller, to the totally depersonalized possibility of banking through e-mail. It is interesting to note that so far telephone banking is proving more popular than e-mail banking. Following the example of First Direct, a subsidiary of Midland Bank U.K., telephone banking is spreading in the United States, with, for example, Chase Manhattan and Chemical announcing, after their merger, the creation of Chase Direct, modeled on First Direct.[3]

Thus, we might claim that in a remarkably short span of time, people have shifted from an interaction involving social skills within quality spaces at given times, to one that can be made at any location, at whatever time, and allows individuals to be totally oblivious to their material surroundings. Is Western society inadvertently sliding into cultural patterns that make us less and less dependent on the physical environment for the necessities of daily life?

CYBERSPACE

The preeminence of cyberspace is what was enthusiastically argued by Mitchell from his book, *City of Bits*, in which he stated:

> The tests the follow re-imagine architecture and urbanism in the new context suggested by...the digital telecommunication revolution, the ongoing miniaturization of electronics, the commodification of bits, and the growing domination of software over materialized form. They adumbrate the emergent but still invisible cities of the twenty-first century. And they argue that the most crucial task before us is not one of putting in place the digital plumbing of broadband communication links and associated electronic appliances ... nor even of producing electronically deliverable "content," but rather one of imagining and creating digitally mediated environments for the kind of lives we will want to lead and the sort of communities that we will want to have.[4]

The previous belief, reinforced by the patterns of his own personal activities, by the examples of Professor Hawking's voice box, and of Yo Yo Ma's electronically enhanced musical capacities,[5] allows Mitchell to see people less as human animals and more as mutating human cyborgs, ready to enter and exit at will, back and forth, from the virtual to the electronic to the physical environment. The argument is that as we seem to find the electronic world useful and enjoyable, we will use more of it, and, as IT is transforming the way we interact with and perceive our surroundings, we could conceive of both the organic and the electronic worlds as equal providers of information.

Within this line of argument it naturally follows that there would be little difference between the two worlds and we could and should imagine with the same mental outlook both the physical and the electronically produced space. Thus, Mitchell argued that space and activities physically present and electronically generated are commensurate with each other as when he wrote, "Once we have both a 'real' dimensional world and computer-constructed 'virtual' ones, the distinctions between these worlds can get fuzzed or lost."[6] And, outside of nutrition, it seems that there is little that for him could not be satisfactorily duplicated or accessed though the computer.

This message, fervent with the zeal of an author who, having invested a lifetime of work, finally sees some of the results toward which he was initially working, suffers from the overenthusiasm of two basic assumptions. First, I would challenge our organisms' capacity to modify as quickly as Mitchell assumed. Notwithstanding that the human body is increasingly adjusted through artificial prothesis by modern medicine, our species' genetic imprinting has not changed much in the past few centuries, as recent work in symbiogenesis, global ozone change, evolution, and cognition is showing.[7] Our limitations in adaptation are painfully evident by the insurgence of immunodeficiency illnesses, as is our need, even without fully subscribing to Lovelock's Gaia hypothesis,[8] for a symbiotic relationship with a healthy planet. Second, and more importantly, I would give a higher consideration than Mitchell to the tradition of permanence in human experience, as it appears that we cherish artefacts that speak through generations and physical spaces that convey a particular sense of place and time. These experiences can of course be electronically duplicated, but I would maintain they would not serve, in the virtual world, the same basic human needs that they perform in the organic world. Moreover, if spaces and places are to be made accessible through electronic media, they need first to be created.

Mitchell would argue that it is enough for these places to have a location on the Internet, and here I partially agree. For some places destined to the service industry, this might be enough, but for all those places that derive their meaning from being a representation of society's aspirations and needs, I feel that it would not suffice. The Internet is too precarious and impermanent a medium to allow it to carry the symbols of our society. Humans are ancient animals not only in the physical sense but in the emotional and social sense, too. We need physical proximity for a variety of human interactions and we need to maintain and continue to invent the cultural metaphors of that proximity through the creation of different artefacts. The electronic world is a wonderful added tool to our physical world, not its substitute. Moreover, Mitchell's message could be seen as serving a particular trend in our contemporary society that is not conducive to the development of socially encompassing physical metaphors; that is, the furthering of individualism at the expense of social responsibility.

If a few years ago the urban debate among the cognoscenti was about the erosion of public space,[9] the replacement of meaningful communal places with privately controlled ones, and the linked problems of gentrification and renewal, nowadays these issues are augmented and diverted by an increasing number of citizens who choose to opt out from common living and who buy into the lifestyle offered by private community developments.[10] For these people, the allure of IT as the major provider of links with the outside world is as strong as was Mitchell's necessity to be linked by radio to school as a boy in the Australian outback. The difference, of course, is that I assume that the Mitchell family did not have a choice, whereas the majority of people settling in controlled neighborhoods could remain in the larger community and help with its care.

If Mitchell is right, these people will hardly need to experience even the mall, that poor substitute for street life, as they will mainly shop from home, viewing, customizing, and ordering the merchandise from their individual enclaves. People could become more and more secluded in communities similar in income, race, and lifestyle and almost encouraged not to meet physically with others by the richness of the electronic offerings at their disposal.

Within this scenario, how are we going to learn to coexist with "the different," a prerequisite for the establishment of a pluralist and tolerant society? Traditionally, urban places and architectural spaces have served that purpose, but to further the progressive demise of traditional architecture and the necessity for a virtual one, Mitchell used the well-known rhetorical device of simplifying the argument presented by the opposing view and, with a technique reminiscent of Venturi and Rossi, he reduced architecture to pure *utilitas*; that is, to functional categories, when he spoke of it.[11] However, the meaning of buildings does not solely reside in their usefulness; in addition to the other two Vitruvian categories of *firmitas* (strength) and *venustas* (beauty), architecture has social and cultural implications that go far beyond its built or unbuilt presence.

Why then would people debate so heatedly building and urbanism? Obviously they matter. The tradition, the ideas, and the physical enjoyment conveyed by their experience matter.

GOVERNMENT AND GOVERNANCE

Much of the economic rationale for a priority development of ITs is currently underpinned by a pervasive mentality that believes in the inevitability of the increasing internalization of our world.

Hirst and Thomson presented a very convincing argument against the sweeping myth of globalization and for the importance of the nation state as a central agency for governance, upward toward international agencies and downward toward subnational organizations, and their argument, if applied to IT, shows the necessity of a network of regulations at all levels. Moreover, the authors distinguished between the role of government and that of governance and defined *governance* as "the control of activity by some means such that a range of desired outcomes is attained."[12] The issue of governance is quite relevant to IT as an individualistic, almost anarchist, view of control and regulation seems to be intrinsic to its development.

As with the broadband radio community, those who have pursued IT in the past few years have grown into a network of users who largely like to think of themselves as outside mainstream rules. For example, they perceive the current attempts to police the Internet as intrusions and prefer self-regulation. One of the most popular North American popular press commentators on the subject, Elizabeth Dyson, is quite eloquent in this respect, as when she wrote:

> In this age of political correctness and other intrusions on our national cult of independence, it's hard to find a place where you can go and be yourself without worrying about the neighbors. There is such a place: cyberspace....Yes, community standards should be enforced, but those standards should be set by cyberspace communities themselves, not by the courts or by the politicians in Washington. What we need isn't Government control over all these electronic communities: we need self rule....We haven't created a perfect society on earth and we won't have one in cyberspace either. But at least we can have individual choice and individual responsibility.[13]

Laws would, of course, be both necessary and inevitable as IT grows out of its developmental stage into its full commercial phase, but they might be long in coming if the IT community bypasses national regulation, choosing self-regulation on the road to internationalization.

Self-regulation would obviously be necessary in a situation as fluid as IT, and internationalization is a worthwhile long-term aim, but these strategies might be used to divert energies from national governance, which, I believe, needs to be energetically pursued both as a prerequisite for transnational agreements and to check an IT solely fueled by the market forces. Moreover, as national governments can be effective in regulating the direction and speed of development by underpinning or withdrawing funds and research grants, obviously decisions at a national and regional level have a direct impact on the relationship between the private and the public realm. This is especially true in the absence of a situation of plenty, as the hierarchy of expenditure allocation and the direction of efforts will be a reflection of the cultural conventions and the collective fantasies shaping society's priorities.

I believe ultimately that it will be the way in which market-driven and community forces together regulate access to IT that will determine if IT's developments will only increase the commodification of Western society or prove to be beneficial in other ways. In order for this to occur, local, national, and international forms of governance need to be operational. This failing, we will see its rippling effect in all aspects of our life.

The first to be affected will be the public realm because, unlike the private realm that can partly protect itself through class and wealth, the public realm needs both individual and government patronage. The central question is not only whether the cultural conventions shaping our deployment of IT are progressive, but also if the framework envisaged by the advocates of IT's development as a societal priority is encompassing enough of the multifarious aspects of our contemporary society.

Would individual locational choices be increased or decreased? Would public place be preserved or eroded? These questions are relevant as, traditionally, the location of housing is largely determined by its real estate value and the provision of public places reflects the value that a community attributes to itself. Would the ubiquity resulting from IT's spreading use level financially different locations? Could and should the importance of public physical spaces diminish as their functions are replaced by an electronic meeting forum? What would become of the decision-making pattern of traditional power brokers when their realm of communication becomes the electronic one?

Remembering that public spaces are traditionally loaded with symbolic meanings embedded within the foundations, often the stones themselves, of a given place; that the political history of a society can be read in the architecture and layout of a place; that a space, private or public, is often cherished exactly for its power to evoke and inspire—could electronic sites then satisfy these deep human emotions?

Moreover, most societies believe that if they are to remain democratically healthy, it is important to achieve an acceptable balance between public and private spaces as metaphors for equitable access and as a legacy for future generations. Could IT replace these important functions?

The issue evidently is not whether societies should wholly embrace ITs as a futuristic symbol of progress or take the Unabomber's ideological stance, but, rather, how we might use them, for what purposes and under what form of national and international governance.

SPACE AND PLACE

Place and space in contemporary society have become full of paradoxes even without the added complication of IT. This has been noted by several authors, who, often starting from Marxian or Heideggerian assumptions, have explored location and activities in increasingly complex and dislocated Western societies.[14] They have noted that the meaning of space and place have become more and more blurred, partially because of a phenomenon they have been termed *time-space compression*, which, incidentally, is increasing with IT developments.

From the long-distance call that allows instant access to future or past time zones to the virtual spaces created, transmitted, and modified through the World Wide Web, we understand space-time compression as the extending of the geographical boundaries of social relationships through people's movement and communication in space and in time, and this phenomenon is due as much to the transformation of capital as to socially differentiating factors.

Massey argued against Harvey's and Jameson's pure materialist view and, through a series of well-chosen examples, demonstrated that the hierarchies of access determining social control of space-time compression are as essential to its understanding as are the economic issues. On this she wrote: "Different social groups have distinct relationships to this anyway-differentiated mobility: some are more in charge of it than others: some initiate flows and movement, others don't; some are more on the receiving end of it than others; some are effectively imprisoned by it."[15] Moreover, as control over mobility and communication reinforces individual power, she argued that inherent within time-space compression are politics of access that, whereas reinforcing the societal control of some groups, could weaken or deny that of others. Thus, her question—"whether our relative mobility and power over mobility and communication entrenches the spatial imprisonment of other groups"[16]— appears central to the debate on the impact of IT.

In this respect, it is interesting to note how the debate concerning the bandwidth of the fiber optic cable carrying the new integrated technology, essentially a political issue, has been clouded by technocratic and financial arguments. We understand that the thicker the cable the more signals can be transmitted, possibly at higher cost. But what needs to be considered is whose responsibility it is to provide it for individual computers. Would it be a private or a public service? Would there be discrimination between wealthy and poor neighborhoods? Would this result in yet another statistic documenting the racial divide within the United States like the recent one showing that whereas about 30% of Asian and White households possessed a computer, very few of the rest of the population owned one?[17]

In a not too wild flight of the imagination, it is possible to project that ITs will further increase the divide line between suburban, middle-class neighborhoods and less affluent environs. The inhabitants of the former will have even fewer reasons ever to be present in malls, midtowns, or downtowns, as they can have instant access to work, entertainment, shopping, and vital information from the keyboard at home. The latter, not being able to afford that vital cable connection, will still need to go to the places that give them access to those necessities and thus will have to occupy public spaces they cannot afford to implement, renew, or maintain.

But will those who have been given the choice to access the outside from the safety of their homes remain committed citizens, interested in a public realm they rarely use? Understanding that cyberspace can be no substitute for the real physical experience of localized place making and belonging, perhaps the only way to ensure that some vestige of a public realm is maintained in an increasingly privatized world would be if the capacity of the bandwidth allowed to individual users is not solely determined by their purchasing power and if, in all cases, it is large enough to allow substantial two-way traffic of information. In this way, it could allow users to make the shift from passive viewers to active broadcasters and it also would allow a creative interaction with any received signal, so that perhaps, for the first time in culture, viewers, listeners, and readers could become active participants and not just passive recipients.

The argument made by IT's supporters is that the public realm to which individuals could contribute would then not be limited to their immediate community but extend to far and distant places that might share similar problems and aspirations. This argument needs to be tempered by two observations. First, cyberspace should not be promoted as the overprotective effort of drawing boundaries around similar groups, but rather as the integration of multifaceted individual and community personalities. Thus, if social interactions are perceived in cyberspace not unidimensionally but as a network embracing differences as well as similarities, then we might conceive an integrated set of Internet sites without increasing social disintegration and individual displacement. Second, we ought to remember that we use spatial terms as metaphors within the electronic world and that the status of these metaphors is to remind us of the real thing to make our use of computer software easier.

Thus, place making and belonging is dependent, because of its uniqueness, on a physical sense of place based on both the social interactions and the cultural attributions we give to that place.

This is even more evident if we see both place and space making as continuing dynamic processes. Ultimately, it would be the word *relationship* that would stand out as pivotal for a new understanding that would lead both to progressive policies and new approaches to spatial issues, with ITs forming a constitutive, pervasive, and necessary addition of both the public and the private realms.

CONCLUSIONS

There are causes for concern if one believes that the possibility of enhancing the democratic pluralism of society is highly dependent on both the physical and the metaphorical views of the public realm.

It is possible that the impact of ITs, if unchecked by democratic wishes or pursued only for capital gain, would increase the privatization of the public realm, but it could also be anticipated that concerted criticism and a clear vision could determine more precisely the kind of service we want IT to perform.

As ITs progress, offering a closer approximation of reality, in the absence of national governance, international agreements, and strong interdisciplinary consensus as to what needs to be studied or proposed for our cities, uncalculated urban decay among spots of renewal appears increasingly inevitable, with any kind of generalized urbanity no longer a realistic possibility.

At this point in time, the impact of the information revolution is still to be decided. Cyberspace, the big, new, rapidly modifying factor on our perception of what constitutes place and space, might, with careful monitoring, enhance our life, or it could ensure for the majority alienating living models and contribute to socially unresponsive developments.

It then becomes imperative that we start considering both form and place making as processes and both space and cyberspace as parts of a larger social and formal event.

NOTES AND REFERENCES

[1] See "Reluctant Conscripts in The March of Technology," *The New York Times*, 17 September 1995, p. 16; R. C. Post, *High Performance. The Culture and Technology of Drag Racing* (Baltimore, Johns Hopkins University Press, 1994).

[2] For example, Smith Corona ceased production of typewriters in 1995.

[3]See "5,000,000 Clients No Branches. Phone Banking Is Catching On," *The New York Times*, 3 September 1995, p. 10.

[4]W. J. Mitchell, *City of Bits: Space, Place, and the Infobahn* (Boston, MIT Press, 1995), p. 5.

[5]*Ibid.*, p. 28.

[6]*Ibid.*, p. 20.

[7]For updated information on this continuously evolving subject it is useful to access the Internet/Bitnet Health Resource List available through FTP at ftp.sura.net in directory PUB/NIC as file MEDICAL.RESOURCES.XX (XX = date of last update). For a popular account of the relationship between contemporary science and the Gaia hypothesis see E. Royte, "Attack of the Microbiologists," *New York Times Magazine* 14 January 1996, pp. 21-23.

[8]See J. Lovelock, *The Ages of Gaia. A biography of Our Living Earth* (New York, Bantam Books, 1988), where he argued that all terrestrial phenomena are caused by life.

[9]For an early critique of the relationship between IT and suburbanization see L. Winner, "Silicon Valley Mystery House," In M. Sorkin (Ed.), *Variations on a Theme Park. The New American City and the End of Public Space* (New York, Hill & Wang, 1992), pp. 31-60. For a social criticism about the effects on the U.S.'s recent urbanization see U. Greinacher, "The New Reality: Media Technology and Urban Fortress," *Journal of Architectural Education, 48*, 1995, pp. 176-184.

[10]In 1970 there were 4,000 people in the United States living in community associations; in 1990 there were 66,000; the number is expected to double in the next decade. Source: USA Community Association Institute.

[11]Aldo Rossi and Robert Venturi, in their influential books, depicted the whole of the Modern Movement as a singular "existent-minimum" endeavor in their effort to debunk it. See A. Rossi, *L'Architettura della Città* (Padova, Marsilio Editori, 1966); R. Venturi, *Complexity and Contradiction in Architecture* (New York, Museum of Modern Art, 1966).

[12]P. Hirst & G. Thomson, "Globalization and the Future of the Nation State," *Economy and Society, 24*, pp. 408-442.

[13]E. Dyson, "If You Don't Love It, Leave It," *New York Times Magazine*, 16 July 1995, pp. 26-27.

[14]See D. Harvey, *The Conditions of Postmodernity* (Oxford, Blackwell, 1989); D. Massey, *Spatial Divisions of Labour: Social Structures and the Geography of Production* (Basingstoke, Macmillan, 1984); F. Jameson, "Postmodernism and the Cultural Logic of Late Capitalism," *New Left Review, 14*, pp. 53-92.

[15]D. Massey, "Power-Geometry and a Progressive Sense of Place," in J. Bird, B. Curtis, T. Putnam, G. Robertson, & L. Tickner (Eds.), *Mapping the Futures. Local Cultures, Global Change* (London, Routledge, 1993), p. 61.

[16]*Ibid.*, p. 63.

[17]An ethnic breakdown of computer ownership shows that African American households have the lowest rate of ownership: Black, 11.1%; Hispanic, 13.1%; American Indian, Inuit, 20.7%; White, 28.6%; Asian, Pacific Islanders, 39.1%. Credible statistics about the use of the Internet are difficult to find. Some demographers have formed the Survey Working Group, which will coordinate existing statistics and make them available on the Web (http:www.zilker.net/swg/).

chapter 13

Myths of Information:
The Cultural Impact of New
Information Technologies

Anne Balsamo
School of Literature, Communication, and Culture
Georgia Tech

INTRODUCTION: LIVING IN THE INFORMATION AGE

S peculating about the nature of the information age is a popular
pastime, not only for academics who are fascinated by the possibility that we have entered a new historical era, but also for journalists writing for the popular press who see themselves as covering the
cyberspace beat. No fewer than 50 scholarly books have been published
since the mid-1980s that all seek in different ways to elaborate the central dimensions of the information age based mostly on a discussion of
the use of new information technologies.[1] The range of perspectives
represented in these books is daunting. Where Dordick and Wang, for
example, provided a retrospective cross-cultural perspective on the
information explosion of the past 20 years, Silverstone and Hirsch
examined the way in which people consume information in domestic
spaces.[2] Although the various authors disagree about the exact nature of
the social transformations that undergird in this new age, there is wider
agreement on the principle that something significant has shifted for us
collectively as a society tied to the rapid proliferation of information.
The opinions about the consequences of this shift also vary. Some schol-

ars argue that the information age inaugurates a crisis of democracy, whereas for others it presents a series of interesting business opportunities. There is a reason people persist in referring to this transformation as a revolution of sorts—the use of the term is a rhetorical strategy for announcing a time of dramatic change. The question that emerges is: "What exactly has changed?"

To begin to address this question, I have sought to itemize the underlying set of beliefs that circulate in contemporary U.S. culture about the power of new information technologies. This study involves an extensive review of various mass media discussions about the information age, including a survey of numerous popular and academic books on the topic, and a review of the fictional treatment of information technologies in science fiction books and films. If the information age is a global movement, its epicenter is in the United States where its defining characteristics include:

- An economic philosophy that asserts that information access represents power, and relatedly, that we have moved from a gold standard economy to an information standard global economy.[3]
- A business logic that focuses on the accumulation, production, and management of data.
- Media claims that availability and access to information technologies represent an increase in choice and freedom for individual citizens.
- Political projections that computer-mediated communication networks can solve the problems of democracy in the United States.
- A quasi-religious hope that technology can save us from our own excesses.

These characteristics express the key dimensions of an emergent cultural sensibility whose central concerns focus on the nature of technologically manufactured information and the impact of new digital communication technologies on the everyday life of U.S. residents. These beliefs function as a set of contemporary mythologies that circulate in everyday life via print, film, television, and electronic communication networks about the meaning of a whole range of new technologies.

This chapter discusses two guiding myths of the information age. These myths express two distinct but related stories about the impact of new information technologies on individuals and on our collective political life:

1. The belief that new information technologies will empower individuals, transforming both work and leisure.

2. The belief that new information technologies will augment demo-cratic practices.

These myths are neither true nor false; rather, they are collective accounts of our collective life. Cultures create mythologies to help members make sense of the meaning of new phenomenon. Our cultural myths have gone high-tech: Not only do they concern high technology and its role in citizens' lives, they are also disseminated via high-tech channels of communication such as the television, video screens, and the Internet. A closer examination of these myths will reveal several interesting paradoxes. On the one hand, it is clear that we are in the midst of a cultural shift on a par with the great paradigm shifts in the history of science—our understandings of basic philosophical issues are changing. We can track shifts in our thinking about the nature of reality, the nature of knowledge, and even the nature of the human being. On the other hand, there is evidence to suggest that not enough has changed in our thinking about certain philosophical issues, especially as these relate to the concept of information and ideas about originality, privacy, citizen empowerment, democracy, and community. I conclude with a list of questions that emerge from the transformation of one age to another.

MYTH 1: DATA = INFORMATION = POWER: FOR WHOM?

At the heart of our analysis of the transformative power of information technologies is a set of ideas about the nature of information. Business pundits make information into a fetish item—assigning to it magical properties and powerful influence. In business news weeklies, we read how information is the key to greater control, greater knowledge, and greater wealth. John Verity, writing the introduction to the special issue of *Business Week* devoted to the information revolution, had this to say: "However you define it...the capture, manipulation, transmission, and consumption of information in digital form has become a critical function in our economy—and soon, perhaps, in our civilization.[4]

As several of the articles in this special issue of *Business Week* describe, information is the commodity that defines the U.S. economy. It is considered not only a business resource to be managed and protected, but, more importantly, a good to be manufactured and sold.

How does information get turned into a commodity? We know that it is now possible to mass-produce information. In fact, a well-rationalized organizational infrastructure has emerged for the automatic accumulation of information, based on the automatic production of data. Patterns of human activity are translated into bits of data that are, in turn, packaged and sold as information about people's consumption habits, such as consumption patterns, viewing patterns, travel patterns, and eating patterns. Through the use of automated recording devices, data are unobtrusively (some would say covertly) collected from people as they go about their daily business. Aggregate accounts of people's consumption patterns are useful information for businesses that make money from those behaviors, namely those who provide consumer goods and services. The use of mainframe computers enables the recording of mass-produced data about consumer habits, which in turn can be organized as databases that can be searched and sold. Wells Branscomb called this the "information market-place."[5]

The process of gathering information about people's behavior in order to predict and influence that behavior is the conceptual foundation of the advertising industry—and certainly not a new cultural phenomenon. What is new is the fact that the production of information has exceeded the needs of the advertising industry. Just as happens with the mass production of material goods, when production exceeds demand, consumption must be stimulated somehow. This is where those cultural myths of information come into play. Demand for information is stimulated by promoting the notion that individuals—not just businesses and industries—need information in order to get better jobs, gain a competitive edge, enhance their quality of life, and even be responsible citizens. Like advertisements more broadly, these myths first provoke an anxiety and then offer solutions for its arrest.

A topic for another paper is a discussion of the issues surrounding the mass production of information and the resulting public concern for consumer privacy. Suffice it to say that the use of electronically accumulated information is a contested terrain, both legally and ethically. My purpose in this discussion is to elucidate the misconceptions embedded in the myths about information and individual empowerment, focusing here on the nature of information, not from the point of view of a commercial interest, but rather from the perspective of the individuals who are being cajoled to join the information revolution.

When people are solicited to join one of the many online services, they are promised access to new people, new information, new communication services, and new social spaces. For example, America Online's (AOL's) software envelope announces these benefits: "EXCHANGE ideas with people who share your interests; DOWNLOAD over 60,000 files and software programs; SEND and receive e-mail anywhere in the world; CHAT with other members in live conversation; CHECK the latest news, weather and sports instantly; ACCESS the World Wide Web the easy way!" In short, connectivity (via an AOL account) provides access to interactive networks and electronic databases that in turn allow access to vast storehouses of information.

There are several layers of irony in this solicitation, not the least is the exhortation to chat live online with other members. As is the case for most advertisements for online services, the slick promotions often fail to address two important issues from the user's perspective: the veracity of information and the experience of information overload. Concern about the reliability of information made available through these services is slowly beginning to become an issue for network users. When one searches the Web for simple factual information—a product specification or a zip code, for example—reliable information providers are easy to find—such as the vendor or the appropriate government agency. But when the information sought is less factual and more subjective, how does one verify the accuracy of the information? What kinds of extratextual signals can people rely on to make sense of the veracity of information (i.e., institutional address and professional identity)? Online services already show their concern for the quality of information exchanged through their services. For example, some services instruct chat room moderators to monitor (and censor) the use of improper language. Although it is beyond the capacity of any service provider to guarantee the accuracy or propriety of the information made available through its cyberspatial services, it is also clear that services are interested in maintaining certain informational standards for their clients. To date, these standards have more to do with topics of debate than with the quality of information exchanged. For instance, Branscomb reported that some services have arbitrarily delimited discussions on homosexuality and on internal pricing procedures.[6] No online service provider would be willing to monitor information exchanges based on notions of accuracy or quality; instead, these judgments are left to individual users. However, it is exactly these judgments that are increasingly difficult to render. Given the rate of Internet growth and the phenomenal expansion of the World Wide Web, people are confronted daily with a greatly expanded information landscape. As more and more people become connected to these information networks, the capacity for misinformation also grows. Finding reliable information is not easy, even with the best search engines or the most sophisticated knowledge of network navigation, because the issue is not about navigation; it is about the mistaken belief that information is inherently meaningful, or inherently valuable.

At the most basic level, the production of data does not naturally yield useful information. Second, the accumulation of information is not equivalent to the construction of meaning. Information has no context; data have no telos. The construction of meaning is a complex human

behavior that is dependent on the embodied knowledge of individuals—
in short, embodied literacy. Literacy cannot be reduced to the skills of
data recognition or information accumulation. Literacy is the ability to
make significant connections, to form interpretations, to evaluate situations, and to provide context. Information processing does not promote
deep thinking; rather it is an act of mechanized—albeit highly ritual-
ized—consumption. It is reactive, not reflective. The claim that access to
information networks will empower individuals is based on a misguided
notion that information is equivalent to knowledge, and relatedly that
access is enough. The production of knowledge is a much more complex
process. Information has to be interpreted to be meaningful; interpretation is an analytical process. Simple access is not enough to guarantee
more knowledge, more power, or more insight. What is needed is a
foundation of literacy, where users are taught how to evaluate the quality of the information, to make connections between different categories
of information, and to assess the veracity of information based on an
understanding of the conditions of its production. At the base, this
assertion has implications for education—at all levels—from K-12 (precollege) through college. More importantly, it is a reminder that access
to technological networks of information cannot substitute for education about the process of knowledge construction.

MYTH 2: THE INFORMATION REVOLUTION AND
TECHNOLOGICALLY ASSISTED DEMOCRACY

An equally invigorating, if not so widespread discussion taking place in
the popular press concerns the relationship between new information
technologies and democratic practices. Techno-advocates argue that new
information technologies will deliver democracy by making more information available to network-savvy citizens. Again, founding assumptions
such as the beliefs that more information is better and that increased
access is empowering are rarely questioned by these advocates, who end
up arguing, often quite persuasively, that the development of faster
information distribution systems is a moral imperative for the United
States.

According to communication historian James Carey, these claims
made daily in the U.S. press about the information age echo those made
about the telegraph and the railroad 100 years ago—it is, from Carey's
view, the most recent manifestation of an old American dream.[7] In fact,
as Carey carefully demonstrated these ideas are woven deeply into the
founding documents of this country, such that we can understand, following Carey's lead, how the United States was built in part on a dream

of technologically assisted democracy and the promise of an information revolution.

> The United States was, to flirt with more deterministic language, the product of literacy, cheap paper, rapid and inexpensive transportation, and the mechanical reproduction of words—the capacity, in short, to transport not only people but a complex culture and civilization from one place to another, indeed between places that were radically dissimilar in geography, social conditions, economy, and very often climate.[8]

In his historical study of the Federalist Papers, Carey illuminated how James Madison (the "author" of the Federalist Papers) attempted to resolve the contradictions facing the new union produced by its geographic and cultural diversity and displacement.

> The problem of continental democracy was to be solved by the press and the art of transportation engineering. A constitutionally protected technology would amplify the debate of democracy and serve as a check on government. Engineering and communication would bind the nation together, collect representatives to public functions, and disperse them to constituencies, and give a vivid presence to a continent-wide public discourse.[9]

Reading carefully, we can hear the resonance with more recent proclamations made about the civic role of the information highway in revitalizing U.S. democracy. Note the familiar sound of this paraphrase: The problem of modern democracy will be solved by the Internet and the art of information engineering. The difference is that, in 1996, geographic dispersion is more virtual than real (a matter of time, not space); the notion of a national union has been replaced with the idea of political parties, ruling ideologies, and economic interests; constituencies are more commonly identified as audiences and target market groups; and there is no form of public discourse that is not technologically mediated.

Although additional issues relating to the notion of electronic democracy are posed in terms of information access, the infrastructure of communication networks, and the education of technologically literate citizens, it is clear that there is still a strong belief in the civic service potential of information technologies. The difference in our thinking about the information revolution and the role of new communication technologies now from at a previous moment in U.S. history concerns the particular form of technology under discussion. What remains similar is the underlying set of beliefs about the capability of information technologies to produce desired social changes, to reinvigorate an ideal of human community, and to overcome misuses of power and political advantage.

Social change is produced when people act in concert with one another to accomplish an agreed-upon objective. The question that remains to be addressed in the light of these claims is: How (exactly) does access to greater amounts of information enable people to act in socially responsible ways such that desirable social changes are enacted? It seems just as likely that such access could be counterproductive, disabling, and overwhelming to a person's ability to discern important information and act accordingly. Indeed, some social critics argue that the information explosion has done more harm than help to the democratic process because, when confronted with the sheer volume of information available through various media, people cannot find the information they need to make insightful decisions. What this myth fails to address is the "Tower of Babel" effect that happens when each citizen's voice now becomes a broadcast channel. How is rational debate and discussion supposed to take place over the din of voices that take the form of textual junk mail? Does more bandwidth guarantee more democratic discussion or more confusion? Adding to the difficulties is the fact that rational debate among informed citizens, the key process of democracy, is often sabotaged by the manufacture of pseudoscientific findings in the form of opinion polls and market research, which, as additional sources of information have the net effect of confusing people about the issues being debated.

As the myth would have it, more information enables people to make better choices. In many cases, though, access to more information does not mean that better decisions are being made, or that people better understand the nuances of the issues being debated. Furthermore, the myth of technologically assisted democracy obscures the process whereby choices are constructed for people. Whereas the guiding myth of the information age proclaims that citizens have access to all the information they need, what is rarely discussed is the mechanism whereby information is encoded, manipulated, packaged, and selectively disseminated. In short, we often fail to appreciate how our choices are already constructed for us by the kind of the information made technologically available.

Another factor that complicates the issue is the fact that there are few identifiable agents of misinformation misbehaving with our databases. The process of encoding and manipulating information is a consequence of the information processing infrastructure: When information-handling responsibilities are dispersed among several agents, such as survey writers, journalists, advertising professionals, or information managers, it is extremely difficult to determine who is the responsible agent for the selective encoding and dissemination of information. The cultural purpose this myth serves is to focus attention on the amount of information and to deflect attention from questions about the kind and the quality of information disseminated through new communication technologies.

CONCLUSION: AN IDENTITY CRISIS OR PARADIGM SHIFT

Cultural myths about the information age often sound more like hopeful projections of where we want to be than realistic accounts of where we are. Although there is certainly something different about U.S. culture, wrapped around the notion of information most statements about the impact of new information technologies record mundane truths: These new technologies do provide people with access to more information. What other impacts can we observe? The following statements suggest a set of questions that I argue should be considered in discussions of the consequences of the information revolution. They concern issues of information ownership, the relationship of individuals to personal information, ideas about originality, and the nature of human beings in a technological era.

Information Ownership

When information is treated as a commodity in a legal sense, we are forced to rely on a system that is not designed for such a nonmaterial commodity form. What are some of the difficulties of applying a system of rules and regulations built for the regulation of durable goods and tangible services to information as a commodity? How does one account for the production conditions of information so as to determine issues of ownership, veracity, and context? What rights do individuals have vis-à-vis the information they produce in the course of their daily lives? What is the relationship between individuals and descriptions of their identities (collected as demographic data), descriptions of their behaviors (collected as taste indices) and descriptions of their economic exchanges (collected as consumption patterns)?

Originality and Authorship

When information can be electronically replicated with little or no deterioration in the quality of the reproduction, what happens to the notion of the original? What is the relationship between the individual who produces the original information (the code, the work) and the multiple copies made of it? How do collaborative working relationships change the nature of work compensation? How does one assign authorship to work that is collaboratively produced? What is the nature of the work that guarantees an owner? Why can't other people's material—in whatever form—be borrowed, transformed, and revised?

Human Identity

At a basic level, our thinking about the human being is changing. The individual has been redefined in terms of biological information systems and clusters of biomechanical parts. This is to say, we are starting to think of the human being through the information paradigm. Biological information systems can be decoded; biomechanical parts can be replaced with technological components. What does this do to our notion of the human being? What rights do individuals have vis-à-vis the biological and genetic information they embody? What is the notion of privacy in the information age? How is privacy being redefined as a property of data access and identity codes?

Given the projections about the continued development of digital technologies, it is clear that additional cultural changes are on the horizon. To address these adequately, we will have to refashion our thinking about knowledge, truth, and democracy. Changes in educational programs and pedagogies will also be required. Notions of literacy will have to be expanded and refined. My criticism of these guiding myths is that we are not yet enough of an information age. Too much information is never collated; too few people are taught how to use information intelligently and responsibly; too much time is spent accumulating information and not enough on seeking its meaning. The cost of this revolution is high, in that it not only requires that we abandon outworn notions of individuality, originality, and information as a commodity, but also notions of personal privacy and democratic debate. The purpose of the myths of the information age is to convince us that there is no price to pay. However, if we were forced to consider the price, I wonder if we would be so enthusiastically willing to embrace the changes.

NOTES AND REFERENCES

[1] A sample includes: J. Beniger, *The Control Revolution: Technological and Economic Origins of the Information Society* (Cambridge, MA, Harvard University Press, 1986); J. Berleur, A. Clement, R. Sizer, & D. Whitehouse (Eds.), *The Information Society: Evolving Landscapes* (New York, Springer Verlag, 1990); G. Brown, *The*

Information Game: Ethical Issues in a Microchip World (London, Humanities Press, 1990); M. Castells, *The Information City: Information, Technology, Economic Restructuring and the Urban Regional Process* (Oxford, Blackwell, 1989); J. Collins, *Architecture of Excess: Cultural Life in the Information Age* (New York, Routledge, 1993); T. Forester (Ed.), *The Information Technology Revolution* (Cambridge, MA, MIT Press, 1985); T. Forester (Ed.), *Computers in the Human Context: Information Technology, Productivity and People* (Cambridge, MA, MIT Press, 1989); O. H. Gandy, *The Panoptic Sort: A Political Economy of Personal Information* (Boulder, CO, Westview Press, 1993); N. K. Hayles, "Text Out of Context: Situating Postmodernism Within an Information Society," *Discourse*, 9, 1987, pp. 24-36; L. Levidow & K. Robins (Eds.), *Cyborg Worlds: The Military Information Society* (London, Free Association Books, 1989); S. Lubar, *Infoculture: The Smithsonian Book of Information Age Inventions* (Boston, Houghton Mifflin, 1993); D. Lyon, *The Information Society: Issues and Illusions* (Cambridge, Polity Press, 1988); D. Lyon, *The Electronic Eye: The Rise of Surveillance Society* (Minneapolis, University of Minnesota Press, 1994); V. Mosco, *Pushbutton Fantasies: Critical Perspectives on Videotex and Information Technology* (Norwood, NJ, Ablex, 1982); M. Poster, *The Mode of Information: Poststructuralism and Social Context* (Chicago, University of Chicago Press, 1992); N. Postman, *Technopoly: The Surrender of Culture to Technology* (New York, Knopf, 1992); T. Roszak, *The Culture of Information* (Berkeley: University of California Press, 1986); P. Sieghart (Ed.), *Microchips With Everything* (London, Comedia, 1983); J. Slack & F. Fejes (Eds.), *The Ideology of the Information Age* (Norwood, NJ, Ablex, 1987); N. Weinberg, *Computers in the Information Society* (Boulder, CO, Westview Press, 1990); K. Woodward (Ed.), *The Myths of Information: Technology and Postindustrial Culture* (Madison, WI, Coda Press, 1989); S. Zuboff, *In the Age of the Smart Machine* (New York, Simon & Schuster, 1989).

[2] H. S. Dorick & G. Wang, *The Information Society. A Retrospective View* (Newbury Page, CA, Sage, 1993); R. Silverstone (Ed.), *Consuming Technologies: Media and Information in Domestic Spaces* (London, Routledge, 1992).

[3] A. Pennings, *Electric Money and the Politics of Global Cyberspace* (Minneapolis, University of Minnesota Press, forthcoming).

[4] Special issue of *Business Week* on "The Information Revolution," Summer 1994.

[5] A. Wells Branscomb, *Who Owns Information: From Privacy to Public Access* (New York, Basic Books, 1994).

[6] *Ibid.*

[7] J. Carey, *Communication Culture: Essays on Media and Society* (Boston, Unwin Hyman, 1989).

[8] *Ibid.*, pp. 2-3.

[9] *Ibid.*, p. 6.

chapter 14

Less Labor, Longer Lives:
Time to Share

Alan L. Porter
School of Industrial and Systems Engineering
Georgia Tech

Ann Bostrom
School of Public Policy
Georgia Tech

INTRODUCTION

Momentous change in the focus of economic activity is a common feature of the agricultural, industrial, and information revolutions.[1,2] "What people do" shifted first from hunting and gathering to farming, then from farming to factory work, and now from manufacturing to services. In 1900, 36% of the U.S. labor force worked on the farm, dropping to under 3% today. Many farmers moved into manufacturing, which still occupied 34% of the workforce in 1960, but is down to 16% today, and may drop to as little as 5% by 2020 (our target time frame in this analysis). Meanwhile, the service sector—which includes a broad range of occupations, from taxi drivers to computer technicians—has expanded tremendously. Most American workers today—about four out of five—do not directly produce goods (see Table 14.1).

When, where, and how people work are all changing. Flex time, multiple job-holding,[3] and distributed work (telecommuting) are increasing.

TABLE 4.1. Employed Persons by Industry and Occupation, Ages 16 and Over

Industry	% of Total Employed (1224.5 Million)	Managerial and Professional Specialty	Technical, Sales, and Administrative Support	Private Household, Other Service Occupations	Precision Production, Craft, and Repair	Operators, Fabricators, and Laborers	Farming, Forestry, and Fishing
Agriculture	2.9	*	*	*	*	*	2
Mining	0.5	*	*	*	*	*	*
Construction	6.0	2	*	*	3	1	*
Manufacturing	16.2	4	3	*	3	7	*
Transportation and Public utilities	6.9	1	2	*	1	2	*
Wholesale and retail trade	20.7	2	11	4	1	3	*
Finance, insurance, and real estate	6.6	2	4	*	*	*	*
Services	35.4	16	8	8	2	2	*
Public administration	4.8	2	1	1	*	*	*

Note: *Less than 0.5%. From Employment and Earnings, Table A19, July 1995, in percentage of total employed.

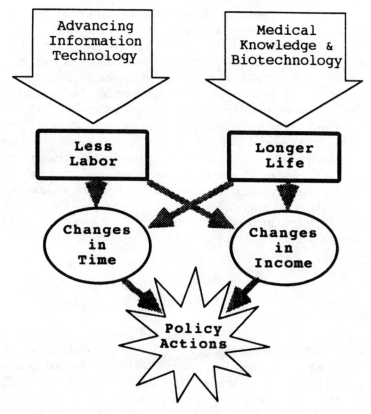

FIGURE 14.1.   Changing Times

The baby boom and cultural diversification are reshaping the labor force: The proportion of the adult population in the labor force increased from 61% in 1969 to 66% in 1991,[4] with more women working than ever before.[5]

What, then, will happen to work over the next quarter century? Figure 14.1 presents our conceptual framework, which keys on two major changes taking place:

- Less labor—Reduced need for labor as we now know it, due to increasing productivity, driven largely by advanced information handling.
- Longer life—Increased longevity, driven by enhanced health care and prosperity.

In turn, these changes in work and longevity will alter how we share wealth and how we spend our time. Together, they challenge the well-being of information age societies: "Neither the continuity of our social security systems nor the competitiveness of our firms can be guaranteed in the long run without a completely different organization of paid work."[6] "For the first time since his creation, man will be faced with his real, his permanent problem...how to occupy his leisure."[7]

Such changes remake civilizations. They recast family and community life, beliefs and values, business and politics, and culture. Even the definition of labor as economic activity and leisure as what remains may lose currency as the nature of human activities changes. In the next four sections of the chapter, we explore these key changes (focusing on U.S. statistics, but largely generalizable over the developed world): declining demand for labor, increasing life spans, and the influence of these on how money and time are used. The final section explores the implications.

LESS LABOR

"The new technology has fewer parts and fewer workers and produces more product."[8] The U.S. Bureau of Labor Statistics (BLS) calculates that the value of manufactured goods will rise by 41% over the next 15 years, but the number of workers in manufacturing will fall by 3%.[9] As Aronowitz and DiFazio put it, modern manufacturing plants (e.g., electronics, steel) have a "ghost-like" quality in that live workers are scarce and seemingly marginal to the production processes.[10] Manufacturing, whether in the United States or elsewhere, offers fewer jobs.

For 40 years after World War II, labor found a new home in the service sector. That is now changing. Moreover, as Table 14.1 illustrates, what workers actually do—in agriculture, manufacturing, or services—can now more usefully be broken into information work (knowledge work, symbolic processing) and other work. Occupations spread along a continuum from mainly information work to mainly physical work. Most jobs mix information and other work (e.g., the UPS driver, farmer, factory machine operator, and bank clerk who use computers to perform certain tasks). Advancing technology chips away at physical labor needs (e.g., robotics), human interaction tasks (e.g., self-service modes of automatic teller machines or phone answering systems), and, above all, at information work. Computing and telecommunications enable fewer people to accomplish more information work.

As functions blur, it becomes more difficult to measure the extent of information work. Over 57% of workers fall into the first two categories of Table 14.1, which are primarily information work. Many other workers also spend some portion of their time doing information work. Thus, we estimate that 60% of all work today is information work.

The information revolution entails development and implementation of a spectrum of information technologies. We have increasing computing power, data storage, and telecommunications—at decreasing cost. Looking ahead, here is a sampling of pertinent projections for the coming quarter century:[11]

- Broadband network of networks, providing voice, data, and graphics worldwide.
- Automation commonplace inside and outside the factory.
- Ubiquitous computing (witness its prevalence in the automobile).
- Virtual reality technologies commonplace for training, recreation, planning, and product design.

For years, we have heard that office work productivity had not increased despite increasing investments in information technology.[12] However, we are now seeing that the increasing information technology base, combined with systems integration, learning, and restructuring, yields profound increases in effectiveness and efficiency. That means that less labor is needed per unit of information work. Over the next couple of decades, productivity gains are expected to continue in all sectors except construction and mining, with the greatest gains in communications.[13]

Recent job losses provide a litany of bad news for U.S. labor. For instance:

- U.S. oil refinery production and maintenance workers down from 200,000 in 1960 to 50,000 in 1991.
- Loss of half of the 500,000 coal miners.
- Loss of almost a quarter of all U.S. factory, construction, and transportation jobs in the past 25 years;
- Government employment flat since 1980.
- Jobs down 30% to 40% in commercial banking and financial institutions.
- Secretarial and receptionist jobs down 750,000 from 1989 to 1994.
- A "management massacre" over the past decade in Fortune 500 companies.[14]

The "electronic collar" is squeezing out blue- and white-collar jobs, in both production and services. Despite years of a strong economy, current U.S. unemployment holds at around 6%. Were discouraged workers who have stopped looking for work included, unemployment might approach 12%, comparable to rates in Western Europe. Projections for decades ahead, unless we intervene, range to a shortfall of 50,000,000 jobs in the United States.[15] Job displacement is pervasive.

Despite this, the labor force has grown significantly, both in numbers and as a proportion of the population. Continued entrepreneurial growth is expected in health and social services, training, and leisure activities. Whereas demand for highly motivated information professionals projects strongly, the less skilled are becoming easier to replace. We see a bifurcation of work into more integrated, challenging assignments, on the one hand, and simpler ones on the other, leaving a nasty gap in the middle where once lived a robust middle class. Multiple job-holding and other nontraditional work arrangements are also increasing.

Contingent work (nonpermanent employment or contract work) and distributed work (e.g., remote information-processing operations, work at home) present new challenges. For example, contingent workers are about 20% less likely to have health insurance than other workers, and less likely to get their coverage from their employers.[16] Interestingly, both contingent and distributed work are conducive to a preindustrial age village, blending work with home environments. Contingent work is estimated at 5% of job holders.[17] Estimates on U.S. contingent and distributed work together range in the tens of millions, with 30 million telecommuters projected by 2001,[18] increasing to 40% of the workforce by 2020.[19]

Is the job obsolete? Bridges argued that the job, invented only in the 19th century for the factory, is too rigid for the elastic tasks demanded in the information age.[20] Looking ahead, one can imagine the complete automation of work. Production would take place in fully automated factories; service would be handled by computers with appropriate intelligence. We need not go that far to envision ever more work done by automata, leaving many people with no job per se, with its regular work hours and pay.

LONGER LIFE

Shifting gears, it appears that population ageing may soon replace population growth as a key policy concern.[21] We are living longer. In 1960, 17 million Americans (9%) were 65 and older; in 1995, 33 million (12.5%) were; and some 53 million (16%) 65 and up are projected for 2020—a tripling.[22] Interestingly, this profound growth in the elderly population assumes only marginal life-span extension.[23]

Why are we living longer now than in the past? Mainly because of public health measures and antibiotics that have reduced death at younger ages. Since 1900, annual U.S. death rates per 100,000 have plummeted for infectious disease: from 200 to under 20 for pneumonia/flu; from 200 to essentially 0 for tuberculosis; and from 150 to essentially 0 for diarrhea. U.S. infant mortality per 100,000 has dropped since 1950 from 4,000 to less than 1,000. So, we are mainly living longer because we are not dying younger. However, because we are living longer, we are more subject to heart diseases and cancer (mortality doubled from 66 to 131 per 100,000 from 1900 to 1988).[24]

What are future prospects? The immediate targets are clear—in low mortality rate countries like the United States, cancer and cardiovascular disease account for three of four deaths after age 65.[25] We are trying: low-fat diets, reduced smoking, better individual medical records, targeted drug treatments, understanding DNA repair mechanisms, and detecting the genetic links to human disorders. Of course, new diseases (like AIDS), wars, or a catastrophic failure of the public health system could undermine these gains. A key issue is whether medical science can up the upper limit. Unfortunately, tales of long-lived peoples (e.g., in the Caucasus) are not credible: We have no documented populations where individuals routinely live beyond 100.[26] However, we should at least recognize the possibility that genetic engineering or molecular engineering (nanotechnology) might boost the upper limit on life dramatically, thereby, swelling the ranks of the senior population.

We are now extending life by squaring off the age distribution of the population—that is, getting more people closer to an unchanging upper age limit—rather than stretching the tail by upping it. Although demographers disclaim the likelihood of life expectancies averaging much more than 85 by 2020, we are closing on that now: Japanese women can expect to live beyond 81 (men about 76). Put another way, we are presently moving toward a rectilinear age distribution where more than 90% of the people born will live past 65, with two thirds surviving past 85.[27] Conservatively, the average life expectancy should be 85 in 2020.

What should we expect for those aged 65 to 85, and those older than 85? Can we keep ourselves healthier, so that morbidity and disability beset only the very end of life, or will we simply extend the time during which the debilitating diseases of aging get expressed? Active retirement, or osteoporotic fractures and Alzheimer's? One ominous indicator is that currently only 9% of those aged 65 to 69 need help with any personal care, but 45% of those 85 and older do.[28]

Taken together, increasing longevity and changing work patterns imply major consequences for income distribution and how we spend our time.

MONEY, MONEY, MONEY

The industrial age has deeded us with three premises that do not fit the information age. The labor theory of value holds that the key factor of production is labor, which, in turn, serves as the main mechanism for income allocation. However, technology is displacing labor as the prime factor of both production and service provision. That undercuts the legitimacy of allocating income primarily on the basis of paid labor. Imagine an extreme in which 10% of the population could provide for society's material needs—if only those 10% are paid, how do we provide for the other 90%? For decades, labor collected two thirds of the nation's income; that share is shrinking.[29] Even more problematic is continuing to expect the job to provide for medical care, disability, life insurance, and old age income.

The second dubious premise is the work ethic—the Protestant-led (although not monopolized) construct that idle hands do the devil's work. Work has not always been so emphasized; ancient Hebrews and Greeks saw it almost as a curse.[30] The work ethic helped to make 19-century factory workers diligent. Its influence remains strong; indeed, the work ethic largely determines our self-worth—our job provides our primary identity. Those lacking a paying job—either unemployed or keeping house—are seen as less worthy (in both others' and their own eyes).[31] That is a difficult value scheme for a society that simply does not need a lot of labor to meet its economic needs.

The third nasty holdover is consumerism—the drive for ever more material goods. Consumerism is promoted by government policies to induce spending (e.g., tax credits for accruing debt) and heavy advertising to induce us on to the treadmill of "keeping up with the Joneses." Families struggle to keep up, now making two incomes (for two adults) the norm. Not all societies place such a value on material goods. Medieval Europeans worked enough to acquire the essentials, then took off; Buddhist economics values doing with less.

Increasing productivity offers choices that intersect with these values; in essence, we can produce more or enjoy more leisure time. Notice that if we step away from consumerism, we weaken the engine driving capitalism. Lower demand would beget lower production. Were we to legitimize activities other than the job and devise alternative ways to allocate wealth, we could rethink the whole economic value structure.

Income distribution is increasingly uneven, with the rich getting richer. The elderly pose particular income problems. Household incomes for those 65 and older are only 39% of those for people aged 45 to 54.[32] One third of total health care expenses are for the 12.5% aged 65 and older. The dependency load is increasing; in 2025 there will be 32 elderly for every 100 people of working age.[33] Social security and retirement programs were established when fewer reached age 65 and those who did had a far shorter life expectancy. Any additional increases in longevity tilt the imbalance severely.

TIME

"Time is money"—yes and no. We use time to fulfil our needs and desires. How we do so varies—over history, by work status, by sex, and by age. Time, particularly free time, is "extraordinarily badly shared."[34] But some societies prefer time to goods:

> The lives of so-called primitive peoples are commonly thought to be harsh—their existence dominated by the "incessant quest for food." In fact, primitives do little work. By contemporary standards, we'd have to judge them extremely lazy. If the Kapauku of Papua work one day, they do no labor on the next. Kung Bushmen put in only two and a half days per week and six hours per day....The key to understanding why these "stone age peoples" fail to act like us—increasing their work effort to get more things—is that they have limited desires....They are materially poor by contemporary standards, but in at least one dimension—time—we have to count them richer.[35]

Hunter-gatherers also tend to be sharers, which provides a disincentive to extra work.[36]

Shifting to agricultural society, Schor estimated work in medieval England at 28 to 31 hours per week (averaged over the year) for male peasants in the years 1200 to 1300. Work hours were irregular, breaks frequent, work highly seasonal, and holidays abundant (roughly 1 of 3 days were holidays).[37]

The industrial revolution brought year-round activity, fewer holidays, the time clock, and lots more work—four estimates average to an astounding 65 hours per week in England and the United States in 1840 to 1850.[38] That is double the time at work of earlier, agricultural societies.

What we do can be categorized in many ways.[39] We propose five main activity categories, in addition to personal needs and care (e.g., sleeping, eating).

- Market work: The job; paid labor (for others or oneself) for extrinsic reward (i.e., pay, profits, benefits). We include commuting here.
- Community work: Volunteering; labor on behalf of a community primarily for intrinsic reward (e.g., care of the elderly or the environment, church service, political activity).

- Home work: Nonmarket (unpaid) labor to meet domestic needs (providing meals, child care, home maintenance, shopping, etc., for oneself or immediate family).
- Learning and communication: Self-improvement activities, both formal (e.g., classes) and informal (e.g., library and reading, communication and conversations, thinking).
- Play: Mainly personal gratification, including physical and mental recreations (e.g., entertainment, TV, social activities, sports, movies, visiting).

These categories are not neat. We frequently multitask (e.g., by reading professional journals while watching TV) or do one task for multiple purposes. To illustrate the effects of the information revolution, in this section, we estimate the time spent on these activities a quarter century ago, now, and in 2020—a quarter century hence. These are rough estimates, as the data are relatively sparse and inconsistently categorized.

In a 24-hour day, personal care—eating, sleeping, and grooming—holds pretty constant at about 10 hours per day.[40,41] That leaves 14-hour days, or roughly 100-hour weeks, to spread among the five categories of interest. To facilitate comparisons, we focus on weekly available hours, averaging in vacation weeks from yearly hourly totals.

First, consider fully employed adults (age 20-64) in the late 1960s; Table 14.2 offers rounded estimates of how they spent their time.[42] The table also roughly estimates how seniors spend their time, taking advantage of John Robinson's 1985 surveys. This gives us vital clues, unfortunately confounded, as to how time allocation shifts as we age and do less market work, and as the information revolution advances.

The work week has remained essentially stable in the ballpark of 40 hours for decades, but trending upward a bit in the United States since 1969 for men, particularly in higher positions, and women, more of

TABLE 14.2. Time Allocation (Hours per Week)

	Working Adults (About 1969)		Seniors (About 1985)	
	Men	Women	Men	Women
Market work	44	31	9	6
Home work	12	25	23	31
Community work	1	1	3	3
Learning (communication)	8	9	11	11
Play	35	34	47	42
Additional personal care			7	7
Total	100	100	100	100

TABLE 4.3.   General Demographics for the United States (in Millions)

	1970	1995	2020
Total population	203	263	326
under 18	70	69	78
18 to 64	114	161	195
65 and older	20	34	53
Labor force (including armed forces)	84	132	171
Unemployed	3	7	17
Employed	81	125	154

Note: U.S. Department of Labor, Bureau of Labor Statistics, Employment and Earnings, July 1995; Statistical Abstract of the U.S., 1970, Tables 7, 8, and 316; 1994, Tables 13, 16, 614, and 615. The projection for the 2020 labor force participation is based on a simple quadratic regression model fitted to the data provided in these tables (estimated labor force $= 83.6 + 2.25 \times \text{year} - 0.01 \times \text{year}^2$, ad. $R^2 = 0.995$, 1970 = year 0). Ten percent unemployment is assumed.

whom are working full time. Work hours also reflect time off—with paid days off (vacation, holidays, sick leave) increasing from about 14 per year in the United States in the late 1940s to 23 in 1980, dropping back to 20 days in 1990.[43] The American 2 to 3 weeks of vacation pale compared to the 5 weeks typical in Europe. Work hours vary by country, but not drastically—recent tallies for 10 big cities spanning developing to highly developed nations average only 2% more than Chicago (1,933 hours per year), ranging from 11% less (Frankfurt) to 19% more (Seoul).[44]

These numbers are based on fully employed adults. Male (16 years and over) adult labor force participation rates have been declining— 87% in 1948, to 80% in 1969, to 77% in 1990. Conversely, female rates have been increasing—33% in 1948, to 41% in 1967, to 56% in 1987, projecting to 65% in 2020. Table 14.3 provides the larger picture—note that employed adults were only 40% of the population a quarter century ago.

What those not in the labor force in 1970 were doing gets more speculative. Of the 57 million not working regularly, about 35 million (mostly women) were keeping house, about 7 million were in school,[45] and others might have liked a job but were not looking, or were ill or retired. There were also about 62 million under 16 years of age, presumably learning or playing.

Many influences are changing the time spent on these activities, notably the following.

1. Market Work

- Strong, long-term downward pressures for society as a whole, although averages have recently gone up for those working.
- Commuting time has remained fairly constant, although tele-commuting could decrease travel-to-work time.
- Productivity increasing, perhaps more than consumption.
- Trend toward earlier retirement, but retirees then returning to some form of work.

2. Community work
   - Increasing numbers of single-person households, single-parent families, and elderly, creating great social needs.
   - Volunteering has been on the decline. Historically, housewives have done most of the volunteering, and they are now working.
   - Volunteers continue to draw primarily from the 18 to 64 age group; estimates of how many adults do any volunteer work vary from 20 to 50%.[46]

3. Home work
   - Fewer children mean less work. The increase in single adult households means less housework: Married men and women in 1985 did about 40% more housework than their unmarried counterparts.[47]
   - Better technology can save time. Overall housework—including outdoor chores, home repairs, and bills, as well as laundry and meals—has declined in recent decades; women did about 8 hours less housework in 1985 than they did in 1965, whereas males did about 5 hours more.[48]

4. Learning
   - More opportunities and information age demands should increase formal and informal education and training for all ages.
   - Increasing adult participation in education.
   - Increasing use of information technology to facilitate learning.[49]

5. Play
   - Leisure, as the surplus of time once needs are met, is driving upward; spare time is up from 34 to 40 hours per week between 1965 and 1985.[50]
   - However, involuntary leisure accompanies un- and underemployment.

- More production seems to drive consumption time up (shopping is counted as home work); consumption expenditures have doubled from 1947 to 1985 in constant dollars.[51]
- Were materialism to decline, free time could increase doubly (less time for production and for consumption).
- Per capita service expenditures in 1989 were 2.6 times those of 1950, boosting free time.[52]

Changes are highly interdependent. For instance, information age knowledge work pushes us to learn, and the World Wide Web provides a common source for learning, work, and play opportunities together.

This assessment of how time use is changing provides a springboard for predicting time allocation in 2020. Table 14.4 consolidates into one high work and one low work projection (for men and women) some 25 independent predictions made by graduate students based on the preceding information.

Here are two corresponding snapshot scenarios of work and leisure in 2020:

- *Less work*: In the United States over the past decades, productivity has increased in all sectors. Rapid development in the rest of the world has meant more competition, continuing pressure for productivity increases and squeezing markets for U.S. goods and services. On top of this, increasingly healthy and long-lived seniors are reentering the labor force after retirement. Advances in productivity, globalization, and longevity all reduce work and increase leisure for prime-age individuals.
- *More work*: Recent decades witnessed a net gain of jobs as new information products and services were created, and as demand for educational, social, and leisure services increased. The proportion of the U.S. population participating in the labor force increased dramatically (including many seniors), although unemployment rates remained similar to those of the mid-1990s. Increases in a fiscally and physically active senior population and in global economic development have created new and bigger markets for health care, information, and other services. These trends portend plenty of work for all who want it.

People living longer in a more productive economy could mean happy or sad times. Indeed, either of the scenarios could be tinted bright or dark. One critical feature is income distribution—potentially low demand and/or low pay for low-skill workers could mean a harshly two-tier society. Another is what we do with increased time—do we self-indulge or do we study and volunteer more? Treating time and money as commensurables transforms a resource that is equally distributed (we all get 24 hours per day) into one that distinctly favors the wealthy. Even Marcuse, so concerned with the impacts of technology, saw promise in the prospect of free time from the mechanization of labor.[53]

Anomie could spread if we experience "nothing to do, nowhere to go" (Studs Terkel interviewee in *Not Working*). The absence of a regular job could debilitate millions, unless we revise the work ethic. Revolution could appeal to the poor if they lack realistic prospects of crossing the chasm to the middle class. "Gray power" is apt to fight bitterly against facing the actuarial realities of Social Security and other reforms. Diversity will further complicate the picture in 2020 in a United States that is 15% Hispanic, 13% Black, and 6% Asian—each group with different cultural orientations to time, money, and change. The challenge is for us to set effective policy now to foster a positive future.

POLICY ACTIONS

Less labor per economic unit (goods or services) and longer life pose opportunities (i.e., more time) and threats (i.e., by undermining our industrial age income allocation mechanisms). What are we to do? We must begin by recognizing two central issues:

- The demise of the norm of universal jobs for men is changing how wealth is allocated, how our society cares for those without wealth (young, old, disabled, or disenfranchised, and how we spend our time.
- Our present economic structures cannot cope with the expanding senior population's economic, health, and social needs.

As a society, we have not even begun to recognize or act on either.

Configuring sensible policy actions is a challenge; generating acceptance is even tougher. For every policy action there is a reaction. We posed legal requirements to pay overtime to spread work, but employers shifted to more salaried workers, urging them to work longer hours "free." The remaining hourly workers got hooked on lucrative time-and-a-half overtime. The net result: Work became even more concentrated. Were we to legislate reduced job hours, the most motivated (and able) would be likely to take second jobs. Boost minimum wages in America and clerical information work telecommunicates abroad. As political Entity 1 offers tax breaks to attract industry and jobs, Entity 2 betters the offers, and so on.

Recognizing these difficulties, let us consider possible actions. These range from incremental to drastic change.

SMALLER, WEAKER STEPS

Leave It to the Market

Allow new industries and globalization to restructure work into flexible units (possibly a largely contingent workforce) and hope individuals adapt.

Retraining

A favorite American palliative to the cruelty of the market has been government training subsidies. These may beg the question of "for what?" if the projection of less labor demand proves right.

Make Work

As former Speaker of the House Tip O'Neill observed, jobs are the primary policymaking criterion. But can government resources allocated this way cope with increased labor productivity in the face of international competition?

Work Sharing

Two basic options are to reduce the work week (e.g., to 32 hours, but beware moonlighting) and/or to reduce the labor force by eliminating teenage work, boosting parental leave, or enforcing early retirement (e.g., in China, many workers retire at ages 50, 55, and 60). Each raises other concerns, particularly the last, when life expectancy pushes 85.

Individual Entrepreneurship

Bridges suggested a number of measures to support work independent of the job such as:

- Do away with Internal Revenue Service and local code disincentives against SoHo's (single operator, home office).
- Provide both business skills training and incubator support to facilitate entrepreneurship).[54]

BIGGER, BETTER STEPS

Safety Net

A key to solving the dual dilemmas of less labor and longer life is to provide for basic human needs independent of the job.[55] National health insurance and basic income provision for all could be made a right, like public education. In return, government and industry should be immunized against any job retention or make-work pressures. Business should pay for wanted work, nothing else; it should hire and fire at will.

One option would be to tie income to the revenues generated from business taxes (e.g., a value-added tax)—society's share from technology-generated wealth. So, if the economy slips, basic income the following year falls, increasing the incentive for individuals to generate more revenue (i.e., work more). Note that this structure does not actively promote consumption, and so invites use of enhanced productivity for time instead of more. It also largely resolves the senior population income issue by providing them the same income share as others, and covering their health care.

Community Work Expansion

Given that technology is supplanting labor as the major contributor to production and service, we need to reorient our reward system. Pay for market jobs is out of line with pay, and recognition, for community work (the modal value of which is zero—volunteering). Needs include providing health care and educational and recreational programs for seniors (e.g., elder hostels). Unmet needs of youth (child care and education) and other socially needy (e.g., handicapped and criminal) invite work Environmental needs and community building are underserved. As women move into market work, they volunteer less, leaving community needs unmet. On the other hand, community work offers an attractive outlet for our (we hope) healthier and longer-lived seniors. We need policies that direct resources toward our young and old, and other social needs, rather than into selling more cars and TVs.

Value Changes

The preceding paragraph points toward a *care economy*. The sense of community in being with others is deeply rewarding. Were we to redirect our energy from consumption to community goals, we could fulfill human need with fewer material goods, allowing a more sustainable economy. Such a shift requires intervention, for the market cares for market outputs, not social goods. Maybe our future entails social restructuring so that we become "sharers" like our hunter-gatherer ancestors? (However, the demise of communism reminds us of the importance of individual incentives.)

Maslow's familiar hierarchy of human needs serves to remind us that money is only an indirect reinforcer—it enables us to obtain the means to meet real needs. Were society to provide for basic needs (survival and security), higher needs (belonging, esteem, self-actualization) might provide our motives to work. This is consistent with the following definition of work: "Work is purposeful *human* activity directed toward the satisfaction of *human* needs and desires."[56]

The drudgery of jobs can and should be left to machines, not—as in the past—to slaves or to the poor. We should design work that is as challenging, fun, and fulfilling in itself as is feasible. Our work activities will then be creative and caring. The challenge is to evolve a new value system that lets go of the inadequate industrial era premises (i.e., capitalism, Marxism, and "material-ismo")[57] to accommodate this future. Slaughter noted signs of growing support for related values such as sustainable society with qualitative growth, a stewardship ethic, and rebirth of the sacred.[58]

CHOICES

In sum, we need a serious paradigm shift. To quote Bridges, "What stands in our way is a whole system designed to serve the job."[59] If we are bold, what stands ahead is the prospect of much better integrated human activities, of work integrated with learning and play. As de Jouvenal envisioned, "In the expectation, perhaps, of the advent of a society where paid work—the foundation of yesterday's entire social organization—will no longer be anything more than one activity among many, integrated with the others."[60]

What can we do to bring about these changes? Suggestions follow.

1. Find our who really does what now. We need the Bureau of Labor Statistics, the Census, and other agencies to report community work, home work, learning and play, comparably to market work (job) data. Further time diary studies are sorely lacking.
2. Document how community work is compensated, or not; then move to compensate it adequately; explicitly recognize it as more important than market work (e.g., awards, media attention to "heroes").

3. Remove tax incentives encouraging consumption and favoring big business over individual businesses.
4. Cut the working week to a 32-hour standard and increase vacation time.
5. Study, plan, and act now to meet the needs of the growing senior population.
6. Desist from artificial job creation.
7. Discuss alternatives to the work ethic.
8. Build a viable safety net independent of the job, including national health care and reformed Social Security.
9. Consider a national income plan as an alternative to unemployment and welfare support, and study how to fund it with a value-added tax or alternative means other than the individual income tax (which is job-oriented).
10. Continue to seek ways of controlling worldwide population growth; for example, by increasing opportunities for women to participate in meaningful activities other than childbearing.

Should we fail to act, poverty, hardship, class schisms, and social disruption may dominate the United States in 2020. Perhaps we will face a scenario such as Kurt Vonnegut depicted in *Player Piano*, in which a majority undercaste of nonworkers counter their impoverished boredom by planning revolution. One key is to let go of the job as the centerpiece of income distribution and meaning of life. Another is to recognize that our present income and activity arrangements cannot work with 62 million folks aged 65 and over by 2020.[61] If we act briskly and creatively, we can integrate seniors into a caring society. Fluid work activity patterns can blend with lifelong learning and other activities both to meet basic needs and to provide rich opportunities for deeper fulfilment.

NOTES AND REFERENCES

[1] A. Toffler & H. Toffler, *Creating a New Civilization* (Atlanta, Turner Publishing, 1995), p. 31.
[2] J. Gershuny, "Are We Running Out of Time?," *Futures*, January-February 1992, pp. 3-22.
[3] F. Stinson, Jr., "Multiple Jobholding up Sharply in the Eighties," *Monthly Labor Review, 113*, 1990, p. 3.
[4] *Handbook of Labor Statistics*, Bureau of Labor Statistics Bulletin 2340, August 1989, Table 2; Employment and Earnings, January 1992, U.S. Dept. of Labor, Bureau of Labor Statistics, Table A-1. Note: The percentage of men in the labor force dropped from 79.8% in 1969 to 75.9% in 1991. The percentage of women in the labor force increased from 42.7% in 1969 to 57.4% in 1995.

[5] A. Bostrom, "Working Women," *Transition, 58*, 1992, p. 168.

[6] H. de Jouvenel, "Time and Society," *Futures*, 25, 1993, p. 491.

[7] J. M. Keynes, quoted by F. Best (Ed.), *The Future of Work* (Englewood Cliffs, NJ, Prentice-Hall, 1973), p. iii.

[8] S. Aronowitz & W. DiFazio, *The Jobless Future* (Minneapolis, University of Minnesota Press, 1994), p. 3.

[9] R. M. White, "Technology, Jobs and Society: The New Challenges of Change," *Cosmos*, 1994, p. 65.

[10] Aronowitz & DiFazio, *op. cit.*, Ref. 8, p. 108.

[11] J. F. Coates, "The Highly Probable Future: 83 Assumptions About the Year 2025," *The Futurist, 28*, 1994, pp. 51-58.

[12] E. Brynjolfsson, "The Productivity Paradox of Information Technology," *Communications of the ACM, 26*, 1993, pp. 66-77.

[13] S. Dortch, "Productive Projections," *American Demographics,* June 1995, pp. 4-6.

[14] Aronowitz & DiFazio, *op cit.*, Ref. 8, pp. 33, 301, 322, 326.

[15] A. L. Porter, "Work in the New Information Age," *The Futurist, 20,* 1986, pp. 9-14.

[16] R. D. Hershey, Jr., "Survey Finds 6 Million, Fewer Than Thought, in Impermanent Jobs," *New York Times,* 19 August 1995, pp. 15, 17 (survey in February, 1994); J. B. Schor, *The Overworked American* (New York, Basic Books, 1991), p. 66.

[17] Hershey, *op. cit.*, Ref. 16.

[18] *NBC Nightly News,* 22 March 1994.

[19] Coates, *op. cit.*, Ref. 11, p. 19.

[20] W. Bridges, *Job Shift: How to Prosper in a Workplace Without Jobs* (Reading, MA, Addison-Wesley, 1994), pp. 1-3.

[21] S. J. Olhansky, B. A. Carnes, & C. K. Cassel, "The Aging of the Human Species," *Scientific American, 268*, 1993, p. 46.

[22] U.S. Census Bureau, "Population Projections of the United States, by Age, Sex, Race, and Hispanic Origin: 1992 to 2050," *Current Population Reports,* Series P-25-1092, Washington, DC.

[23] P. A. Morrison, "Applied Demography: Its Growing Scope and Future Direction," *The Futurist,* March-April, 1990, p. 13.

[24] T. P. Miles & J. A. Brody, "Aging as a Worldwide Phenomenon," In D. E. Crews & R. M. Garruto (Eds.), *Biological Anthropology and Aging* (New York, Oxford University Press, 1994), pp. 3-15.

[25] Olshansky *et al.*, *op. cit.*, Ref. 21, p. 49.

[26] T. R. Turner & M. L. Weiss, "The Genetics of Longevity in Humans," In Crews & Garruto, *op. cit.*, Ref. 24, p. 94.

[27] Olshansky et al., *op. cit.*, Ref. 21, p. 48.

[28] C. F. Longino, Jr., "Myths of an Aging America," *American Demographics, 16,* 1994, p. 38.

[29] K. Bradsher, *New York Times,* 25 June 1995, p. E4.

[30] A. L. Porter, "The Work Ethic—An Idea Whose Time Has Gone?", *Business, 31,* 1981, pp. 15-22.

[31] *Ibid.*

[32]"American Pies," *American Demographics*, February 1995, pp. 24-31.

[33]Longino, *op. cit.*, Ref. 28, p. 38.

[34]de Jouvenel, *op. cit.*, Ref. 6, p. 492.

[35]Schor, *op. cit.*, Ref. 16, p. 10.

[36]R. Hawkes, "On Sharing and Work," *Current Anthropology, 33*, pp. 404-407.

[37]Schor, *op. cit.*, Ref. 16, pp. 44-48.

[38]*Ibid.*, pp. 45, 51.

[39]Time studies in the United States have included categories for paid work, household work, child care, obtaining goods and services, personal needs and care (includes sleeping), education and training, organizational activities (includes religious and political activities), entertainment and social activities, recreation, and communication. Travel is included in all our five categories. J. P. Robinson, *Estimating Activity and Location Time Expenditures From Human Activity Pattern Data, Report 6: Summary Comparisons* (Survey Research Center, Department of Sociology, College Park, MD, University of Maryland).

[40]J. P. Robinson, "How Americans Use Time," *The Futurist*, September-October 1991, p. 27.

[41]About 11 hours per day for those over 65: J. P. Robinson, "Quitting Time," *American Demographics*, May 1991, pp. 34-36.

[42]The table is a composite estimation. It draws on Schor, *op. cit.*, Ref. 16, for market and home work; on Robinson, *op. cit.*, Ref. 40, for leisure, averaged for 1965 and 1975, with "clubs and organizations" counted as community work, and 20% of "reading" time plus "adult education" called learning. "Commuting" is included in market work

[43]Schor, *op. cit.*, Ref. 16, pp. 32, 79-80.

[44]IEEE (Institute of Electrical and Electronics Engineers), *The Institute*, June 1995, p. 8D.

[45]*Statistical Abstract of the US*, 1970, *op. cit.*, Ref. 45, Table 316.

[46]H. V. Hayghe, "Volunteers in the US: Who Donates the Time?," *Monthly Labor Review*, February 1991, pp. 17-23.

[47]Schor, *op. cit.*, Ref. 16, pp. 8, 38, 84, 87, 102; Robinson, *op. cit.*, Ref. 40, p. 24; J. P. Robinson, "Who's Doing the Housework," *American Demographics*, December 1988, pp. 25-28, 63.

[48]Gershuny, *op. cit.*, Ref. 2, pp. 14-20. The declining use of paid domestic help in the middle classes from about 1950 to the 1970s combined with the decline of housework time in the lower classes to produce fairly flat composite numbers, camouflaging decreases attributable to the introduction of domestic technology. Some increases are apparent in the 1980s, but these are for child care and shopping, not other housework Women's domestic work goes down with their increased participation in economic activities, whereas men's domestic work has increased modestly, leading to an overall decline in unpaid domestic work.

[49]*Statistical Abstract of the US*, 1994, *op. cit.*, Ref. 45, Tables 229, 254, and 273, based on Current Population Survey.

[50]Robinson, *op. cit.*, Ref. 40, p. 25.

[51]Schor, *op. cit.*, Ref. 16, p. 110.

[52]*Ibid.*, pp. 110, 112.

[53] H. Marcuse, *One Dimensional Man* (Boston, Beacon, 1964), pp. 230-231.

[54] Bridges, *op. cit.*, Ref. 20, pp. 178-192.

[55] *Ibid.*, pp. 187-189.

[56] F. Best, *The Future of Work* (Englewood Cliffs, NJ, Prentice-Hall, 1973), p. 2.

[57] Toffler & Toffler, *op. cit.*, Ref. 1, p. 61.

[58] R. A. Slaughter, "Looking for the Real Megatrends," *Futures, 25,* 1993, pp. 827-849.

[59] Bridges, *op. cit.*, Ref. 20, p. 179.

[60] de Jouvenal, *op. cit.*, Ref. 6, p. 493.

[61] The issue is more intense elsewhere: From 1982 to 2000, China's population increase is likely to be 19%; its over-60s increase, 72%. See C. Holden, "New Populations of Old Add to Poor Nations' Burdens," *Science, 273,* 1996, pp. 46-48.

chapter 15

Technology, Jobs, and Society: The New Challenge of Change*

Robert M. White
National Academy of Engineering

Richard H. White
Institute for Defense Analyses

INTRODUCTION

Social structures and practices are greatly influenced by technological advance mediated through economic change. The elements of change appear disparate in their causes, but immigration, job insecurity, two-tier wage compensation systems, and the migration of high-skill jobs overseas are all linked to the underlying forces of technological advance. These are the issues that have come to dominate political discussion. The formulation of public policies to address them depends on understanding underlying causes and the expectations we have for the future.

What will society look like a quarter of a century hence in the year 2020? More importantly, how will society evolve during that period?

*This chapter represents the views of the authors and not the views of the National Academy of Engineering or the Institute for Defense Analyses.

Although present trends set directions in which the future is evolving, they cannot set the outcomes. History is replete with failed predictions and extrapolations, even over short time periods of the order of a decade. Lord Kelvin, one of the great scientists in the United Kingdom expressed the view that, "heavier than air machines are impossible," in 1885. Twenty years later, the Wright brothers flew at Kitty Hawk. In 1943, Thomas Watson, then Chairman of IBM, said, "I think there is a world market for maybe five computers." Today the number of computers worldwide of all types is in the tens of millions. In more recent times, Ken Olson, president and founder of the Digital Equipment Corporation as late as 1977 was quoted as saying, "There is no reason anyone would want a computer in their home." Today personal computers have become common household appliances.

More sobering has been the inability to foreshadow social and political discontinuities that influence the path of technology development. Were we trying in the 1970 to predict the nature of the world we live in today, we might have missed some of the most important driving events that shape the present. We would have missed the ubiquitous nature of the personal computer and the transformations it has wrought in almost every field of human activity. We would have missed the growth of some of the most dynamic new products and services: software, bioengineered pharmaceuticals, mobile wireless communications, noninvasive medical diagnostic devices, compact discs, and the Internet, among others. We would have missed the political upheavals engendered by the collapse of the Soviet Union and the rise of the economic power of Japan and the countries of Southeast Asia. We would have missed the oil embargoes of 1973 and 1979 and detente with China. Not only would we have missed such events, we would have been wrong about others. We would have misjudged the growth of nuclear power. What happened to the promise of almost unlimited and cheap energy?

Technological and economic transformations occur with great rapidity. In 1970, videocassette recorders (VCRs) in U.S. households were too few to be recorded by the Census Bureau. By 1994 there were 74 million U.S. households equipped with VCRs. Cable television is much the same story. In 1970, cable television had penetrated only 4 million households, but by 1994 the penetration had exceeded 59 million. Cellular phones did not exist in 1970, but by 1994 there were 24 million subscribers in the United States. Compact discs were nonexistent in 1970, but by 1994, 882 million CDs were shipped. The same story is found in the automobile industry. Twenty-five years ago the United States imported only 408,000 passenger cars and trucks from Japan annually. By 1994 we were importing 3,250,000 cars and trucks annually. The value of the vehicles imported into the United States had gone from $4 billion to $35 billion in that period.[1]

THE SPACE/TIME CONSEQUENCES OF
TECHNOLOGICAL ADVANCE

Although trends are not destiny, the future unfolds in a nonlinear fashion from present conditions. The basic functions and needs of society, however, change slowly. In 2020 citizens will still want and need to conduct elections, to travel, to educate new generations, to have access to health care, and to be entertained, play, and carry on meaningful personal and family relationships, to say nothing of the need for food and shelter. Most importantly, we will need jobs—good-paying jobs for our citizens.

One does not need to be a technological determinist to recognize that the primary driving force for economic, demographic, and social change is technological advance. Today three enabling technologies are having pervasive effects: information technology, biotechnology, and materials technology. These are supplemented by advances in space, energy, and environmental technologies. These technologies are at the beginning of their transforming trajectories. No area of human activity is now immune to the changes being wrought by these enabling technologies.

One of the fundamental consequences of advancement in these technologies is that time and space dimensions of all human activities radically change. In a sense, time delays disappear as we enter a feedback world in which events of all kinds are communicated, and in many cases acted on, almost instantaneously. Space dimensions shrink as remote operations become possible, and rapid movement from one part of the world to another is a reality. National borders become permeable, and national sovereignty weakens as the actions of multinational enterprises are superimposed on nation states. Markets have long been global, but access to them becomes central to corporate profitability. Concepts of resources change as intellectual content becomes a dominant input to the production of goods and services. The intellectual framework that shapes the mores and practices of business, of education, institutional management, and everyday life has changed and with it the nature of work, the availability of jobs, and the very character of social and economic systems have also changed.

THE CHANGING GLOBAL
INDUSTRIAL COMPETITION

The shrinking world in time and space drives the economies of all nations to be integral parts of a dynamic global technological and economic system. It is technology that has permitted the creation of a global capital pool that is now accessible to qualified enterprises anywhere in the world. The management of industrial enterprises located anywhere in the world can now oversee production and service components that can be globally dispersed.

The global competitiveness of enterprises now depends on the meshing of diverse and interacting influences in new ways. The factors that determine the costs of production of goods and services, more than in the past, now relate to the differences in wage rates throughout the globe; market access now becomes a key determinant of economic viability; and the costs of compliance with environmental, health, and other regulations becomes a significant factor. Intellectual property considerations, the availability of technology, and an educated labor force become important in determining the location of an operation.

The goals of multinational enterprises become independent of the national goals of the country in which their headquarters is based. The CEO of the Coca-Cola Company describes his corporation as an international entity that just happens to be headquartered in the United States. The result is that national sovereignty weakens as control of financial and economic relations with other nations are determined by corporate rather than governmental decisions. Indeed, U.S.-based multinational corporations have been able to maintain their shares of the world market for goods and services; they merely supply those markets from different locations. The share of the world market serviced by U.S.-based corporations has remained at 20% to 21% for decades. The trade deficit in goods and services results from the fact that U.S.-based production has lost world market share.

CHANGING CORPORATE STRUCTURES

Technology now permits corporations to evolve into new kinds of entities that do not own or control all or even most of the means of production and distribution. These corporations are becoming foci for the assembly of capital deployed to gain strategic advantage using many modes to achieve acceptable returns on investment. Management of enterprises can now oversee the activities of globally dispersed units and operations of the individual units can serve the special market needs of variouscountries and be located where the combination of all the factors affecting profitability can be taken into account.

We are witnessing the emergence of the new international corporation. The aerospace industry provides a good example. Because of the need for market access, especially in countries with rapidly developing economies, it is not only wage rate competition that is important in decisions about offshore production, but market access. Technology now makes it possible for a U.S. company like Boeing Aircraft to have the fuselages of some of its aircraft manufactured in Japan, landing gear in Israel, 737 tail sections in China, and nose and wing elements in Korea to gain aircraft sales to national airlines in these countries.

The penalties for the United States are in the transfer of technology and know-how that accompany such manufacture. They are also in the loss of high-wage manufacturing jobs to overseas locations. For the Boeing Corporation, such moves are essential to survival as a global supplier of passenger aircraft, and indeed as an employer of highly skilled workers. Witness the recent announcement by Boeing that it is increasing its workforce in Seattle to enable it to cope with a rush of orders from abroad for its new aircraft.

The pharmaceutical industry evidences the cost advantages of global suppliers. Generic drugs now account for 40% of prescription drugs sold in the United States. Most of the key ingredients come from foreign suppliers, as do 60% of the components of brand-name drugs.[2]

The implications for defense industries and national security are also profound. In a world in which the conception, design, development, production, and distribution of goods and services is an integrated global endeavor, traditional national security concerns such as foreign dependency take on a new meaning. In the past this nation was considered at risk whenever there was a possibility that a militarily important technology was available to our adversaries, or only available from overseas sources. The unfolding future will turn this probability into a certainty—global industrial integration portends the same for defense and civil industries. Defense prime contractors may do their system integration in the United States, but their supplier networks will inevitably extend to take advantage of both domestic and foreign core competencies.

The virtual corporation is becoming a reality. The future can be seen in the operations of a small biomedical company in the Washington area: Alpha 1 Biomedicals, Inc. has only six employees. It literally contracts out everything—its research, toxicology studies, and production. Universities do its research, commercial laboratories do its toxicology studies, and three different drug companies do its manufacturing.[3]

Make or buy decisions have always been a way of life for corporations. There is nothing new in contracting out for parts, retaining in the corporation the key design, systems engineering, product assembly, key technological, and marketing functions. However, many of these functions now migrate abroad. It is the extent and rationale for outsourcing of functions that is a new phenomenon. A harbinger of the future is in the fact that Nike, Inc. does no manufacturing in the United States. The same is true of Mattel, Inc. and mostly true of Apple Computer.

TECHNOLOGICAL PRODUCTIVITY AND CORPORATE RESTRUCTURING

Globalization and its attendant effects on the economic system are the overriding feature of the new global economy resulting from technological advance, but a second pervasive effect is in the restructuring of enterprises. We have already entered the downsizing world—something once reserved for business downturns. Today downsizing in production, service, and management of corporations in large part results from increases in productivity brought about by the introduction of new technology. New technologies permit the realization of increased productivity from matters of scale as well as the specialization of products and services associated with small enterprises.

In the past, firms were thought of as vertically or horizontally integrated, or both. Today, the extent of integration has become less important than the ability to rapidly reconfigure an enterprise to take advantage of internal or external core competencies. New terms have sprung up. We now describe the competitive character of a firm according to whether it is agile or virtual or lean or flexible or a combination of these traits.

The evidences of gains in technological and management productivity are in the almost continuous announcements of corporate layoffs. The American Management Association, whose members employ 25% of U.S. workers, reports that for every new hire another employee is fired. In the first 9 months of 1995, more than 300,000 jobs were eliminated, according to Challenger, Gray, and Christmas, Inc. of Chicago, an organization that keeps track of such matters. Salaried workers in middle management were hardest hit. The productivity effect is evidenced in the 1993 merger of the Bank of America with the Security Pacific Corp. In that year, the Bank of America announced record profits of about $1.5 billion, simultaneously cutting 7,500 jobs.[4]

We are in the embrace of truly historic events related to technological productivity and employment. During the past year, AT&T announced that it is offering job buyouts to 77,800 managers, half of its supervisory workforce. It expects about 10% of these workers to take up the offer. In addition, it announced, as 1996 arrived, that it plans to lay off 40,000 workers, the majority of whom are in white-collar managerial positions. It is information technology that enables the elimination of these jobs. The Bethlehem Steel Co. will stop making steel in its hometown in Pennsylvania for the first time since 1873. Some 1,800 steel workers will be laid off. Nationwide, the total number of steel workers in the United States has declined from about 550,000 to 171,000 in the 45-year period between 1950 and 1995 as old technology is displaced by new technology that makes modern U.S. mini steel mills competitive in the world marketplace.[5]

Layoffs in the 4-year period from 1992 to 1995 on the part of some of the largest U.S. corporations tell the same story. IBM has laid off 122,000 employees, AT&T 123,000, General Motors 99,000, Boeing 61,000, the U.S. Postal Service 55,000, Sears Roebuck 50,000, Digital Equipment 29,800 etc. The list goes on and on.[6] The American Management Association concluded that the employment predicament is different from anything seen since the invention of the factory 200 years ago. Only 6% of its member firms that cut payrolls in 1994 rehired laid-off workers. The new workers tend to be in the professional and technical fields. Middle managers make up 5% to 8% of the workforce but account for 15% to 20% of the job losses. Very few of the firms gave poor business conditions as their reason for downsizing. Poor business conditions have in the past been the major reason for downsizing. In 1990, 43% of firms cited business conditions as the reason for downsizing; by 1992 only 21% gave this reason; and in 1994 only 6% of firms gave this reason.

An important consequence for the world of work that our children will encounter is the attenuation of firm loyalty by workers. They will no longer be able to count on a lifetime of work for a single corporation. They will need to be comfortable with change, with a life's work for many entities with loyalty only to themselves and their careers. This prospect was outlined by James Meadows, one of AT&T's vice presidents for human resources, in connection with the planned layoff of 40,000 AT&T employees. "People," he said, "need to look at themselves as self-employed, as vendors who come to this company to sell their skills." He then went on to say, "We have to promote the whole concept of the work force being contingent." We are giving rise to a society that is increasingly "jobless, but not workless."[7] The sociological ramifications of this kind of job insecurity are poorly understood.

The paradox of technological advance is that it creates employment as well as displaces and destroys it. It would be easy to gain the impression from news headlines that technological advance and employment do not mix. The opposite has been true historically. The issue is whether past history is a useful guide to the future. The race between the job creation and destructive power of technologicaladvance has always been out of balance, but from a historical perspective, technology has been a net job creator.

The creation of jobs depends on the formation and expansion of new industries or new markets, usually both. Technological changes have now moved rapidly to create them. The software industry hardly existed 25 years ago. In 1993 it provided employment for 435,000 individuals. By 1993 it was a $32 billion industry. This story is repeated endlessly. In the past decade, new and growing corporations have been increasing their workforce. MCI has grown from 12,445 employees to 47,500 today. Sprint has increased its workforce from 27,415 workers to 51,500. Cable operators and those responsible for conceiving and producing television programs have increased their workforce in the past two decades from 23,538 in 1978 to 112,239 today, according to the FCC. The cellular telephone industry, since its inception in the 1980s new employs 300,000 workers, directly and indirectly, according to the Cellular Telecommunications Industry Association.[8]

Technological advance transformed agricultural practices in the United States. The productivity of United States agriculture enabled the 30% of the workforce on farms at the turn of the century to be reduced to 3% of the workforce on farms today. That displaced workforce, with considerable disruption and pain, became employed in manufacturing and service industries as new technology created new enterprises and services. The process continues today but the circumstances are fundamentally altered because of the globalization of the economy and the fact that technological advance in one country frequently results in job creation in another as advances are quickly exploited.

Market access is one reason for job and technological migration, but wage rate advantages are among the most important driving forces. It is not only wage rates for production workers, but also for highly skilled technical workers that propels jobs overseas. The Council on Competitiveness reported that skilled workers in the United States are facing increased competition from abroad. The jobs at stake are white-collar jobs in high-tech positions in computer programming, design, and financial services. The Council cited advances in computer and communications technology as the basic reason. Much of this kind of work is going to China, India, Singapore and Taiwan as well as to low-wage countries in Eastern Europe at a fraction of U.S. wages. The cost of hiring an English-speaking computer programmer in India is only $15,000 to 18,000 per year as compared with $150,000 to 120,000 for an American programmer. Programmers in Bulgaria are paid salaries that range from $10,000 to $20,000 per year. This is one fifth of the compensation for programmers in the United States.[9]

EVOLVING TECHNOLOGICAL AND COMMERCIAL VISTAS

Other enterprises, in addition to those applying advances in information technology, are emerging from the other dimensions of the technological revolution in mind-boggling diversity. One of the most rapidly growing is the biotechnology industry. As the private sector rushes to capitalize on the scientific discoveries in molecular biology, the world market for biotechnology products is predicted to grow from $5.7 billion in 1992 to almost $94 billion in the year 2000.[10]

The commercial vistas opened by technological developments in information and telecommunications combined with parallel developments in space, energy, and materials technology seem almost limitless. Highly automated factories are proliferating in all segments of manufacturing. Computer processing in the banking, insurance, and retail industries are rendering many routine clerical jobs obsolete. Automated home banking and shopping are already with us. Internet access providers represent an entirely new industry with initial public offerings of their stock at very high multiples of their present earnings.

The technological promise is much more. For example, the Global Positioning System of earth orbiting satellites, first developed for military purposes, combined with new wireless communication systems to permit wholly new kinds of applications to a wide range of industries. Precision farming becomes possible as satellite-linked tilling and sowing machines respond to microchanges in soil characteristics. Transportation systems are rapidly evolving as automated navigation of automobiles and other vehicles opens up the possibility of "smart" highways. Health care is becoming radically transformed as it becomes possible to diagnose illnesses and provide advice from a distance. The conduct of remote surgery is now a possibility. Monitoring environmental conditions such as ground water contamination becomes possible with the sensor revolution wedded to new information-processing systems. Remote sensing from satellites at altitude revolutionizes our ability to predict weather and ocean conditions as well as survey the biosphere and the earth's resources. The possibilities are endless.

THE GROWING INCOME INEQUALITY

Ever new and innovative applications of these technological advances can be anticipated along with the creation of new industries. Comparisons between employment in low- and high-tech industries is no cause for comfort. Luttwak pointed out that Intel, Microsoft, Apple Computer, and Genentech, representing a sampling of firms in the semiconductor, software, computer, and biotechnology industries, employ about 62,500 workers in the United States. This is about the same number of employees as Home Depot, Inc., the hardware company. Most of the Home Depot jobs are low paying by comparison with those in the high-tech companies.[11]

These technological and economic forces have now given rise to growing income inequality in the United States. There is perhaps no more important feature of the U.S. economic system than the emerging two-tier compensation system. One tier provides high-paying career tracks for technologically adept workers, the other relatively low-paying ones. The conventional wisdom is that the answer to the problem is better education for our children, enabling them to ride the first-tier track to the "good" life. The problem with the conventional wisdom is not that it demands better educational opportunities, but that it assumes that the jobs will be there to employ all who are well-educated and trained. A good education to meet the demanding needs of the new high-tech industries is a sine qua non. It is, however, a necessary, but not a sufficient condition to enable our young people to compete for good jobs.

The Organization for Economic Cooperation and Development reported that the difference between the best paid 10% of American workers and the worst is wider than for any other large industrial nation.[12] Lester Thurow, the MIT economist, expressed grave concern about this phenomenon. He pointed out that since 1968, economic inequality has been on the rise in the United States. In the 20-year period from 1968 to 1988, the earnings difference between the top 20% of wage earners and the bottom 20% doubled. The share of the total net worth of the top 1% of the population rose from 26% to 31%. By the early 1990s, more than 40% of the wealth was held by the top 1% of the population. This is double what it was in 1970. Since 1979, all of the income growth in the United States has gone to the top 40% of households and nearly all of that to the top 20%. Gains in productivity are not being translated into rising incomes for the great majority of workers. According to Claudia Goldin, a Harvard historian of science and technology, we are in a period of great fortune building based on new technology much like the fortune building in the late 1800s, which was also based on new Technology.[13]

THE KNOWLEDGE ECONOMY AND
THE U.S. WORK FORCE

In the currently unfolding economic system, the intellectual content of goods and services becomes ever more important. Our children will be competing not only with other U.S. workers but with the coming generations of workers in other countries. They will truly live and work in a global, multicultural world. We will measure the abilities of the U.S. multicultural workforce against the global one. Not only will wage rates and work ethics be compared, but, most importantly, education and technological adaptability.

International comparisons portray student educational achievement as a competitive race for intellectual excellence that we are losing. The implications are that the United States will be unable to compete in the new technological world. Acknowledging the importance of strengthening the U.S. educational system, especially in the K–12 grades, great care must be taken in the interpretation of these international comparisons. A very thoughtful article in the journal *Science* by Iris Rotberg questioned the myths raised by these international comparisons. She pointed out that the evaluations are based on the comparison of groups selected in different ways. When highly selected groups in other countries are compared with the achievement of the total body of students in the U.S., inevitably test scores are unfavorable to U.S. students. When comparable selected groups of students are tested, U.S. students are competitive.[14] We must not be misled by invidious educational international comparisons of U.S. student achievement. Nor can we be complacent about the U.S. educational system.

THE CHANGING WORKFORCE DEMOGRAPHICS

By the year 2020, the workforce in the United States will have a significantly different composition than that of today. We have reasonably reliable projections of the composition of the population and what it is likely to be in 2020. Out of the total present population of 260 million, about 73% is White, 12% is African American, 10% is Hispanic, and 3.5% is Asian. By 2020 we can expect a shift to 64% White, 13% African American, 16.5% Hispanic, and 6.5% Asian out of a population that will have grown to 325 million. Our children will live in a nation much different from the one we have today.[15]

If present trends in income and education persist into the future, our children could live in a socially differentiated society, driven by great social tensions driven by income inequalities. African Americans and

Hispanics by and large work in the low-wage tier of the economy. Every indicator confirms this unfortunate truth. Per capita income of African Americans in 1993 hovered between 50% and 60% of that of Whites and Asians. Median family income reveals the same phenomenon.

If education is essential to participation in the high-wage tier, indicators of educational levels and achievement among African Americans and Hispanics suggest the nation has a formidable problem. Baccalaureate and professional degrees are measures of the educational attainment that will be in demand in a technology- and knowledge-based world. From 1981 to 1992, Whites, who comprised 80% of the total U.S. population of 226 million in 1980, acquired 86% of bachelors degrees and 90% of professional degrees. Although the percentage of such degrees acquired by Whites decreased to 83% for both professional and bachelors degrees by 1992, their numbers also decreased to 74% of the total U.S. population. The relative educational position of Whites changed little in the intervening years.

African Americans showed no improvement over this period of time in their position relative to their percentage of the total population, although the absolute number of degrees in each class awarded to African Americans increased. At roughly 11% of the population, only 6.5% and 4% of baccalaureate and professional degrees were acquired by African Americans, respectively. Hispanics made small gains in their relative position. The big gainer was the Asian population which saw its numbers in the total population more than double between 1980 and 1994 to about 8.5 million, whereas the number of bachelors degrees more than doubled, from about 19,000 to 47,000—and the number of professional degrees about doubled, from 2,700 to 4,500.[16]

It is impolitic to dwell on the different skills and achievements of the different ethnic groups in the United States, but the implications for U.S. society are worrisome. Quite apart from the availability of jobs, high-paying jobs and rewarding careers will require high levels of educational achievement. Managerial and technical jobs and professional and highly skilled support jobs will be open only to those who have had the requisite education. Today, Whites and Asians are heavily represented among the students seeking higher education. African Americans and Hispanics are heavily represented among the students who do not pursue higher education. In one group many members are trained to exploit the opportunities of the new economy, in the other fewer are trained and able to prosper. This unfortunate ethnic correlation with economic opportunity could become a flashpoint in U.S. society. The remedy is nowhere in sight.

THE AMERICAN DILEMMA

The dilemma now being faced by the U.S. economy is that there is a growing conflict between the need to provide high skills to enable industry to compete in the international marketplace through productivity gains, as at the same time low wage rates in other countries prevent higher salaries in the United States. The facts seem to bear this dilemma out. Productivity has been going up in the United States without resulting wage gains. The average productivity of American workers increased 30% between 1987 and 1992, whereas average real wages fell by 13%. Productivity is increasing because of technological innovation and not education. The problem is that wages fall or at least do not increase if there is an abundance of workers competing for these jobs. This Marxian assessment seems borne out by the realities of the global job market. This abundance is created by the globalization of industry as well as large scale immigration. In turn, globalization and increased immigration can be traced directly back to technological changes.[17]

It is a law of nature that water flows downhill, and it is a law of nature that intellectual knowledge diffuses and leaks. Laws may slow the diffusion, but they cannot stop it. In modern economic terms, technological know-how migrates from countries with high know-how to countries with low know-how. Japan and the other Asian countries demonstrate that technological comparability can be achieved in less than half a century. We are witnessing this process at work today. At present rates of economic growth and technological progress, we can expect China and other nations that place a high value on education and the harnessing of technology for economic growth to be significant economic powers. The competition, however, will not only be in the efficient production and marketing of goods and services; it will be a new kind of competition for intellectual advantage.

IMPLICATIONS FOR THE FUTURE

Presumably we are interested in the shape of the future because we may be able to take actions now that can either enhance the attractive aspects of the future, or perhaps more importantly, because action in the near future can forestall some of the more ominous directions in which technology appears to be driving society. We have recognized the impossibility of predicting the future 25 years from now, but we do have a good sense of the directions that present trends are taking us. We have noted the power of technology to shape the economy and its corollary implications for the demographic problems that the country is likely to encounter.

Because we cannot see the future clearly, we need to be prepared with various action scenarios that could address the multiple issues that confront the country. There is a wide range of social and economic measures that can be brought to bear. We here point only to some important principles involving science and technology that should guide action, whatever scenario unfolds.

1. The overriding principle is the need to appreciate the formidable power of science and technology. The country must remain at the forefront internationally in scientific and technological research and education. To do this, it must take whatever steps are necessary to see that the education of our young people can produce the world-class scientists and engineers that industry and government need. Science and technology literacy for the population as a whole will be necessary if the United States is to remain globally competitive. Recently the National Academy of Sciences and Engineering and the Institute of Medicine completed a multiyear study at the request of the Secretary of Education, culminating in the publication of National Science Standards. It is a fine publication and for the first time sets out what students should know about science and technology and when they should know it. These standards, or variants of them tailored to various school districts, must be adopted everywhere in this country's school systems.[18]

2. We will need to adopt policies that are incentives to investment in science and technology—both in the public and private sectors. The role of the federal government in the support of basic and applied research is directly raised as an issue. Whether such incentives are incorporated in the tax code, provided through direct government investment, or in the reformulation of present disincentives to investment in science and technology, are political decisions for the Congress and the administration in power. We need to remember that throughout the history of the United States, we have oscillated between strong and weak roles for the federal government. We have seen many successes and failures. The preeminence of our agricultural, aeronautic, and biotechnology industries can be largely attributed to strong government roles. On the other hand, we have had our share of failures, such as supersonic transport, nuclear breeder reactors, and the Synthetic Fuels Corporation.

3. The migration of jobs must be a two-way phenomenon with traffic both ways being roughly equal. On the one hand we do not wish to restrict U.S. multinational corporations from taking advantage of

the global labor, economic, or capital markets if that is. what is required for their viability. On the other hand, we will need to adopt policies that will assure that the United States retains a fair share of the attractive jobs in the world. It may be that the free market will naturally achieve this result. It will take several years before we can conclude whether it can or not. The evidence is mixed at the present time. Set against the migration of jobs overseas, there has been a counterflow of jobs as foreign-based corporations employ U.S. workers at all levels, from production to design to research in the United States. Automobile transplants of foreign automobile companies now employ hundreds of thousands of U.S. workers. Ten percent of all industrial research and development in the United States today takes place in U.S. subsidiaries of foreign corporations.

4. The United States must remain an attractive country in which to do business of all kinds—from routine production and services to the most esoteric research and development. The public policies that will encourage this at both the federal and state levels will consist of a complex mix of actions. Certainly, we will need to have an attractive and well-trained workforce and associated educational institutions, but we will need much more. Not unimportant will be the maintenance and improvement of the complex infrastructure of roads, airports, and communication systems in the United States, which are already among the best in the world.

5. The emerging two-tier compensation system for workers must be addressed. The problem is several-fold. It is clear that educational opportunities for economically depressed citizens must be increased, but this will not suffice. There is a problem in the distribution of the benefits of the technological productivity explosion. We have traditionally used the tax code to make a more equitable distribution of the wealth generated by productivity gains, and we will have to keep this approach under consideration. How we do this will be a politically charged issue, but the alternative of socially explosive income inequities is an even less attractive situation.

6. It will be necessary to keep a close eye on general unemployment levels in the United States Technological productivity gains historically have resulted in shorter work weeks. Our fathers and grandfathers worked a normal 60 hours per week. Today the average work week is 40 hours or somewhat less. Shortening work weeks is possible in a globally competitive world only if gains in productivity can compensate. Already in Europe 4-day work weeks have been adopted, for example in the automotive industry in Germany. The fact is that over the past 40 years, unemployment in the United States has ranged from a low of 4% to a high of 8%. Although eco-

nomic ups and downs have principally been responsible for the fluctuations in unemployment, there has been a systematic trend upward that economists refer to as the natural level of unemployment. This natural level has risen from 4% to 6% in the intervening half century—about .5% per decade.

We do not pretend to have the answers to the very difficult issues we have raised. We do know that they will need to be addressed. The task will not be easy but the future well-being of our nation will directly depend on how we address these issues.

NOTES AND REFERENCES

[1] Department of Commerce, Economics and Statistics Administration, Bureau of the Census, *Statistical Abstract of the United* States, 115th Edition, 1995, pp. 596, 575, 571, 578.

[2] K. Bradsher, "Inequalities in Income Are Reported Widened," *New York Times*, 29 October, 1995

[3] K. Day, "Now the Virtual Company," *Washington Post*, 29 October, 1995, p. H1.

[4] K. Downey Grimsley, "The Ax That Cuts Both Ways," *Washington Post*, 5 November. pp. H1, H4

[5] H. El Nasser, "PA Steel Town Left Behind by Time, Progress," *USA Today*, 17 November, 1995, p.

[6] *Washington Post*, 3 March 1996, p. 26, from *People Trends*, Challenger, Gray and Christmas.

[7] "Don't Go Away Mad, Just Go Away," *New York Times*, 13 February 1996, pp. C1, C4.

[8] M. Mills, "A Puzzling Job Picture in Telecommunications." *Washington Post*, 6 January. 1996, p. D1.

[9] M. Lind, *The Next American Nation*, Michael Lind, 1995, The Free Press.

[10] I. Hauchler & P. M. Kennedy, (Eds.), *New Technologies* (New York, Continuum Publishing, 1994).

[11] "Success in America," *Washington Post*, 27 November.1994, p.

[12] Bradsher, *op. cit.*

[13] S. Pearlstein, "Winner Take All," *Washington Post*, 19 November. 1995, p.

[14] I. Rotberg, "Myths About Test Score Comparisons," *Science*, December 1995, p.

[15] Department of Commerce, Economics and Statistics Administration, "Bureau of Census Current Population Reports," *Statistical Abstract of the United States*, 115th Edition, 1995

[16] "Digest of Educational Statistics," U.S. National Center for Educational Statistics, *Statistical Abstract of the United States*, 115th Edition, 1995.

[17] M. Lind, *op. cit.*

[18]National Research Council, *National Science Education Standards* National Academy Press, 1995.

part VI
Predictions

Here we add a postscript. The purpose of this is to peer into the future, about which few things are certain. Among them is that technology, especially information technology, will have an influence. We asked our colleagues in the Georgia Tech Faculty Program on the Information Revolution: Its Current and Future Consequences *to look into their crystal balls. What they saw has surprisingly little to do with technology.*

chapter 16

Predictions

SOFTWARE DEPENDENCY WILL BECOME A BIG PROBLEM

Traditional approaches to the use of information systems have led to a naive dependence on these systems. In the future, information systems will continue to support more complex and critical functions, resulting in even more dependence on these systems. It is my prediction that such dependence will result in an information-systems-based crisis with national and/or global implications.

Further, use of these systems will have a negative impact on quality of life. Whether or not continued integration of information systems into organizational processes leads to the optimization of these processes, information technologies will not decrease the length of the work day. Rather, they will allow organizations to claim more hours of the worker's day as these technologies continue to become accessible and mobile. Work will permeate more and more aspects of our lives.

Judith P. Carlisle
Assistant Professor
Dupree School of Management, Georgia Tech

WHO WILL WIN THE NEW POWER STRUGGLE?

The ongoing computer revolution, the Internet, and other new information technologies have resulted in a remarkable array of new applications. Technology-driven socioeconomic change is occurring. However, there will be many struggles between forces for central control (as has been encouraged in the industrial age and existing power bases) and those for individuality (as is encouraged by the two-way communications of the Internet and similar technologies).

Already the power of technology for free exchange of information has been seen in the breakup of the Soviet Union. Although there will be considerable pressure by many governments and by commercial and social interests to "regain control," the fact is—and will remain—that technology-aided information exchange will remain "free."

The Genie is out of the bottle!

Frederick B. Dyer
Principal Research Scientist, Emeritus
Georgia Tech

MOST LIVES WILL REMAIN UNTOUCHED

In the years ahead, the vast majority of people in the world will go about their daily lives largely untouched by the information revolution. The requisite massive expenditures on technology infrastructure, operations, and personal equipment will not be justified in developing countries until more fundamental needs of adequate food, clothing, shelter, medical care, and basic education are widely satisfied.

Satisfying those needs will absorb most of the income of the increasingly populous third world for the foreseeable future. To be sure, there will be many juxtapositions of the old and the new—as, for example, when a peasant walks half a day over dirt trails to visit a village doctor in a hut equipped with a satellite link to a distant medical center—but those instances will be the exceptions, not the rule, in people's daily lives.

Peter G. Sassone
Associate Professor
School of Economics, Georgia Tech

BEYOND THE HUMAN–MACHINE INTERFACE

Two revolutions have occurred in information technology: We use electronic machines instead of paper to store information, and we have successfully connected these machines together. As a consequence, computer users suffer a lot of "red eye" as they interface with their information machines.

The next revolution will move beyond today's human–machine interface—and liberate all those "red-eyed" users. Machines interfacing with machines—knowledge-based systems, automatic search systems, preprogrammed abstracting systems, and much more—will become commonplace. Look for the coming of the automatic information-finding, classifying, and processing machine!

Donghua Zhu
Visiting Professor
Technology Policy and Assessment Center, Georgia Tech

AN ETHICAL DILEMMA

Ethical issues and concerns have always underscored the utilization, management, and control of information. In the age of information, political and societal tensions will increasingly surface and coalesce, creating significant differences among groups within nations as well as among nations. The quality of information content will be deliberated by the perceived "haves" and the "have-nots." Who controls information will be a major issue for 21st century scholars and politicians.

Don Frank
Assistant Director for Information Services
Georgia Tech

MANAGEMENT OF KNOWLEDGE CAPITAL WILL TAKE OFF

Because knowledge is becoming the key wealth-creating asset, and because high-value knowledge is hard to accumulate in organizations— and even harder to organize and effectively deploy—managers in both the private and public sectors will want to learn how to master the process of knowledge management. They will also want to become innovators in creating knowledge capital in order to achieve competitive advantage. As a consequence, leading schools of business and public administration will make major curriculum changes early in the 21st century.

William H. Read
Professor of Public Policy
Georgia Tech

MERE ACCESS TO INFORMATION
WILL NOT BE ENOUGH

The development of information networks has not followed a purely technological imperative. These networks have been shaped by social networks. New social networks will interact in their own way with the current information infrastructure to lead the next stages in implementation of imformation networks. The Internet, for instance, serves to keep track of the dynamics of various socioeconomic phenomena.

Networks not only bring about change but are the ideal means to monitor change. Because of the importance that this has for both business and government, it is foreseeable that the automatic feeding of transaction information to control and decision centers of various kinds will become ubiquitous.

The key strategic issue in this environment will be the ability to bring processing power, broadly construed, to bear on any point in time and space that circumstances may demand. Mere access to information will not be sufficient. Making something happen with information, from attribution of meaning to rapid incorporation into ongoing decision processes, is what will make a difference.

Juan D. Rogers
School of Public Policy, Georgia Tech

SCIENCE WILL MOVE ONLINE

By 2010 scientific publication will be a fully electronic medium. Journals will no longer be the major means of organizing scientific information. Browsers will help scientific readers to select new papers from across a variety of disciplines and sources. Scientific "papers" will contain digital information of all sorts, including but not limited to text: graphics, movies, audio, simulations, and visualizations. The life cycle of scientific publication will be considerably shortened by electronic media. Collaboration, authorship, submission and review will become more intertwined as science moves online. Quality assurance will be provided by electronic labeling services—entities neither fully academic, corporate, nor governmental in nature.

Scott Cunningham
NCR Corporation, and
Member, Program on the Consequences of the
Information Revolution, Georgia Tech

BUSINESS APPLICATIONS WILL DRIVE THE NET

There are numerous historical examples where an initial period of scientific discovery and invention was followed by a period of intense growth driven by commercialization. These include the colonization of the Americas, the inventions of the industrial age, and now the information revolution.

The Internet will continue to have an increasing and far-reaching impact. There is currently an intense competition among developers of new Internet technologies. One of the issues is who will win these competitions. I predict that the winning technologies will result from the business applications they support, rather than from any engineering parameters. These business applications will develop around better and more competitive ways to manage and use information in the marketplace.

Myron L. Cramer
formerly Principal Research Scientist
Georgia Tech Research Institute
currently, SAIC Corporation

TELECOMMUTING: PERILS LIE AHEAD

Have organizations recognized the potential for harm that can result from allowing employees to interact with the organization's information at sites external to the organization? Currently, an organization has few legal rights to enter the home of an employee to procure its own information that is kept there.

What are the risks? They include, but are not limited to, potential for loss of and damage to valuable company information. The employee's home most likely will not have the same quality of security mechanisms that the organization can afford, leading to potential physical and electronic theft of information. As a consequence, the organization's access to information can be impaired with negative implications.

Michael Smith
PhD Candidate
Dupree School of Management, Georgia Tech

THEY'LL STILL BE HANGING AROUND
THE WATER COOLER

Just as the photocopier and the desktop computer did not eliminate paper, secretaries, and offices (as many had forecast), the devices of the information revolution will not eliminate the interpersonal aspects of commerce and education. For those with access, the pace and volume of human interactions via network will increase enormously, and for many this change will be enriching.

However, the important social aspects of commerce and education—gathering, sharing, learning about behavior, spontaneously connecting with others—that require face-to-face contact will not decrease significantly. People will continue to congregate in classrooms, offices, churches, bars, and shopping malls. The cumulative impact will be a continuing increase in the speed and number of total "information events," and people 50 years from now will wonder why so many in our era thought that the information revolution would increase our leisure.

Richard Barke
Associate Professor
School of Public Policy, Georgia Tech

ELECTRONIC LEARNING IS THE FUTURE

The evidence is clear that there are many problems with the current academic system. The fact of the matter is that college instructional methods have not changed much over the last 50 years. Those institutions that properly assess the changes coming and respond in the appropriate manner will grow and prosper, whereas many others will decline and close-up shop.

The present educational process can be likened to an ancient cottage-shop industry that is neither efficient (costs are growing relative to income) nor effective (does not do a very good job of increasing learning). Clearly college education is ripe for major technological change that makes education both more efficient and effective.

There is no question that electronic learning is going to grow rapidly in importance and dramatically change the college educational process.

Our challenge is to exploit the opportunities being offered by advances in information technology in the context of what we know is right and valuable in the current system.

Farrokh Mistree
Professor of Mechanical Engineering
Director, System Realization Lab
Georgia Tech

AUTHENTICATION TO BECOME MORE IMPORTANT THAN COPYRIGHT

The creative human process of authoring is in part based upon the collection, interpretation, and analysis of existing information. In the future the source, ownership, and authentication of information become significant issues as intelligent processors duplicate these human processes to become both primary and secondary publishers.

Authentication of information sources becomes more important than copyright to ensure these processors do not reuse data that are out of context, thus resulting in false conclusions. As this prediction matures, changes will occur in the publishing business, in educational use of information, and in the purpose and use of libraries.

Robert G. Patterson
Institute for Paper Science and Technology, and
Member, Program on the Consequences of the Information Revolution
Georgia Tech

WINNERS WILL APPLY AND USE TECHNOLOGY

Our physical ability to send, process, and display data is going to increase enormously with cost-effective developments in bandwidth, computing, optical storage, imaging, and display technologies

However, the real challenge of the information revolution is not the development of technology but how to apply and use it. The technology is developing faster than our ability to adopt it. The greatest difficulty is getting people to change. Companies spent huge sums on information technology in the 1980s with limited improvements in productivity.

The winners in the information revolution will be the people and organizations that can adapt change to the way they work and live.

William H. Bellinger
Visiting Professor
Dupree School of Management, Georgia Tech

William M. Riggs
Director
Management of Technology Program, Georgia Tech

ORGANIZING INFORMATION IS NOT THE FUTURE

Organizing information will not be so important in the future; evaluating, validating, and analyzing information will be. Consequently there will be a growing need for information and knowledge analysts whose activities are focused on content, meaning, and value of information. They will need to know how to use the most modern information technologies and at the same time be educators and mentors in a changing learning environment.

Julie Yang
Librarian
Georgia Tech

DECENTRALIZATION IS THE FUTURE

The industrial age was based on the centralized coordination of large numbers of manual laborers and service workers. The knowledge age, in contrast, is based upon the decentralized coordination of large numbers of knowledge workers. One should therefore expect that decentralized mechanisms of all sorts (e.g., products, services, business processes, business strategies, markets, government agencies) will flourish at the expense of centralized ones in the future.

Predictions: The network computer will not be a successful product; governments will lose control of their currencies and the ability to control interest rates; and communications industries that developed as monopolies, oligopolies, or because of sheer size will wither.

Gary S. Tjaden
Director, Center For Enterprise Systems
Georgia Tech Research Institute

NEXT COMES THE INFORMATION [NOT TECHNOLOGY] REVOLUTION

In the 1980s, information technology (IT) took off. Computing went from an occasional activity for specialists to routine in the lives of most technical professionals; then it did likewise for white-collar workers and students; then, for many blue collar workers and on into our homes. In the 1990s, we have gotten networked—first the technical community;

then business and school; then home—via modems, ethernet, some broadband, and wireless. That is an IT Revolution.

Now we are poised for the information revolution. Newly accessible, digitally formatted information is weaving into our daily lives. Technical professionals first, then white-collar workers and students, then most all of us will rebuild our work and home lives around this resource—ubiquitous electronic information.

Alan L. Porter
Director, Technology Policy and Assessment Center
Georgia Tech

Author Index

Subject Index